Statistics Step by Step

An Introduction to Understanding Numbers, Patterns & Probability with Clarity

Robert Gibson

© 2025 by Robert Gibson

All rights reserved.

No part of this publication may be reproduced, distributed, or transmitted in any form or by any means, including photocopying, recording, or other electronic or mechanical methods, without the prior written permission of the publisher, except in the case of brief quotations embodied in critical reviews and certain other noncommercial uses permitted by U.S. copyright law.

This book is intended to provide general information on the subjects covered and is presented with the understanding that the author and publisher are not providing professional advice or services. While every effort has been made to ensure the accuracy and completeness of the information contained herein, neither the author nor the publisher guarantees such accuracy or completeness, nor shall they be responsible for any errors or omissions or for the results obtained from the use of such information. The contents of this book are provided "as is" and without warranties of any kind, either express or implied.

Publisher email: info@tagvault.org

Preface

Welcome to *Statistics Step by Step*. If you've ever felt intimidated by statistics or wondered how data can reveal patterns and truths about the world, this book is for you. Whether you're a student, a professional, or just curious about how statistics influence our lives, this guide will help you navigate the concepts in an approachable and engaging way.

Why Write This Book?
Statistics is all around us. From the news we read, the health studies we trust, and the economic forecasts we rely on, to the algorithms powering our favorite apps, statistics drives decisions in nearly every field. Yet, for many people, it's a topic that feels complex, abstract, or even downright frustrating. I wrote this book because I believe everyone can learn to understand and appreciate statistics with the right approach and explanations.

This book isn't just about numbers—it's about stories. Behind every dataset is a story waiting to be uncovered, and statistics gives us the frameworks to tell those stories accurately and meaningfully. My goal is to demystify the subject, break it down into manageable steps, and show you that statistics isn't just useful—it can also be fascinating.

Who Is This Book For?
This book is designed for anyone who wants to build a strong foundation in statistics, regardless of your background. Maybe you're a student tackling statistics for the first time, a professional looking to sharpen your data analysis skills, or someone who simply wants to make sense of the graphs and charts you encounter every day. No matter where you're starting from, this book will guide you through the basics and beyond.

I've structured the content to be both relatively thorough (but not overwhelmingly so) and beginner-friendly. You won't need a background in advanced math to follow along, but you will need a willingness to explore, think critically, and occasionally practice what you learn.

What Makes This Book Different?
1. **Step-by-Step Approach:** The title says it all—this book is a journey, not a sprint. Each chapter builds on the previous one, so you develop a solid understanding before moving on to more complex topics.
2. **Real-World Examples:** Throughout the book, you'll find practical examples and applications of statistics. Whether it's analyzing election polls, understanding medical studies, or predicting business trends, these examples will show you how statistics is used in everyday life.

3. **Clarity and Simplicity:** I've worked hard to explain concepts in plain language without sacrificing depth. Complex ideas are broken down into clear steps, and technical jargon is kept to a minimum.
4. **Focus on Application:** This isn't just a theoretical guide. Wherever possible, I've included practical advice and tools to help you apply statistical methods to real-world problems.
5. **A Complete Learning Experience:** From foundational concepts like types of data and probability to advanced topics like regression analysis and Monte Carlo simulations, this book covers everything you need to know to become confident with statistics.

What Will You Learn?

By the end of this book, you'll have an understanding of the core principles of statistics and how they're applied. Here's a snapshot of what's in store:

- **Foundations of Statistics:** Learn what statistics is, why it matters, and how it's used to solve problems.
- **Organizing and Visualizing Data:** Discover how to transform raw data into meaningful insights with tables, charts, and visualizations.
- **Probability and Distributions:** Master the rules of probability and understand different types of probability distributions.
- **Inferential Statistics:** Learn how to draw conclusions and make predictions about populations based on sample data.
- **Advanced Topics:** Explore modern methods like Bayesian statistics, time series analysis, and optimization techniques.
- **Real-World Applications:** See how statistics is applied across diverse fields like business, healthcare, and technology.

How to Use This Book

This book is designed to be read chapter by chapter, but you can also jump to the sections that are most relevant to your needs. Each chapter includes clear explanations, practical examples, and, where appropriate, step-by-step guides. Don't hesitate to revisit earlier chapters if you need a refresher—statistics is a cumulative subject, and it's normal to build your understanding gradually.

There's also an appendix with definitions and key terms to help you quickly reference important concepts.

A Word of Encouragement

Learning statistics can be a challenge, but it's also an incredibly rewarding journey. The ability to interpret data, recognize patterns, and make informed decisions is a valuable skill in today's data-driven world. If at any point you feel stuck or overwhelmed, remember that progress is made step by step. With patience and practice, you'll be surprised at how much you can accomplish.

This book isn't just about learning statistics—it's about empowering yourself to think critically and approach problems with confidence. Whether you're analyzing data for work, studying for an exam, or simply curious about how the world works, the knowledge you gain here will serve you well.

Let's Get Started!
I'm thrilled to have you on this journey and excited for the discoveries that await. So grab a pen, open your mind, and let's take the first step into the world of statistics together.

Here's what we have in store:

Topical Outline

Chapter 1: Foundations of Statistics
- What is Statistics? Understanding Its Scope and Purpose
- Types of Data: Qualitative, Quantitative, and Mixed
- Levels of Measurement: Nominal, Ordinal, Interval, and Ratio
- Sampling Methods: Random, Stratified, Cluster, and Systematic Sampling
- Common Statistical Misconceptions and Pitfalls to Avoid

Chapter 2: Organizing and Visualizing Data
- Creating Frequency Distributions
- Histograms, Bar Charts, and Pie Charts
- Box Plots and Scatterplots for Multivariable Data
- Heatmaps and Density Plots: Advanced Visualization Techniques

Chapter 3: Measures of Central Tendency
- Mean: Calculation and Interpretation
- Median: When to Use It and Why
- Mode: Identifying Patterns in Data

Chapter 4: Measures of Dispersion
- Range: Quick Insights into Variability
- Variance and Standard Deviation: Digging Deeper
- Coefficient of Variation: Standardizing Comparisons
- Percentiles and Interquartile Range

Chapter 5: Probability Basics
- Definitions: Experimental vs. Theoretical Probability
- Rules of Probability: Addition and Multiplication
- Independent and Dependent Events
- Conditional Probability and Bayes' Theorem

Chapter 6: Probability Distributions
- Discrete vs. Continuous Distributions
- The Binomial Distribution: Success/Failure Scenarios
- The Normal Distribution: Properties and Applications
- The Poisson Distribution: Modeling Rare Events
- Nonparametric Distributions

Chapter 7: Sampling Distributions and the Central Limit Theorem
- Sampling Distribution of the Mean
- The Role of the Central Limit Theorem
- Practical Applications of Sampling Distributions
- Sampling Distribution of Proportions

Chapter 8: Hypothesis Testing Fundamentals
- Null and Alternative Hypotheses: Setting the Stage
- Types of Errors: Type I and Type II Errors
- Significance Levels (p-values) and Decision-Making
- Power Analysis: Determining Sample Size Requirements

Chapter 9: Inferential Statistics
- Confidence Intervals: Interpreting Margins of Error
- t-Tests: Comparing Two Groups
- ANOVA: Analyzing Differences Among Multiple Groups
- Z-Tests: Comparing Means with Large Sample Sizes

Chapter 10: Correlation and Regression Analysis
- Pearson's Correlation Coefficient: Measuring Relationships
- Simple Linear Regression: Prediction with One Variable
- Multiple Regression: Expanding the Model
- Residual Analysis: Diagnosing Model Fit

Chapter 11: Chi-Square Tests
- Chi-Square Goodness-of-Fit Test
- Chi-Square Test of Independence
- Applications in Categorical Data Analysis

Chapter 12: Nonparametric Statistics
- Introduction to Nonparametric Methods
- Mann-Whitney U Test and Wilcoxon Signed-Rank Test
- Kruskal-Wallis Test for Group Comparisons

Chapter 13: Advanced Topics in Statistics
- Factor Analysis: Uncovering Latent Variables
- Time Series Analysis: Trends and Forecasting
- Bayesian Statistics: Updating Beliefs with Data
- Monte Carlo Simulations: Modeling Uncertainty

- Optimization: Achieving Optimal Results

Chapter 14: Real-World Applications of Statistics
- Business Analytics: Driving Decisions with Data
- Economics and Finance: Probability Applications in Markets and Economies
- Health and Medical Research: Evidence-Based Practice
- Social Sciences: Understanding Human Behavior
- Engineering and Technology: Optimizing Systems

Appendix
- Terms and Definitions

Afterword

Table of Contents

Chapter 1: Foundations of Statistics ... 1
Chapter 2: Organizing and Visualizing Data ... 15
Chapter 3: Measures of Central Tendency ... 25
Chapter 4: Measures of Dispersion ... 31
Chapter 5: Probability Basics ... 39
Chapter 6: Probability Distributions ... 52
Chapter 7: Sampling Distributions and the Central Limit Theorem ... 68
Chapter 8: Hypothesis Testing Fundamentals ... 81
Chapter 9: Inferential Statistics ... 95
Chapter 10: Correlation and Regression Analysis ... 110
Chapter 11: Chi-Square Tests ... 125
Chapter 12: Nonparametric Statistics ... 135
Chapter 13: Advanced Topics in Statistics ... 147
Chapter 14: Real-World Applications of Statistics ... 167
Appendix ... 187
Afterword ... 190

Chapter 1: Foundations of Statistics

What is Statistics? Understanding Its Scope and Purpose

Statistics is the science of collecting, organizing, analyzing, interpreting, and presenting data. At its core, statistics is about making sense of information in a structured way. Humans have always gathered data—census counts, crop yields, trade records—but statistics provides a formal framework to draw meaningful conclusions from that data. It turns raw numbers into knowledge.

At its simplest, statistics helps answer questions. How often do events happen? What factors influence them? What trends can we predict? For example, a business might use sales data to decide which products to promote, or a government might use population data to allocate resources effectively. **Statistics provides a systematic way to handle uncertainty and make informed decisions.**

One key idea is that statistics is more than just numbers. It focuses on *data*. Data is information, often expressed numerically, but it could also include categories, rankings, or even preferences. For instance, a survey asking people's favorite color produces categorical data, while measuring people's heights produces numerical data.

Statistics operates through two main branches: descriptive statistics and inferential statistics. **Descriptive statistics** summarizes and organizes data to highlight its main features. This includes measures like averages, medians, or visual tools like charts and graphs. For example, summarizing the test scores of a class with an average score of 75% is descriptive. It tells you what's already known. **Inferential statistics**, on the other hand, goes beyond the given data. It uses a sample to make predictions or generalizations about a larger population. If you surveyed 1,000 voters in a country to predict an election result, you're using inferential methods.

The backbone of inferential statistics is probability. Statistics uses probability to account for randomness and uncertainty in data. For example, you may hear that a study is 95% confident that the average income in a city is between $40,000 and $50,000. That "confidence" comes from probability calculations. Without probability, you wouldn't know how reliable your conclusions are.

One concept that ties descriptive and inferential statistics together is variability. Variability refers to how spread out or different the data values are. A dataset with all values close to the average has low variability, while a dataset with widely scattered values has high variability. Understanding variability is critical because no two data samples are ever exactly the same.

In practical terms, statistics is very important for decision-making. Consider medicine: clinical trials use statistics to evaluate whether a new drug works better than existing treatments. By comparing outcomes across different groups of patients, researchers assess effectiveness and safety. Without statistics, such evaluations would be guesswork.

Businesses also depend heavily on statistical methods. Marketing teams analyze customer data to segment markets and predict buying behavior. Supply chains rely on forecasting models to minimize costs. Even sports teams use player statistics to shape strategies and recruit talent. In finance, stock market analysts use statistical models to estimate risks and returns.

One distinguishing feature of statistics is its ability to handle randomness and uncertainty. Random events can skew data, and no dataset perfectly represents reality. Yet statistics allows us to estimate and quantify uncertainty. For example, polling a small group of voters may not yield an exact result for the entire population, but it can provide a reliable estimate, assuming the sample is representative.

Bias, however, is a major concern in statistics. Bias occurs when the data collected or analyzed systematically misrepresents reality. For example, if a survey only includes responses from people who shop online, it may not accurately reflect the views of the entire population. Avoiding bias requires careful sampling and data collection techniques.

Data collection lies at the heart of statistical practice. Data can come from many sources, such as experiments, surveys, historical records, or observational studies. Each method has its strengths and limitations. For instance, experiments provide controlled conditions to test hypotheses, but they can be expensive and time-consuming. Surveys gather information directly from people, but their reliability depends on how questions are worded and whether responses are honest.

An essential part of working with data is understanding its context. Without context, numbers lose meaning. For example, a statistic like "60% of respondents prefer option A" is meaningless unless you know who the respondents are, what options they had, and why the data was collected. This context shapes how the data is analyzed and interpreted.

One challenge in statistics is distinguishing correlation from causation. Correlation means that two variables move together in some way, but it doesn't necessarily mean that one causes the other. For example, ice cream sales and drowning incidents may both increase in summer, but one doesn't cause the other—they're both related to the season. Misinterpreting correlation as causation is a common statistical error.

Another cornerstone of statistics is the concept of sampling. Most of the time, analyzing an entire population is impossible or impractical, so we rely on smaller samples. The trick is to ensure the sample is representative of the population. For example, if you want to study the spending habits of adults in a city, surveying only college students would produce biased results. Random sampling methods are often used to minimize such bias.

When working with statistics, precision matters. Small errors in data collection or analysis can lead to big mistakes in conclusions. For example, rounding off too early in a calculation can distort results. Similarly, improper use of statistical methods—like applying a test meant for large samples to a small dataset—can lead to false conclusions.

Statistics is dynamic and constantly evolving. Modern technology has significantly enhanced statistical analysis. Computers and software like R, Python, and Excel allow us to handle large datasets and perform complex calculations quickly. Machine learning, a branch of artificial intelligence, applies advanced statistical methods to tasks like image recognition and predictive modeling. These advancements make statistics more accessible and impactful than ever before.

Statistics also has a unique way of bringing simplicity to complexity. Consider the weather forecast. Behind a simple statement like "There's a 70% chance of rain tomorrow" are thousands of data points—temperature, humidity, wind patterns—all processed through statistical models. These models turn overwhelming information into something people can understand and act on.

One important principle in statistics is reproducibility. Statistical findings should be verifiable by others using the same methods and data. This principle is especially important in scientific research, where errors or dishonesty can undermine trust. If a study claims that a new treatment reduces symptoms, other researchers must be able to replicate the analysis and confirm the results.

Another vital aspect of statistics is visualization. Data visualizations—charts, graphs, and plots—help communicate findings clearly. A well-designed chart can reveal trends and patterns that raw numbers alone might hide. For instance, a line graph showing sales over time instantly conveys trends, while a scatterplot reveals relationships between variables.

Statistical literacy is becoming increasingly important in everyday life. With the rise of big data, understanding how statistics works helps people evaluate the information they encounter. For example, when reading news about a scientific study, knowing whether the study used a representative sample or accounted for confounding variables can help you judge its credibility. Similarly, understanding the margin of error in a political poll can prevent overconfidence in its predictions.

Ethics has a key role in statistics. Data should be collected and analyzed responsibly, respecting privacy and avoiding harm. Misusing statistics—whether by cherry-picking data, presenting misleading graphs, or ignoring limitations—can have serious consequences. For example, flawed statistical analyses have contributed to financial crises, public health disasters, and policy failures.

Types of Data: Qualitative, Quantitative, and Mixed

Data is the foundation of statistics, and understanding its types is essential for analyzing and interpreting it effectively. Broadly, data can be classified into **qualitative**

(categorical), quantitative (numerical), and mixed data. Each type serves a specific purpose and requires different methods of analysis.

Qualitative Data

Qualitative data, also known as categorical data, represents characteristics, attributes, or categories. Instead of numbers, qualitative data uses labels or names to describe an observation. For instance, a survey asking for respondents' favorite colors collects qualitative data. Examples include gender (male, female, nonbinary), marital status (single, married, divorced), and product categories (electronics, clothing, furniture).

Qualitative data can be further divided into two subtypes: **nominal** and **ordinal**. **Nominal data** consists of categories without any inherent order. For example, blood types (A, B, AB, O) are nominal because no category is ranked higher or lower than another. In contrast, **ordinal data** has a meaningful order but no fixed intervals. Customer satisfaction ratings like "poor," "average," and "excellent" are ordinal because they imply a ranking, but the difference between "average" and "excellent" isn't measurable in numerical terms.

Analyzing qualitative data often involves summarizing it using counts or percentages. For example, in a classroom of 40 students, if 20 prefer online learning, 15 prefer in-person classes, and 5 have no preference, the data can be presented as percentages or pie charts. Visualization tools like bar graphs and pie charts work well for qualitative data, as they display distributions clearly.

Quantitative Data

Quantitative data is numerical and represents quantities or measurements. Unlike qualitative data, it involves values that can be counted or measured. For instance, the height of a group of individuals, the number of cars sold in a month, or the daily temperatures in a city are all quantitative data. This type of data allows for mathematical computations like addition, subtraction, averages, and more.

Quantitative data can be further classified into **discrete** and **continuous** data. **Discrete data** consists of whole numbers or distinct values. Examples include the number of employees in a company or the number of books on a shelf. You can't have 3.5 employees or 2.8 books, so the values are limited to integers. **Continuous data**, on the other hand, can take any value within a range, including decimals and fractions. Measurements like height (5.7 feet), weight (150.3 pounds), and time (2.45 hours) fall under continuous data.

Analyzing quantitative data often involves statistical measures such as mean, median, variance, and standard deviation. Visualization tools like histograms, line graphs, and scatterplots are commonly used to represent quantitative data. For instance, a histogram can show the distribution of test scores, while a scatterplot might display the relationship between two variables, like age and income.

Mixed Data

In real-world scenarios, datasets often contain a combination of qualitative and quantitative data, referred to as mixed data. For example, consider a dataset about patients in a hospital. It may include qualitative variables like gender and diagnosis type, alongside quantitative variables like age, blood pressure, and cholesterol levels. Analyzing such datasets requires methods that handle both types of data simultaneously.

Mixed data is frequently encountered in research, business, and healthcare. For instance, a customer survey might ask both categorical questions ("What is your preferred product category?") and numerical ones ("How much do you spend on this product monthly?"). Analyzing mixed data can involve separate techniques for the qualitative and quantitative aspects before combining insights for a holistic view.

Key Differences Between Qualitative and Quantitative Data

While qualitative and quantitative data are distinct, they are complementary. Qualitative data answers questions like "What?" and "Why?" while quantitative data focuses on "How many?" and "How much?" For example, qualitative data might reveal that customers prefer a specific product, while quantitative data shows how often they purchase it. Together, these insights enable more comprehensive analysis.

One major difference lies in the analysis methods. Qualitative data often relies on descriptive statistics, such as percentages and frequency distributions, while quantitative data allows for more complex computations, like correlation, regression, and hypothesis testing. For example, analyzing customer satisfaction ratings (qualitative) might involve calculating the percentage of "satisfied" respondents, whereas analyzing monthly sales (quantitative) could involve identifying trends using time series analysis.

Challenges in Working with Data Types

Each type of data presents its own challenges. With qualitative data, ensuring clarity and consistency can be difficult. For example, open-ended survey responses may include different spellings or synonyms for the same answer, requiring standardization before analysis. Quantitative data, meanwhile, can suffer from errors like missing values or outliers, which can skew results if not addressed.

Another challenge is determining the appropriate statistical methods for mixed data. For instance, combining numerical and categorical variables in a single analysis, such as exploring the relationship between income (quantitative) and education level (qualitative), may require advanced techniques like regression models for categorical predictors.

Practical Examples

To illustrate the use of these data types, consider the context of education. A school might collect **qualitative data** like students' grade levels (freshman, sophomore, junior, senior) and **quantitative data** like their test scores. The qualitative data helps categorize students into groups, while the quantitative data allows for performance analysis within each group. If the school gathers mixed data, such as students' preferred study methods (qualitative) alongside their grades (quantitative), it can identify correlations between study habits and academic success.

In healthcare, qualitative data like disease categories (e.g., diabetes, hypertension) can be paired with quantitative data like blood pressure readings and age. This combination allows researchers to analyze trends within specific groups and tailor interventions effectively.

The Importance of Recognizing Data Types

Understanding the distinction between qualitative, quantitative, and mixed data ensures proper analysis and interpretation. Using the wrong methods for a given data type can lead to incorrect conclusions. For instance, calculating an average for categorical data (e.g., finding the "average" eye color) is meaningless, while treating numerical data as categorical (e.g., grouping continuous age values into arbitrary ranges) may oversimplify important trends.

Recognizing data types also guides the choice of visualization tools. Bar charts and pie charts suit qualitative data, while histograms and scatterplots are ideal for quantitative data. Mixed datasets might require combined visualizations, such as a chart with bars representing categorical groups and lines showing trends for numerical values.

By understanding the characteristics and distinctions of each data type, you can confidently analyze and interpret data, whether it's collected for research, business, or personal projects. This foundational knowledge ensures that the methods you choose are both accurate and appropriate for the data at hand.

Levels of Measurement: Nominal, Ordinal, Interval, and Ratio

Understanding levels of measurement is critical in statistics because they determine how data can be analyzed and interpreted. The **four levels of measurement—nominal, ordinal, interval, and ratio—each describe a different way to categorize and quantify data.** Knowing these levels helps ensure appropriate statistical techniques are applied to data.

Nominal Level

The nominal level of measurement is the simplest. It involves data that can be classified into categories, but the categories have no inherent order. Examples include eye color (blue, brown, green), marital status (single, married, divorced), and types of pets (dog, cat, bird). Nominal data answers the question, "What type or category does this observation belong to?"

In nominal data, the only statistical operation possible is counting. You can calculate frequencies or proportions within categories, but numerical computations like averages or differences are meaningless. For instance, if a survey reveals that 40% of respondents own dogs, 35% own cats, and 25% own birds, this is a valid use of nominal data. However, it makes no sense to say that "dogs are twice as good as birds" based on these numbers.

Nominal data is often represented visually using bar charts or pie charts. These visualizations emphasize the distribution of categories rather than any numerical relationship between them. For example, a pie chart showing the percentage of students in different academic majors highlights the relative sizes of each group without implying any ranking.

Ordinal Level

Ordinal data introduces order to the categories but still lacks precise numerical intervals. It answers questions like, "Which is higher or better?" Examples include rankings (1st, 2nd, 3rd), satisfaction levels (satisfied, neutral, dissatisfied), and education levels (high school, bachelor's, master's, PhD). While the categories are ranked, the distances between them are not consistent or measurable.

A key characteristic of ordinal data is that it allows for comparisons but not precise calculations. For instance, if a restaurant survey ranks satisfaction as "poor," "average," "good," and "excellent," you can say that "excellent" is better than "good," but you can't quantify how much better. Similarly, in a race, the difference in time between the 1st and 2nd place finishers might not be the same as the difference between 2nd and 3rd place.

Ordinal data can be analyzed using median and mode but not mean. For example, in a group of survey responses, if most people rate their experience as "good," that mode represents the most common sentiment. Visualizations like bar charts are common for ordinal data, but care should be taken to preserve the order of categories. A bar chart showing satisfaction levels, for example, should always display "poor" to "excellent" in the correct sequence.

Interval Level

Interval data takes a significant step forward by introducing consistent and measurable intervals between values. Examples include temperature in Celsius or Fahrenheit, IQ scores, and calendar years. In interval data, differences between values are meaningful, but the concept of an absolute zero is missing. This absence of a true zero makes certain calculations, like ratios, impossible.

Temperature is a classic example. The difference between 20°C and 30°C is the same as the difference between 30°C and 40°C. These intervals are consistent, making addition and subtraction meaningful. However, you cannot say that 40°C is "twice as hot" as 20°C because the zero point on the Celsius scale is arbitrary and does not represent a complete absence of temperature.

The interval level allows for more advanced statistical techniques, such as calculating means and standard deviations. For example, the average IQ score in a group can be calculated because IQ is an interval measure. Visual representations like histograms and line graphs are useful for interval data, as they highlight trends and distributions.

Ratio Level

The ratio level of measurement is the most precise and versatile. It includes all the properties of interval data—consistent intervals, meaningful differences—but adds a true zero point. A true zero indicates the absence of the measured attribute. Examples include weight, height, age, income, and distance. Ratio data answers questions like, "How many times more?" or "What proportion?"

Consider weight: If one object weighs 10 kg and another weighs 20 kg, you can say the second object is twice as heavy as the first. Similarly, an income of $0 represents no income at all, and someone earning $50,000 earns half as much as someone earning $100,000.

Ratio data supports all mathematical operations, including addition, subtraction, multiplication, and division. This flexibility makes it the most powerful level of measurement. For example, you can calculate averages, proportions, and growth rates. In business, ratio data is often used to measure financial metrics like profit margins or return on investment. In health, it is used to track body mass index (BMI) or cholesterol levels.

Visualizations like scatterplots and boxplots are common for ratio data, as they effectively show relationships and variability. For instance, a scatterplot of height versus weight might reveal a positive correlation, indicating that taller individuals tend to weigh more.

Key Differences Between the Levels

The levels of measurement build on each other, each adding more precision and analytical possibilities. Nominal data categorizes, ordinal data ranks, interval data measures consistent differences, and ratio data allows for absolute comparisons. The distinctions between these levels guide the selection of statistical methods.

For example, consider survey data asking participants to indicate their education level (nominal), rank their satisfaction (ordinal), rate their experience on a scale of 1 to 10 (interval), and provide their annual income (ratio). Each type of data requires a specific approach to analysis, visualization, and interpretation. Treating nominal data like interval data—or vice versa—leads to invalid conclusions.

Practical Applications

In education, levels of measurement help analyze student performance. Letter grades (A, B, C) are ordinal, while raw test scores (out of 100) are ratio. Teachers might rank students based on grades while calculating the average test score for the class.

In healthcare, nominal data like blood types (A, B, AB, O) is used to classify patients, while ratio data like blood pressure measurements guides treatment decisions. Interval data, such as body temperature in Celsius, monitors trends over time, and ordinal data like pain levels ("mild," "moderate," "severe") informs diagnosis and care plans.

In business, customer demographics like gender and location are nominal, while satisfaction ratings are ordinal. Financial data, including revenue and expenses, is ratio, supporting profitability analysis. Understanding these distinctions ensures accurate reporting and decision-making.

Common Challenges

Misinterpreting the level of measurement is a frequent error in data analysis. For instance, treating ordinal data like interval data can lead to misleading results. Consider a customer satisfaction survey using a 5-point scale (1 = very dissatisfied, 5 = very satisfied). Calculating the mean score assumes the intervals between points are equal, which may not be true.

Another challenge is converting between levels. For example, grouping continuous data into categories, like turning ages into ranges (e.g., 18-24, 25-34), simplifies analysis but sacrifices precision. Conversely, treating categorical data numerically, such as coding "male" as 1 and "female" as 2, risks implying a numerical relationship that doesn't exist.

Why Levels of Measurement Matter

Levels of measurement are more than theoretical concepts; they form the backbone of statistical analysis. Applying the wrong techniques—such as using a mean to summarize nominal data or ignoring the lack of a true zero in interval data—can undermine the validity of your conclusions. Understanding these levels ensures that data is handled appropriately, allowing for accurate analysis and meaningful insights.

Sampling Methods: Random, Stratified, Cluster, and Systematic Sampling

Sampling methods are essential in statistics because they allow researchers to draw conclusions about a population without needing to study every individual. Choosing the right sampling method ensures that the sample accurately represents the population and minimizes bias. Four commonly used methods—random sampling, stratified sampling, cluster sampling, and systematic sampling—each serve specific purposes depending on the nature of the data and the research question.

Random sampling, also known as simple random sampling, is the most straightforward and widely recognized method. Every individual in the population has an equal chance of being selected. This is often achieved by assigning each member of the population a number and using a random number generator to select participants. For example, if a researcher wants to study college students' study habits, they could compile a list of all students enrolled at a university and randomly select a subset to participate in the study. Random sampling is popular because it eliminates selection bias, assuming the population list is complete and accurate. However, it can be resource-intensive, especially with large or geographically dispersed populations, as obtaining a complete list of potential participants may be challenging.

Stratified sampling addresses some limitations of random sampling by dividing the population into subgroups, or strata, based on a shared characteristic before selecting participants. For example, if a researcher is studying political opinions and knows that the population has distinct age groups, they might divide the population into strata such as "18-29 years old," "30-49 years old," and "50+ years old." From each stratum, individuals are then randomly selected to form the sample. Stratified sampling ensures that all significant subgroups of the population are represented proportionally in the final sample. For instance, if 40% of the population is in the 18-29 age group, then 40% of the sample should also come from that group. This method is particularly effective when researchers suspect that subgroups may differ significantly on the variable of interest. However, stratified sampling requires detailed knowledge of the population and its subdivisions, which can complicate the sampling process.

Cluster sampling simplifies the sampling process when the population is large or spread out across multiple locations. Instead of selecting individuals, researchers randomly select entire groups or clusters from the population. For example, if a national study on high school students is being conducted, schools could be treated as clusters. Researchers would randomly select a subset of schools and include all students within those schools in the sample. Cluster sampling is often used because it reduces logistical challenges and costs, especially in studies that require physical data collection. However, it is less precise than random or stratified sampling because individuals within a cluster may be more similar to each other than to the overall population, leading to increased sampling error. For example, if the clusters are schools, students in a single school might share similar socioeconomic backgrounds, which may not reflect broader diversity.

Systematic sampling provides a straightforward alternative to random sampling by selecting every nth individual from a list after choosing a random starting point. For example, if a researcher has a list of 10,000 employees at a company and wants a sample of 1,000, they would randomly pick a starting point between 1 and 10 and then select every 10th individual. Systematic sampling is simple to implement and works well when the population is already organized in a list or queue. However, it can introduce bias if there is a pattern in the population list that aligns with the sampling interval. For instance, if the list alternates between male and female employees, systematic sampling could unintentionally produce a sample that is predominantly one gender.

Each sampling method has advantages and limitations, and the choice often depends on the specific research objectives, resources available, and characteristics of the population. For example, in a survey of voter preferences across a country, random sampling might be ideal in theory but impractical in practice due to logistical constraints. Stratified sampling could ensure proportional representation of urban and rural voters, while cluster sampling might involve selecting regions or precincts to simplify data collection. Systematic sampling could work if there is a comprehensive voter registry organized alphabetically.

To illustrate these methods, consider a hypothetical study on health behaviors in a city. If the researchers use random sampling, they might generate a random list of addresses and invite residents at those addresses to participate. With stratified sampling, they might divide the population by age, gender, or neighborhood income level to ensure representation across these variables. Using cluster sampling, they could randomly select several neighborhoods and survey all residents within those areas. Systematic sampling would involve selecting every nth household from a city directory.

The quality of any statistical study depends heavily on how well the sample represents the population. A poorly chosen sample can lead to bias and invalid conclusions, regardless of how sophisticated the analysis is. For example, if a study on exercise habits uses a sample drawn exclusively from gym-goers, the results will not generalize to the entire population, as it excludes people who do not exercise in gyms. Similarly, if a stratified sample neglects to include an important subgroup, such as older adults, the findings will be incomplete.

Random sampling is often considered the gold standard because it minimizes bias, but it is not always feasible. Stratified sampling is particularly useful when researchers know that subgroups within the population differ significantly. Cluster sampling works well for large-scale studies with geographic constraints, while systematic sampling is ideal for well-organized, structured populations.

Regardless of the method chosen, ensuring that the sample is representative is paramount. Representation depends not only on selecting the right sampling technique but also on addressing potential issues like nonresponse bias. Nonresponse bias occurs when certain individuals are less likely to participate in the study, potentially skewing results. For example, if a phone survey is conducted during working hours, people who work full-time may be underrepresented, leading to biased conclusions.

Another consideration is sample size. A larger sample reduces sampling error and improves the reliability of estimates, but it also requires more resources. Researchers must balance the desire for precision with practical constraints, such as time, budget, and personnel. For example, a study with a small random sample may yield less precise results than a larger stratified or cluster sample designed to capture key population characteristics.

Technology has made sampling more efficient by enabling the use of software and tools to automate selection processes. Random number generators, database management systems, and geographic information systems (GIS) can streamline sampling for complex studies. These tools reduce human error and increase transparency, ensuring that the sampling process is replicable and unbiased.

In short, sampling methods are the cornerstone of effective statistical analysis. Random sampling ensures fairness but requires access to a complete population list. Stratified sampling balances representation across key subgroups, making it ideal for diverse populations. Cluster sampling reduces logistical barriers in large-scale studies, while systematic sampling offers simplicity and efficiency for ordered populations. Each method serves a unique purpose, and selecting the most appropriate one is a critical step in any research project.

Common Statistical Misconceptions and Pitfalls to Avoid

Statistics is important for understanding the world, but it is also prone to misuse and misunderstanding. Misconceptions about statistics often stem from a lack of clarity in interpreting data, inappropriate methods, or overlooking important principles. Avoiding common pitfalls requires not only technical knowledge but also critical thinking and attention to context.

One widespread misconception is that **correlation implies causation.** Just because two variables are correlated does not mean one causes the other. For example, data might show a strong correlation between ice cream sales and drowning incidents. However, the underlying factor is seasonal temperature: both increase during the summer. Assuming causation in such cases can lead to flawed conclusions and misguided actions. Careful statistical analysis must differentiate between correlation and true causal relationships, often using experimental or longitudinal studies to establish causality.

Another common pitfall is the misuse of **averages.** The word "average" can refer to mean, median, or mode, and each serves a different purpose. The mean is sensitive to outliers, which can skew results. For instance, if you calculate the average income of a group where one person earns $1 million and others earn $40,000, the mean income will appear much higher than what most people earn. In such cases, the median, which represents the middle value, provides a more accurate picture of typical income. Misreporting averages without specifying which measure is used can mislead audiences.

Overgeneralizing from small or unrepresentative samples is another frequent mistake. Suppose a study surveys 50 college students and concludes that most young adults prefer online learning. This sample size is too small and narrowly focused to represent the entire population of young adults. Larger, more diverse samples are necessary for reliable generalizations. Sampling bias, where certain groups are underrepresented, compounds this issue. For instance, conducting a phone survey might exclude individuals without landlines, leading to skewed results.

Misinterpreting **statistical significance** is also a recurring issue. A statistically significant result indicates that the observed effect is unlikely due to chance, but it doesn't measure the size or importance of the effect. For example, a medical study might find that a new drug reduces symptoms with $p < 0.05$. While this result is statistically significant, the actual improvement might be negligible. Confusing statistical significance with practical significance can result in overhyping minor findings.

Ignoring variability in data is another trap. Statistics often involves summarizing data with measures like means and medians, but these summaries hide the variability within the data. For example, two classrooms might have the same average test score, but one may have scores tightly clustered around the average, while the other has a wide range of scores. Failing to consider variability can lead to oversimplified conclusions and missed insights about differences within the data.

The improper use of **percentages** and **proportions** is another area where errors arise. Percentages are useful for comparing data, but they can be deceptive if the base numbers are not disclosed. For example, reporting that a company's sales increased by 50% sounds impressive until you learn that the initial sales were only $100. Proportions should always be presented with their denominators to provide context.

One of the most pervasive issues is **data dredging**, or p-hacking. This occurs when researchers test multiple hypotheses on the same dataset until they find a statistically significant result. While the result may appear valid, it often arises by chance rather than reflecting a genuine relationship. This practice undermines the reliability of findings and is especially problematic in fields like medical research, where spurious results can have serious consequences. Pre-registering hypotheses and adjusting for multiple comparisons can help prevent p-hacking.

Over-relying on visualizations without critical evaluation is another risk. Graphs, charts, and plots can be great ways for communicating data, but they can also mislead if poorly designed or deliberately manipulated. For example, altering the scale of a graph can exaggerate or minimize differences between groups. A bar chart that starts its y-axis at a value other than zero might make small differences appear more significant than they are. Readers should always scrutinize visualizations for accuracy and context.

Confusing precision with accuracy is a subtle but important distinction. Precision refers to how detailed a measurement is, while accuracy refers to how close it is to the true value. For instance, reporting a measurement as 3.45678 grams implies precision, but if the actual value is 4 grams, the measurement is inaccurate. Excessive precision can also create a false sense of reliability. In statistics, it's important to match the level of precision to the quality of the data.

The **failure to account for confounding variables** is a critical error in statistical analysis. Confounding variables are factors that influence both the independent and dependent variables, potentially distorting the relationship between them. For example, a study might find a link between coffee consumption and improved memory, but the confounding variable could be that coffee drinkers are more likely to have active lifestyles, which also enhance memory. Controlling for confounders through techniques like regression analysis is essential for drawing valid conclusions.

Another common misconception is that **bigger samples always lead to better results.** While larger samples reduce sampling error and improve reliability, they can also amplify systematic bias if the sampling method is flawed. For example, increasing the sample size in a biased survey will not correct the bias; it will only make the biased results more precise. Quality, not just quantity, is crucial in sampling.

The inappropriate application of **statistical tests** is another frequent pitfall. Each test is designed for specific types of data and research questions. For example, using a t-test to compare more than two groups is incorrect; ANOVA is the appropriate test in this case. Similarly, applying parametric tests to non-normally distributed data without transformations or nonparametric alternatives can produce invalid results. Understanding the assumptions underlying statistical tests is critical for proper application.

A widespread issue in modern data analysis is **misusing machine learning algorithms** as if they are interchangeable with traditional statistics. While machine learning and statistics share common roots, they serve different purposes. Statistics focuses on inference and understanding relationships between variables, while machine learning emphasizes prediction and optimization. Applying a machine learning model without understanding the statistical properties of the data can lead to overfitting or misinterpretation of results.

The misuse of **outliers** also warrants attention. Outliers can significantly influence statistical measures, such as the mean or correlation coefficient. For example, a single extreme value in a dataset might inflate or deflate the average, leading to misleading conclusions. However, automatically removing outliers without considering their context can also be problematic. Outliers might represent rare but important phenomena, such as a medical breakthrough or a financial fraud case. Carefully assessing whether outliers are errors, anomalies, or legitimate values is a necessary step in data analysis.

Finally, one of the most harmful pitfalls is the **misrepresentation of findings.** Statistics is often used to support narratives, but selectively reporting results or manipulating data presentation undermines its integrity. For example, presenting only favorable results from a study while ignoring negative or inconclusive findings creates a biased view. Transparency in data collection, analysis, and reporting is essential to maintain trust in statistical conclusions.

Avoiding these misconceptions and pitfalls requires a solid understanding of statistical principles, a skeptical mindset, and a commitment to ethical practices. Whether analyzing data or interpreting results, statisticians and consumers must remain vigilant about the limitations and context of the data.

Chapter 2: Organizing and Visualizing Data

Creating Frequency Distributions

Frequency distributions are a method for organizing data to show how often each value or range of values occurs. They make raw data more readable by summarizing it into categories or intervals, highlighting patterns, and revealing trends. By grouping data into meaningful categories, frequency distributions allow you to understand how data points are spread out and where they concentrate.

To create a frequency distribution, the first step is to collect and organize the raw data. Suppose you have a dataset of exam scores for 50 students. These scores might range from 45 to 95. In its raw form, this data is difficult to interpret because it lacks structure. The goal of a frequency distribution is to group the data into intervals, or bins, and count how many values fall within each interval.

The next step is to determine the range of the data, which is the difference between the highest and lowest values. If the highest score is 95 and the lowest is 45, the range is 95 - 45 = 50. Once the range is known, decide how many intervals to use. The number of intervals depends on the size of the dataset and how detailed you want the distribution to be. A common guideline is to use between 5 and 20 intervals. For this example, let's use 10 intervals.

To calculate the width of each interval, divide the range by the number of intervals. In this case, 50 ÷ 10 = 5, so each interval will span five points. The intervals might look like this: 45-49, 50-54, 55-59, and so on up to 95. It's important to ensure that the intervals are mutually exclusive, meaning no value can belong to more than one interval, and they should cover the entire range of the data.

Once the intervals are defined, count how many data points fall into each interval. This can be done manually by scanning through the dataset or using software tools like Excel or Python. For instance, if three students scored between 45 and 49, the frequency for that interval is 3. Repeat this process for all intervals.

The resulting table is a basic frequency distribution. It typically has two columns: the intervals and their corresponding frequencies. You can enhance it by adding relative frequencies, which express each frequency as a percentage of the total number of observations. For example, if there are 50 students and 3 scored between 45 and 49, the relative frequency for that interval is (3/50) × 100 = 6%.

A cumulative frequency distribution is another variation that shows the running total of frequencies up to each interval. For instance, if the first interval has a frequency of 3, and the second interval has 5, the cumulative frequency for the second interval is 3 + 5 = 8. Cumulative distributions are especially useful for identifying medians or percentiles.

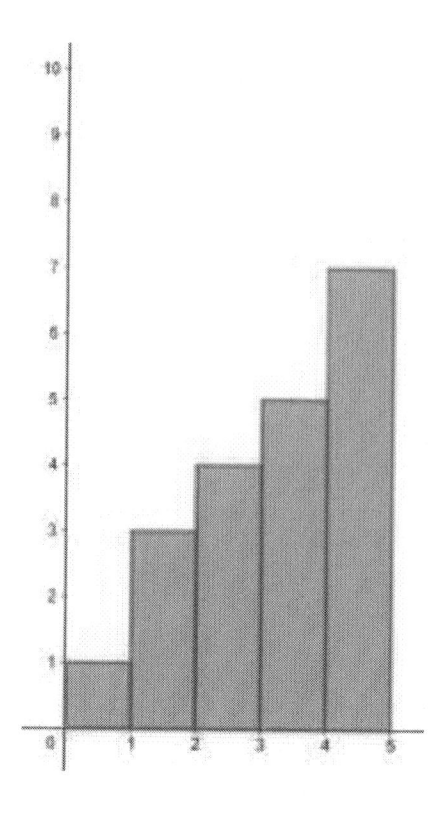

Frequency distributions are not limited to numerical data. Categorical data can also be organized into frequency tables. For example, if you surveyed 100 people about their favorite color and recorded responses like red, blue, green, and yellow, you could create a frequency distribution showing how many people chose each color. Unlike numerical data, categorical data does not require intervals, as each category is distinct.

Visualizing frequency distributions makes them easier to interpret. The most common visualization is a histogram, which uses bars to represent the frequencies of numerical data. Each bar corresponds to an interval, and the height of the bar reflects the frequency. For categorical data, a bar chart serves a similar purpose but represents categories instead of intervals.

One key consideration when creating frequency distributions is the choice of interval width. If the intervals are too wide, important details may be lost, as multiple data points get grouped together. For example, in a dataset of incomes, grouping all values between $30,000 and $70,000 into one interval might obscure meaningful differences. On the other hand, intervals that are too narrow can result in a fragmented and overly complex table. Finding the right balance is essential.

Frequency distributions can also highlight patterns like skewness. A dataset that has a long tail on the right side of its distribution is positively skewed, while one with a long tail on the left is negatively skewed. Recognizing these patterns helps in understanding the overall shape of the data.

Another practical use of frequency distributions is in identifying outliers. Outliers are data points that fall far outside the expected range. For instance, if most exam scores are between 45 and 95, but one student scored 20, this score is an outlier. Including outliers in a frequency distribution can distort the overall picture, so it's important to handle them carefully.

Frequency distributions are a fundamental starting point for further statistical analysis. They provide a structured way to examine the data before calculating measures like the mean, median, or standard deviation. For example, if the frequency distribution of exam scores shows that most students scored in the 60-70 range, the mean score should reflect this concentration. If the mean is significantly different, it may indicate the presence of outliers or errors in the data.

Software tools have simplified the process of creating frequency distributions. Programs like Excel have built-in functions for grouping data and calculating frequencies. Statistical software like R and Python can automate the process and handle large datasets efficiently. For instance, in Python, the `pandas` library provides functions to group data into intervals and generate frequency tables.

Histograms, Bar Charts, and Pie Charts

Visualizations like histograms, bar charts, and pie charts are essential tools for representing data. Each type has specific uses and advantages depending on the nature of the data and the message you want to convey. These visualizations help transform raw data into intuitive, easily understandable formats, making it easier to spot patterns, trends, and relationships.

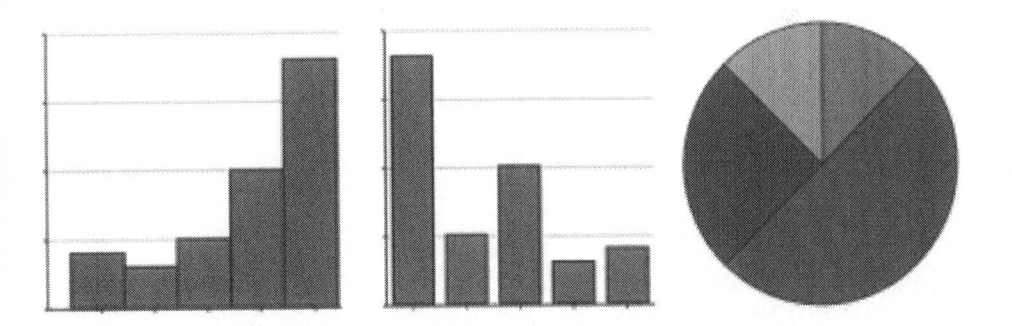

A **histogram** is used to represent the frequency distribution of numerical data. It consists of adjacent bars, where each bar corresponds to an interval (or bin) of data values. The height of the bar reflects the frequency of data points within that interval. For example, in a dataset of students' test scores ranging from 40 to 100, a histogram might show how many students scored between 40-50, 50-60, and so on.

The key feature of a histogram is that the bars are continuous, meaning there are no gaps between them. This reflects the continuous nature of the underlying data. Histograms are particularly useful for identifying the shape of the data distribution, such as whether it is symmetric, skewed, or uniform. For instance, a histogram of heights might show a bell-shaped curve, indicating a normal distribution.

The choice of bin width is critical when creating a histogram. If the bins are too wide, important details may be lost, as the data is overly generalized. Conversely, if the bins are too narrow, the histogram may appear fragmented, making it harder to identify meaningful patterns. For example, when analyzing monthly sales data, using a bin width of $1,000 might clearly show trends, while $100 bins could result in a cluttered, overly detailed chart.

A **bar chart**, unlike a histogram, is used for categorical data. Each bar represents a category, and the height of the bar reflects the frequency or proportion of data points in that category. For instance, in a survey of favorite fruits, a bar chart might show how many people chose apples, bananas, or oranges. Unlike histograms, the bars in a bar chart are separated by gaps to emphasize that the categories are distinct and not part of a continuous scale.

Bar charts are versatile and can be used for absolute frequencies, relative frequencies (percentages), or even comparisons between groups. For example, a side-by-side bar chart could compare the number of males and females in different age groups. They are also useful for displaying rankings, such as the top-selling products in a store or the most common causes of traffic accidents.

When designing a bar chart, it's important to maintain consistent scales and proportions. A misleading bar chart might exaggerate differences by truncating the y-axis or using uneven bar widths. For example, starting the y-axis at 90 instead of 0 could make small differences in frequency appear much larger than they are. Proper labeling and scaling ensure that the chart accurately represents the data.

Pie charts are used to show proportions or percentages within a whole. They represent data as slices of a circle, where each slice corresponds to a category, and the size of the slice reflects the relative proportion of that category. For example, a pie chart might show the market share of different smartphone brands, with each slice representing a brand's percentage of the total market.

Pie charts are best suited for datasets with a small number of categories, as too many slices can make the chart difficult to read. For instance, a pie chart showing four product categories works well, but one with 15 categories becomes cluttered and hard to interpret. Pie charts are often criticized for making precise comparisons difficult, especially when slices are of similar size. In such cases, a bar chart might be a better choice for clarity.

One effective variation of the pie chart is the **donut chart**, which is essentially a pie chart with a hole in the center. Donut charts are often used to display additional information in the middle, such as the total percentage or an overarching category. For example, a donut chart showing the breakdown of customer satisfaction levels might include the total number of survey responses in the center.

Another consideration when using pie charts is ordering the slices. Organizing them from largest to smallest, starting at the 12 o'clock position, makes the chart more readable. Additionally, using contrasting colors helps distinguish the slices, especially when they are close in size.

When deciding between these visualization types, consider the nature of your data and the story you want to tell. Use **histograms** for numerical data to explore distributions, such as test scores, weights, or rainfall amounts. Choose **bar charts** for categorical data or when comparing groups, such as survey responses or product sales. Opt for **pie charts** when illustrating proportions within a whole, like budget allocations or demographic breakdowns.

While these visualizations simplify complex data, they can also mislead if not used carefully. A histogram with improperly chosen bins might hide patterns or exaggerate trends. A bar chart with inconsistent scales can distort comparisons. A pie chart with too many slices can confuse rather than clarify. Always prioritize accuracy and clarity in your visualizations to ensure they effectively communicate the data's meaning.

Technology has made creating these visualizations more accessible. Software like Excel, Tableau, R, and Python offers tools to generate histograms, bar charts, and pie charts with minimal effort. For example, Python's `matplotlib` library allows for precise control over chart design, including customization of labels, colors, and scales. These tools also make it easier to experiment with different chart types and select the one that best represents your data.

Box Plots and Scatterplots for Multivariable Data

Box plots and scatterplots are critical visualization tools for examining relationships and distributions in multivariable data. While both serve distinct purposes, they are complementary in helping you understand patterns, variability, and outliers in datasets. These plots enable analysts to move beyond simple univariate summaries and explore connections between multiple variables.

A **box plot** (also called a box-and-whisker plot) provides a visual summary of the distribution of a dataset. It displays the minimum, first quartile (Q1), median, third quartile (Q3), and maximum values, along with potential outliers. The "box" itself represents the interquartile range (IQR), which is the middle 50% of the data, spanning from Q1 to Q3. The line inside the box marks the median, and the "whiskers" extend from the box to the smallest and largest values within 1.5 times the IQR. Data points beyond this range are plotted individually as outliers.

Box plots are highly effective for comparing distributions across multiple groups. For example, a study comparing test scores among students in different grade levels can use a box plot for each grade. The plot immediately reveals differences in medians, variability, and the presence of outliers. If the median test score for 10th-grade students is higher and their box is narrower, this indicates both higher performance and less variability compared to other grades.

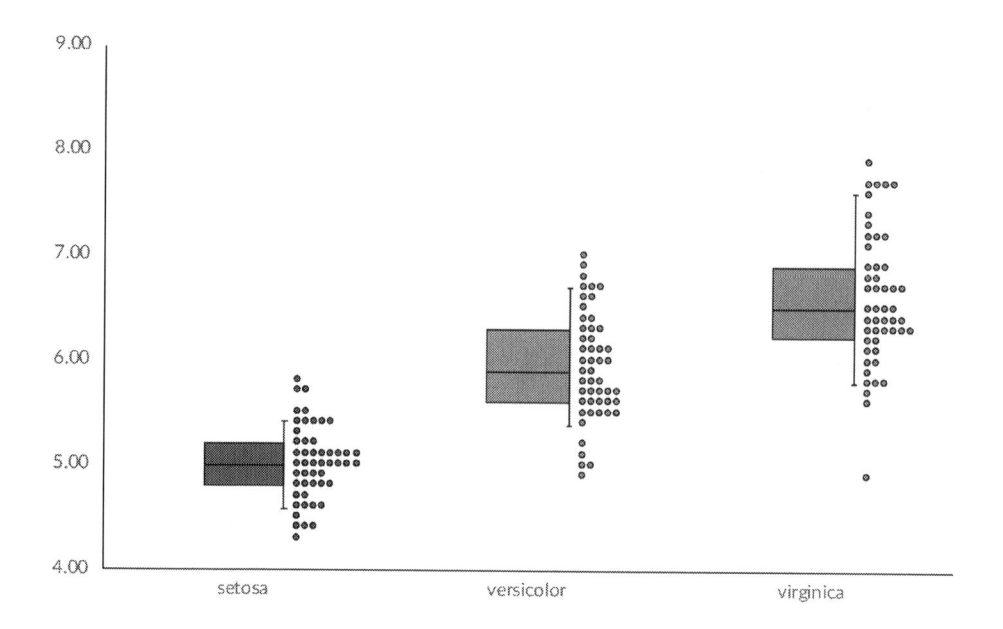

One of the key advantages of a box plot is its ability to highlight **asymmetry and skewness** in a dataset. For instance, if the median line is closer to Q1 than Q3, the distribution is positively skewed. Similarly, whiskers of unequal lengths can indicate asymmetrical spread. These visual cues help analysts understand the overall shape of the data without requiring detailed calculations.

Box plots also excel in identifying **outliers**, which can significantly impact statistical analysis. For example, in a box plot of salaries in a company, an outlier might represent an executive's salary, which is far higher than other employees. Identifying these outliers early can guide decisions on whether to exclude or further investigate them.

Scatterplots are another essential visualization tool, particularly for exploring relationships between two numerical variables. Each point on a scatterplot represents an observation, with its position determined by values on the x-axis and y-axis. For example, in a dataset of house prices and square footage, a scatterplot would show each house as a point, with square footage on the x-axis and price on the y-axis.

The primary purpose of a scatterplot is to reveal relationships, such as trends or correlations, between variables. If the points form an upward-sloping pattern, it indicates a positive relationship—for instance, larger square footage typically correlating with higher house prices. Conversely, a downward slope suggests a negative relationship, such as age of a car and its resale value. When points are scattered without any discernible pattern, it indicates little or no correlation.

Scatterplots are particularly useful for detecting **clusters** or **subgroups** within the data. For instance, in a scatterplot of income versus education level, distinct clusters might emerge for different industries or demographic groups. Recognizing these clusters can guide further analysis or inform segmentation strategies.

Outliers are also easily identifiable in scatterplots, appearing as points that deviate significantly from the main pattern. For example, in a scatterplot of monthly sales versus advertising spend, an outlier might represent a promotional campaign that yielded unusually high sales. Such outliers can indicate errors, rare events, or opportunities for deeper investigation.

Adding a **trendline** to a scatterplot enhances its interpretability by summarizing the overall relationship between variables. A linear trendline, for example, indicates a constant rate of change, while a curved trendline might suggest more complex relationships. Including the equation of the trendline and the R-squared value provides additional information about the strength and direction of the relationship.

Scatterplots can also incorporate **color, size, or shape** to represent additional variables, transforming them into multivariable visualizations. For example, a scatterplot of students' study hours (x-axis) versus test scores (y-axis) could use color to represent different teaching methods or size to indicate class attendance. These enhancements make scatterplots versatile tools for exploring complex datasets.

When comparing box plots and scatterplots, the choice depends on the specific analysis. Box plots are ideal for summarizing distributions and comparing multiple groups, while scatterplots are best for investigating relationships between numerical variables. For instance, a box plot might show that one sales team has consistently higher performance than others, while a scatterplot could reveal that sales performance is strongly correlated with marketing expenditure.

Despite their simplicity, both box plots and scatterplots require careful interpretation. Box plots may obscure certain details, such as the specific number of data points in each quartile, and scatterplots can be misleading if data points overlap heavily. Using transparency or jittering in scatterplots can help mitigate this issue by making overlapping points more distinguishable.

Technology has made creating these plots more accessible. Tools like Python's `matplotlib` and `seaborn` libraries, R's `ggplot2`, and Excel provide robust options for generating box plots and scatterplots. These tools allow for customization, such as adding labels, adjusting axis scales, and incorporating additional variables. For instance, in Python, the `seaborn` library's `boxplot` function can produce polished box plots with options to overlay swarm plots for more granular detail.

In short, box plots and scatterplots provide complementary perspectives on data. Box plots summarize distributions and highlight variability, skewness, and outliers, while scatterplots explore relationships, patterns, and clustering.

Heatmaps and Density Plots: Advanced Visualization Techniques

Heatmaps and density plots are advanced visualization tools that provide detailed insights into data distributions and relationships. Both are particularly effective when dealing with large datasets or when you want to examine patterns that might not be immediately apparent using simpler visualizations like histograms or scatterplots. These methods excel at highlighting concentrations, trends, and anomalies in multivariable data.

A **heatmap** is a grid-based visualization where individual cells are color-coded to represent the magnitude or intensity of a variable. Heatmaps are versatile and can be used for a variety of purposes, from showing correlations between variables to analyzing spatial data. For example, in a dataset of website traffic, a heatmap might display the number of visitors at different times of day, with darker colors indicating higher traffic.

To create a heatmap, you need at least two categorical or continuous variables to define the axes and a third variable to determine the color intensity. Suppose you are analyzing sales data for a retail store. The x-axis of the heatmap could represent days of the week, the y-axis could represent store locations, and the color intensity could indicate total sales. By glancing at the heatmap, you might quickly identify that Saturdays show the highest sales across most locations.

As another example, if one were to generate a heatmap on a pandemic outbreak in the US, it might look like:

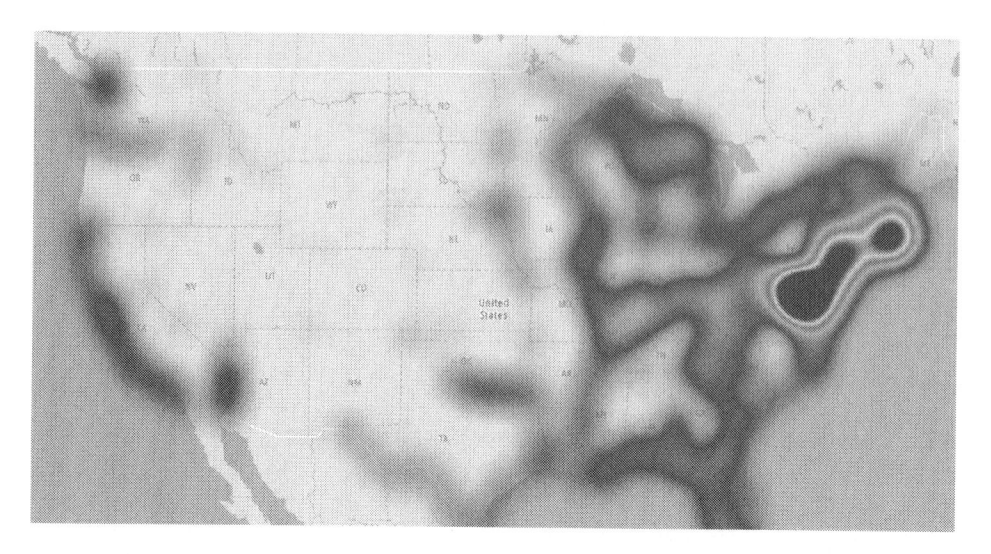

Heatmaps are particularly useful for visualizing **correlation matrices**, which show the relationships between multiple variables. In this context, each cell represents the correlation coefficient between two variables, and the color indicates the strength and direction of the relationship. For example, a positive correlation might be represented by shades of blue, while a negative correlation is shown in shades of red. This visual summary allows you to identify strongly correlated or independent variables at a glance.

One of the strengths of heatmaps is their ability to handle large datasets effectively. For instance, a genomic heatmap might show the expression levels of thousands of genes across different conditions, with each cell representing the expression of one gene in one condition. Clustering algorithms can further enhance the analysis by grouping rows and columns based on similarity, revealing underlying patterns in the data.

However, heatmaps also have limitations. The choice of color scale is critical, as poor design can make differences difficult to interpret. For instance, using too many colors or overly subtle gradients might obscure important details. It's also essential to provide clear labels and legends so that viewers can understand what the colors represent.

Density plots, on the other hand, are used to visualize the distribution of a continuous variable or the joint distribution of two variables. They are an alternative to histograms but provide a smoother representation of the data. Unlike histograms, which group data into discrete bins, density plots use a kernel density estimation (KDE) method to create a continuous curve that reflects the underlying distribution.

For example, a density plot of students' test scores might show a single peak if most scores are clustered around the mean, or multiple peaks if there are distinct groups within the data. This smooth representation makes it easier to identify subtle patterns, such as bimodality, that might be hidden in a histogram.

When dealing with two variables, a **2D density plot** provides a way to visualize their joint distribution. For example, in a dataset of house prices and square footage, a 2D density plot would show where data points are most concentrated, with darker regions indicating higher densities. This is particularly useful when working with large datasets where individual points might overlap heavily in a scatterplot, making patterns hard to discern.

One advantage of density plots is their flexibility. You can adjust the bandwidth, which controls the smoothness of the curve. A smaller bandwidth produces a plot that closely follows the data, revealing fine details, while a larger bandwidth creates a smoother curve that highlights broader trends. For example, in financial data, a small bandwidth might capture daily fluctuations, while a larger bandwidth could show long-term trends.

Density plots also allow for comparisons between groups. For instance, you could overlay density curves for male and female participants in a dataset to compare their height distributions. The overlap or separation between the curves provides a clear visual representation of group differences. Adding color or shading can further enhance the comparison, making it easier to distinguish between groups.

Heatmaps and density plots are particularly effective when used together in multivariable analysis. For instance, a heatmap can summarize correlations between variables, while density plots can reveal the distribution of individual variables or their relationships. In a marketing dataset, a heatmap might show which customer demographics are most correlated with high spending, while density plots reveal the spending patterns within those demographics.

Despite their advanced capabilities, these visualizations require careful interpretation. Heatmaps can oversimplify data if not designed thoughtfully. For example, using overly large grid cells might hide important nuances, while overly small cells can make the chart look cluttered. Similarly, density plots can be misleading if the bandwidth is not appropriately chosen, as this affects the accuracy of the curve.

Creating heatmaps and density plots has become more accessible with modern software tools. Python's `seaborn` library offers user-friendly functions like `heatmap` and `kdeplot` to generate these visualizations. R's `ggplot2` package provides similar capabilities, with options for customization and layering. Excel and Tableau also support heatmaps, though they are less suited for advanced density plotting.

These visualizations are important in fields where data is complex and multidimensional. In biology, heatmaps are used to study gene expression patterns or protein interactions. In urban planning, they analyze traffic flows or population density. Density plots, meanwhile, are popular in economics for studying income distributions or in environmental science for modeling weather patterns.

Combining heatmaps and density plots, you can gain a deeper understanding of your data, uncover hidden patterns, and communicate findings more effectively. These techniques are useful for anyone working with large or complex datasets as a way to transform numbers into clear, actionable visuals.

Chapter 3: Measures of Central Tendency

Mean: Calculation and Interpretation

The mean, often referred to as the average, is one of the most widely used measures of central tendency in statistics. It provides a single value that summarizes a dataset by indicating its central location. While simple in concept, the mean has significant applications in various fields, from finance to healthcare to education, making it an essential statistical tool.

To calculate the mean, you add all the values in a dataset and divide the sum by the number of values. For example, consider a dataset of five test scores: 70, 80, 85, 90, and 95. The mean is calculated as follows:

$$(70 + 80 + 85 + 90 + 95) \div 5 = 420 \div 5 = 84$$

The mean score is 84, which represents the central point of the dataset. This straightforward calculation makes the mean easy to use, especially with smaller datasets. However, for larger datasets, tools like calculators, spreadsheets, or statistical software simplify the process.

One of the mean's strengths is that it uses every value in the dataset. By including all values, the mean accounts for the total distribution of data, making it a comprehensive measure of central tendency. For example, in a dataset of monthly sales figures, the mean reflects the overall sales performance over the period.

However, this inclusivity also makes the mean sensitive to extreme values, or outliers. For instance, consider the dataset 10, 12, 14, 16, and 100. The mean is:

$$(10 + 12 + 14 + 16 + 100) \div 5 = 152 \div 5 = 30.4$$

In this case, the mean (30.4) is much higher than most of the values because the outlier (100) skews the calculation. In such situations, the mean may not accurately represent the dataset's central tendency. This sensitivity to outliers is a limitation that analysts must consider when interpreting the mean.

The mean is particularly useful for datasets with symmetric distributions, where values are evenly spread around the center. In a perfectly normal distribution, the mean coincides with the median and mode, providing a clear representation of the data's center. For example, in a dataset of heights with a bell-shaped distribution, the mean accurately reflects the average height.

In contrast, in skewed distributions, the mean shifts toward the tail of the distribution, potentially misrepresenting the central tendency. For instance, in a dataset of household incomes, where most values cluster around $50,000 but a few exceed $1,000,000, the mean will be much higher than the majority of incomes. In such cases, the median might be a better choice to describe the central value.

The mean is also central to many statistical formulas and methods, including variance and standard deviation. Variance measures the average squared deviation of each value from the mean, while standard deviation is the square root of variance. These metrics depend on the mean as a reference point for understanding data dispersion. For example, in quality control, the mean helps identify whether a process consistently produces products within acceptable limits.

Weighted means are a variation used when certain values in a dataset carry more importance than others. For example, in calculating a student's grade point average (GPA), course grades are weighted by the number of credit hours. If a student earns an A in a 4-credit course and a B in a 3-credit course, the weighted mean is calculated as:

$$[(4 \times 4) + (3 \times 3)] \div (4 + 3) = (16 + 9) \div 7 = 25 \div 7 \approx 3.57$$

This weighted mean accounts for the relative importance of each course, providing a more accurate representation of the student's academic performance.

The arithmetic mean, discussed so far, is just one type of mean. The **geometric mean** is used for datasets involving ratios or percentages. It is calculated by multiplying all the values together and taking the nth root, where n is the number of values. For example, to find the geometric mean of 2, 4, and 8:

$$\text{Geometric mean} = (2 \times 4 \times 8)^{\wedge}(1/3) = 64^{\wedge}(1/3) = 4$$

The geometric mean is particularly useful in finance, where it is used to calculate average growth rates. For instance, if a stock's annual returns over three years are 10%, 20%, and -5%, the geometric mean provides a more accurate measure of performance than the arithmetic mean, as it accounts for compounding effects.

Another variation is the **harmonic mean**, used when dealing with rates or ratios. It is calculated as the reciprocal of the arithmetic mean of reciprocals. For example, in a dataset of speeds (40 km/h, 60 km/h, and 80 km/h), the harmonic mean is:

$$\text{Harmonic mean} = 3 \div [(1/40) + (1/60) + (1/80)] \approx 54.55 \text{ km/h}$$

The harmonic mean is often used in fields like transportation and finance, where rates are a key focus.

Interpreting the mean requires understanding its context and limitations. For example, if a company reports that its employees' average salary is $75,000, this figure might not reflect the typical experience if a few executives earn millions while most employees earn far less. In such cases, supplementary measures like the median or mode provide a fuller picture.

Technology has made calculating and interpreting the mean easier. Software like Excel, R, and Python offer built-in functions to compute the mean for datasets of any size. For example, in Python, the `mean()` function from the `statistics` module can quickly calculate the mean, even for large datasets.

The mean is also fundamental in inferential statistics, where it serves as a key parameter for estimating population characteristics. For example, in hypothesis testing, the sample mean is compared to the population mean to determine whether observed differences are statistically significant. Similarly, confidence intervals use the mean to estimate the range within which the true population mean is likely to fall.

Despite its limitations, the mean remains one of the most commonly used measures of central tendency because of its simplicity, versatility, and mathematical properties.

Median: When to Use It and Why

The median is a measure of central tendency that represents the middle value in a dataset when it is arranged in ascending or descending order. Unlike the mean, which calculates an average, the median directly identifies the central point of the data. This makes it particularly useful in datasets with skewed distributions or outliers, where the mean may be misleading.

To calculate the median, begin by sorting the dataset. If the number of data points is odd, the median is the value at the middle position. For example, in the dataset 10, 20, 30, 40, and 50, the median is 30, as it is the third value in the ordered list. When the number of data points is even, the median is the average of the two middle values. For instance, in the dataset 15, 25, 35, and 45, the median is $(25 + 35) \div 2 = 30$.

The median is particularly useful for datasets with skewed distributions. In a positively skewed dataset, such as household incomes, the mean can be disproportionately affected by a few high-income earners, making it much higher than most individuals' incomes. For example, in a dataset with incomes of $30,000, $35,000, $40,000, $45,000, and $1,000,000, the mean is $230,000, which is not representative of the typical income. The median, in this case, is $40,000, providing a more accurate reflection of the central value.

In negatively skewed datasets, where the tail extends to the left, the same principle applies. For example, consider a dataset of exam scores: 10, 10, 15, 20, and 95. The mean, influenced by the high score of 95, is $(10 + 10 + 15 + 20 + 95) \div 5 = 30$. However, the median is 15, which better represents the central tendency of the majority of scores.

The median's robustness against outliers is one of its key advantages. Outliers can heavily distort the mean, but the median remains unaffected as it depends solely on the order of the values. For example, in a dataset of housing prices—$200,000, $250,000, $300,000, $350,000, and $2,000,000—the median is $300,000, which accurately reflects the typical home price. The mean, on the other hand, would be significantly inflated by the $2,000,000 outlier.

When analyzing ordinal data, the median is often the preferred measure of central tendency because it accounts for the inherent order of the values. For instance, in a customer satisfaction survey with responses like "very dissatisfied," "dissatisfied," "neutral," "satisfied," and "very satisfied," the median identifies the middle response, offering a clear summary of the central tendency without assuming equal intervals between categories.

The median is also effective in comparing distributions across groups. For example, in a study comparing salaries by gender, the median for each group can highlight differences without being skewed by outliers, such as extremely high salaries in executive positions. This provides a more accurate picture of the central tendency for each group.

While the median is robust and insightful, it has limitations. It does not account for the magnitude of values in the dataset beyond their position. For instance, in the dataset 1, 2, 3, 4, and 100, the median is 3, which ignores the significant difference between the outlier (100) and the other values. In such cases, additional measures like the mean or interquartile range (IQR) may provide complementary insights.

The median is particularly relevant in fields where data is naturally skewed. In real estate, the median home price is often reported instead of the mean, as a few high-value properties can distort the average. Similarly, in healthcare, the median waiting time in emergency departments is more informative than the mean, as a few exceptionally long wait times can inflate the average.

The concept of the median extends to more complex statistical analyses. In regression analysis, the median is used in robust regression techniques, such as least absolute deviations (LAD) regression, which minimizes the sum of absolute differences rather than squared differences. This makes LAD regression less sensitive to outliers than ordinary least squares (OLS) regression.

The median is also used in constructing box plots, a common visualization tool in exploratory data analysis. The line inside the box represents the median, while the box spans the interquartile range (IQR), providing a clear picture of the dataset's spread and central tendency. Outliers are plotted individually, further emphasizing the median's stability in the presence of extreme values.

Calculating the median becomes more complex in large datasets, especially when the data is not readily ordered. In such cases, statistical software like Excel, R, or Python simplifies the process. For example, in Python, the `median()` function from the `statistics` module quickly computes the median, even for datasets with thousands of entries. For grouped data, interpolation methods can estimate the median when exact values are unavailable.

The median also has a role in defining percentiles. The median is the 50th percentile, meaning half the data lies below it and half above it. Percentiles extend this concept to other points in the distribution, such as the 25th percentile (Q1) or the 75th percentile (Q3), which are essential in summarizing data variability and identifying central trends.

Despite its strengths, the median should not be used in isolation. Combining it with other measures, such as the mean and standard deviation, provides a fuller understanding of the data. For instance, if the median and mean are close in value, it suggests a symmetric distribution. A large difference between the two, however, indicates skewness.

Mode: Identifying Patterns in Data

The mode is the value that appears most frequently in a dataset. Unlike the mean and median, which summarize central tendencies by calculation or position, the mode directly identifies the most common value or values. This makes it particularly useful for categorical data, though it can also be applied to numerical datasets.

To find the mode, simply count the frequency of each value in the dataset. For example, in a dataset of shoe sizes—6, 7, 7, 8, 8, 8, 9—the mode is 8, as it occurs more often than any other size. If two or more values occur with equal frequency, the dataset is bimodal or multimodal. For instance, in the dataset 4, 4, 5, 5, 6, both 4 and 5 are modes.

The mode is particularly useful for **categorical data**, where other measures of central tendency, like the mean or median, are not applicable. For example, in a survey asking respondents about their favorite color, the mode identifies the most popular choice. If 50 people prefer blue, 40 prefer red, and 30 prefer green, the mode is blue. This information can guide decisions, such as product design or marketing strategies.

In numerical datasets, the mode is often used to identify clusters or common values. For example, in a dataset of house prices, if the mode is $300,000, it indicates that this price point is most common. While the mean and median provide measures of central tendency, the mode highlights specific values that dominate the dataset.

One key strength of the mode is its simplicity. It requires no calculations or assumptions about the distribution of the data. This makes it accessible and intuitive, especially when analyzing small datasets or quick summaries. For example, in a classroom of 30 students where 12 have brown eyes, 10 have blue eyes, and 8 have green eyes, the mode is brown eyes. This simple observation can provide meaningful insights without requiring advanced statistical tools.

However, the mode has limitations. It is less stable than the mean or median, as small changes in the dataset can alter the mode. For instance, in the dataset 2, 2, 3, 4, 5, adding a single value of 3 creates a bimodal distribution (2 and 3). This sensitivity to minor changes can make the mode less reliable for larger or more complex datasets.

In some datasets, the mode may not exist or may not provide useful information. For example, in a dataset of unique values—1, 2, 3, 4, 5—there is no mode, as no value repeats. Similarly, in continuous data with many unique values, such as measurements of height or weight, identifying the mode is impractical. In such cases, grouping the data into intervals (e.g., 60-65 inches, 65-70 inches) and finding the modal class can provide more meaningful insights.

The mode is particularly valuable in **skewed distributions** where the mean and median may not capture the dataset's most common value. For example, in a dataset of hourly wages—$10, $12, $12, $15, $50—the mode is $12, reflecting the most frequent wage. This is especially useful for identifying the most typical or standard value in a dataset with extreme outliers.

In business, the mode is often used to analyze customer preferences or behaviors. For example, a retailer might track the most commonly purchased product size, color, or style to optimize inventory. If size medium consistently appears as the mode for clothing sales, the retailer can adjust production or ordering to match demand.

In **healthcare**, the mode is used to summarize common outcomes or characteristics. For example, in a study of patient symptoms, the mode might identify the most frequently reported symptom, guiding diagnostic or treatment priorities. Similarly, in pharmacology, the mode can highlight the most common dosage prescribed for a medication.

Visualizing the mode can be helpful for interpretation. Bar charts are a common way to display categorical data, with the tallest bar representing the mode. For numerical data, histograms can indicate the mode by showing the interval or bin with the highest frequency. For example, in a histogram of ages, the mode corresponds to the tallest bar, which represents the most common age group.

Technology simplifies the process of finding and interpreting the mode. Software like Excel, R, and Python includes built-in functions to calculate the mode. In Python, the `mode()` function from the `statistics` module quickly identifies the mode for small datasets, while libraries like `pandas` handle larger or more complex datasets.

Despite its simplicity, the mode is often most effective when used alongside other measures of central tendency. While the mode highlights the most frequent value, the mean and median provide context for the overall distribution. For example, in a dataset of monthly sales—$10,000, $10,000, $20,000, $30,000, $1,000,000—the mode ($10,000) identifies the most common sales figure, but the mean and median reveal the impact of the outlier.

Whether analyzing categorical or numerical data, understanding the mode helps pinpoint dominant values, providing insights into the most frequent characteristics or behaviors within a dataset.

Chapter 4: Measures of Dispersion

Range: Quick Insights into Variability

The range is the simplest measure of dispersion in a dataset. It gives a quick sense of the spread by showing the difference between the highest and lowest values. While basic in its calculation, the range provides useful initial insights into how widely data points are distributed.

To calculate the range, subtract the smallest value in the dataset from the largest value. For example, if you have the test scores 45, 55, 65, 75, and 95, the range is 95 - 45 = 50. This value indicates that the test scores span 50 points. The calculation is straightforward, making the range easy to understand and apply in various contexts.

The range provides an immediate snapshot of the dataset's variability, but it has limitations. One of its main drawbacks is its sensitivity to outliers. For instance, consider the dataset 10, 20, 30, 40, and 1000. The range here is 1000 - 10 = 990, but this extreme value of 1000 does not represent the majority of the data points. In such cases, relying solely on the range can give a distorted view of variability. Analysts often combine the range with other measures, like the interquartile range or standard deviation, to get a fuller picture.

Despite its limitations, the range is useful in certain situations, particularly when a quick estimate of variability is sufficient. For example, in manufacturing, the range can be used to monitor product quality. If a machine produces items with weights ranging from 48 to 52 grams, the range is 4 grams. If this range suddenly widens to 10 grams, it might indicate a problem with the machine, prompting further investigation.

The range also has practical applications in fields like weather forecasting and sports analytics. In weather, the range might indicate daily temperature fluctuations. If the highest temperature is 85°F and the lowest is 65°F, the range is 20°F, showing the day's variability. In sports, the range can highlight performance consistency. For example, if a basketball player scores between 15 and 25 points per game, the range is 10 points, suggesting relative consistency compared to a player with a range of 30 points.

Another consideration is the impact of sample size on the range. In smaller datasets, the range is more likely to be influenced by random variations. For example, in a sample of five people's heights, the range might vary significantly depending on the tallest and shortest individuals. In larger datasets, the range tends to stabilize as the sample becomes more representative of the population. However, it remains sensitive to extreme values regardless of sample size.

The range is often used in conjunction with grouped data. For example, in a frequency table showing ages of survey respondents grouped into intervals like 20-29, 30-39, and so on, the range is the difference between the upper boundary of the highest interval and the lower boundary of the lowest interval. If the intervals are 20-29 and 80-89, the range is 89 - 20 = 69. This approach is particularly useful when working with large datasets where individual values are impractical to analyze.

While the range itself is simple, variations like the interquartile range (IQR) add more depth. The IQR focuses on the middle 50% of the data, excluding outliers, providing a more robust measure of variability. For example, in the dataset 10, 12, 14, 16, 100, the range is 90, but the IQR is based on the middle 50% of values (12, 14, and 16), offering a clearer view of the typical spread.

Another variation is the mid-range, which is the average of the maximum and minimum values. For the dataset 45, 55, 65, 75, and 95, the mid-range is (95 + 45) ÷ 2 = 70. While the mid-range doesn't directly measure variability, it provides a sense of central tendency that complements the range.

Variance and Standard Deviation: Digging Deeper

Variance and standard deviation are fundamental measures of dispersion in statistics. They quantify how spread out data points are around the mean, offering insights into the variability within a dataset. While the range provides a simple snapshot of variability, variance and standard deviation offer a more precise and nuanced understanding.

To calculate the variance, start by finding the mean of the dataset. Next, subtract the mean from each data point to find the deviations. Then square each deviation to eliminate negative values, sum them up, and divide by the number of data points (for a population) or by the number of data points minus one (for a sample). This process captures the average squared deviation from the mean.

For example, consider the dataset 4, 6, 8, 10, and 12. The mean is (4 + 6 + 8 + 10 + 12) ÷ 5 = 8. The deviations from the mean are -4, -2, 0, 2, and 4. Squaring these deviations gives 16, 4, 0, 4, and 16. The sum of these squared deviations is 40. For a population, the variance is 40 ÷ 5 = 8. For a sample, it would be 40 ÷ (5 - 1) = 10.

The variance has a limitation: its units are squared, making interpretation less intuitive. For example, if the dataset represents test scores, the variance is in squared points, which is not meaningful in practical terms. To address this, we use the standard deviation, which is simply the square root of the variance. In the example above, the standard deviation for the population is $\sqrt{8} \approx 2.83$, and for the sample, it is $\sqrt{10} \approx 3.16$.

The standard deviation has the same units as the original data, making it easier to interpret. A standard deviation of 2.83 for test scores indicates that, on average, scores deviate from the mean by about 2.83 points. This provides a clearer sense of how much variability exists within the dataset.

Variance and standard deviation are especially useful for comparing datasets. Consider two datasets: A = {50, 52, 54, 56, 58} and B = {40, 50, 60, 70, 80}. Both have the same mean (54), but their variability differs. Dataset A has smaller deviations from the mean, resulting in a lower standard deviation, while dataset B has larger deviations and a higher standard deviation. This distinction is critical in fields like finance, where comparing the volatility of investments is essential.

The standard deviation is also a cornerstone of the normal distribution, a key concept in statistics. In a normal distribution, about 68% of data points lie within one standard deviation of the mean, 95% within two standard deviations, and 99.7% within three standard deviations. For example, in a dataset with a mean of 50 and a standard deviation of 5, approximately 95% of values fall between 40 and 60.

Variance and standard deviation are widely used in real-world applications. In quality control, they measure product consistency. For instance, if a factory produces bottles with a mean volume of 500 mL and a small standard deviation, the volumes are consistent. A larger standard deviation indicates greater variability, potentially leading to customer dissatisfaction.

In finance, standard deviation measures the risk or volatility of investments. A stock with a high standard deviation in its returns is considered more volatile and riskier than one with a low standard deviation. For example, if Stock A has a mean annual return of 8% with a standard deviation of 2%, and Stock B has the same mean return but a standard deviation of 6%, Stock B is more volatile.

Variance is also critical in analysis of variance (ANOVA), a statistical method used to compare means across multiple groups. ANOVA partitions the total variance in a dataset into components, such as variance within groups and variance between groups, to determine whether group means differ significantly.

While variance and standard deviation are robust measures, they have limitations. Both are sensitive to outliers, which can inflate their values. For instance, in the dataset 10, 12, 14, 16, and 100, the mean is 30.4, and the deviations from the mean are large because of the outlier (100). In such cases, robust alternatives like the interquartile range (IQR) or trimmed standard deviation may be more appropriate.

Another consideration is that variance and standard deviation assume equal importance for all deviations, regardless of their magnitude. Squaring the deviations amplifies the impact of larger deviations, making the measures more sensitive to extreme values. This is particularly relevant when analyzing data with skewed distributions.

Technology simplifies the calculation of variance and standard deviation. Software tools like Excel, R, and Python have built-in functions to compute these measures quickly, even for large datasets. In Python, for example, the `statistics` module includes `variance()` and `stdev()` functions for variance and standard deviation, respectively.

Variance and standard deviation are also integral to inferential statistics. In hypothesis testing, they help assess whether observed differences between groups are due to chance. Similarly, in confidence intervals, the standard deviation determines the width of the interval, reflecting the uncertainty of the estimate.

Despite their mathematical complexity, variance and standard deviation are important in understanding and comparing data variability. They provide a detailed view of how data points spread around the mean, offering insights into consistency, volatility, and overall data structure.

Coefficient of Variation: Standardizing Comparisons

The coefficient of variation (CV) is a measure of relative variability that standardizes the comparison of data variability across different datasets or contexts. It expresses the standard deviation as a percentage of the mean, allowing comparisons regardless of the units or magnitude of the data. The CV is particularly useful when comparing datasets with different scales or units, such as heights in centimeters and weights in kilograms, or when the mean and standard deviation vary widely.

To calculate the CV, divide the standard deviation by the mean and multiply the result by 100 to express it as a percentage. For example, in a dataset where the mean is 50 and the standard deviation is 10, the CV is:

$$CV = (10 \div 50) \times 100 = 20\%$$

This value means the standard deviation is 20% of the mean, giving a sense of how much variation exists relative to the average value. Unlike standard deviation, which is in the same units as the data, the CV is unitless, making it ideal for comparisons.

The CV is especially valuable in comparing variability across datasets with different units or magnitudes. For instance, if Dataset A has a mean of 100 and a standard deviation of 5, while Dataset B has a mean of 500 and a standard deviation of 50, the standard deviations suggest Dataset B is more variable. However, calculating the CVs provides a clearer picture:

- CV for Dataset A = $(5 \div 100) \times 100 = 5\%$
- CV for Dataset B = $(50 \div 500) \times 100 = 10\%$

These results show that Dataset B has greater relative variability, despite having a larger standard deviation.

The CV is widely used in finance to compare the risk and return of investments. A lower CV indicates that the investment offers a relatively stable return compared to its mean performance, while a higher CV suggests more risk relative to the expected return. For example, if Stock A has a mean return of 8% and a standard deviation of 4%, and Stock B has a mean return of 15% with a standard deviation of 10%, their CVs are:

- CV for Stock A = (4 ÷ 8) × 100 = 50%
- CV for Stock B = (10 ÷ 15) × 100 ≈ 66.7%

Although Stock B offers higher returns, it also has greater relative risk, as reflected by its higher CV.

In manufacturing, the CV is often used to assess process consistency. For example, if a production line generates parts with a mean diameter of 20 millimeters and a standard deviation of 0.5 millimeters, the CV is:

$$CV = (0.5 \div 20) \times 100 = 2.5\%$$

A low CV like this indicates that the production process is highly consistent. If the CV increases, it signals that the process variability has risen, potentially requiring intervention.

The CV is also helpful in scientific research, particularly in experimental studies where comparisons between variables are necessary. For instance, in biology, the CV can compare variability in physiological measurements like blood pressure or enzyme activity across different groups. If one group has a mean blood pressure of 120 mmHg with a standard deviation of 10 mmHg (CV = 8.33%) and another has a mean of 140 mmHg with a standard deviation of 15 mmHg (CV = 10.71%), the latter group exhibits relatively greater variability, even though the standard deviation is higher in absolute terms.

Despite its usefulness, the CV has limitations. It is undefined when the mean is zero and becomes less meaningful when the mean is close to zero because dividing by a very small number inflates the CV. For example, if a dataset has a mean of 0.1 and a standard deviation of 0.05, the CV is:

$$CV = (0.05 \div 0.1) \times 100 = 50\%$$

While technically correct, this high CV may exaggerate the variability's significance. In such cases, other measures of dispersion, like the standard deviation, may be more appropriate.

The CV is also sensitive to changes in the scale of measurement. For example, if weights measured in kilograms are converted to grams, the mean and standard deviation both increase by a factor of 1,000, but the CV remains the same. This scale invariance is a strength, as it ensures the CV's comparability across different units.

In probability and statistics, the CV is particularly relevant in assessing relative variability in probability distributions. For example, in a Poisson distribution, where the mean equals the variance, the CV decreases as the mean increases. This property highlights the decreasing relative variability in datasets with larger means, such as high-volume production processes.

Calculating and interpreting the CV requires caution when working with skewed or non-normal data. In datasets with significant skewness, the mean may not adequately represent the central tendency, and the CV may misrepresent the relative variability. For example, in income distributions with a long right tail, the mean can be heavily influenced by extreme values, inflating the CV.

The CV is also sensitive to outliers, as these affect both the mean and the standard deviation. For instance, in a dataset of salaries—$30,000, $35,000, $40,000, and $1,000,000—the mean and standard deviation are disproportionately affected by the outlier ($1,000,000), leading to a misleadingly high CV. In such cases, trimming outliers or using robust measures like the median absolute deviation (MAD) can provide a more accurate assessment of variability.

In practice, technology makes calculating the CV straightforward. Statistical software like Excel, R, and Python simplifies the process. In Excel, the CV can be calculated using the formula (STDEV(range) / AVERAGE(range)) * 100. In Python, the CV can be computed using libraries like NumPy, where np.std(data) / np.mean(data) * 100 yields the CV. These tools are particularly useful for large datasets or complex analyses.

The CV's versatility extends to comparing datasets in fields as diverse as medicine, economics, and engineering. For example, in clinical trials, the CV helps compare the efficacy of different treatments relative to their variability. In economics, it evaluates income inequality by measuring the dispersion of wages or wealth within populations. In engineering, the CV assesses variability in material properties like tensile strength or electrical conductivity.

Percentiles and Interquartile Range

Percentiles and the interquartile range (IQR) are measures of dispersion that describe how data is distributed across a range. They help identify patterns, variability, and outliers by focusing on relative positions within the dataset. These tools are particularly useful when analyzing skewed data or comparing groups.

Percentiles divide a dataset into 100 equal parts, with each percentile representing a specific rank or position. For example, the 25th percentile (P25) is the value below which 25% of the data falls, while the 90th percentile (P90) indicates that 90% of the data is below that value. Percentiles are often used to interpret individual values in the context of the overall dataset. For instance, if a student's test score is at the 80th percentile, they performed better than 80% of their peers.

To calculate percentiles, the dataset must be ordered from smallest to largest. The rank of the percentile is determined using the formula:

$$P = (n \times r) \div 100$$

Here, P is the position in the dataset, n is the number of data points, and r is the desired percentile. If the calculated position is an integer, the value at that position is the percentile. If it's not, the percentile is interpolated between the two closest values.

For example, in a dataset of 10 values—5, 8, 12, 15, 20, 25, 30, 35, 40, and 50—the 25th percentile corresponds to position (10 × 25) ÷ 100 = 2.5. Interpolation between the second value (8) and the third value (12) gives P25 = 10. Similarly, the 90th percentile corresponds to position (10 × 90) ÷ 100 = 9, so P90 is 40.

Percentiles are particularly useful in standardized testing and performance evaluations. For instance, in college admissions, percentiles rank applicants based on test scores, helping schools understand how a candidate compares to others. Similarly, in health, percentiles are used to track child growth, such as height and weight percentiles for age groups.

The interquartile range (IQR) is a related measure that focuses on the middle 50% of the data. It is calculated as the difference between the third quartile (Q3, or the 75th percentile) and the first quartile (Q1, or the 25th percentile):

$$IQR = Q3 - Q1$$

The IQR provides a robust measure of variability, as it excludes the extreme values in the tails of the dataset. For example, consider the dataset 10, 12, 14, 16, 18, 20, 22, 24, and 26. Here, Q1 is the 25th percentile (14), and Q3 is the 75th percentile (22). The IQR is 22 - 14 = 8, indicating the range of the central half of the data.

Because the IQR focuses on the middle portion of the data, it is less affected by outliers than the range or standard deviation. For example, in the dataset 10, 12, 14, 16, 18, 20, 22, 24, and 1000, the range is 1000 - 10 = 990, heavily influenced by the outlier (1000). However, the IQR remains 22 - 14 = 8, providing a more stable measure of variability.

The IQR is widely used to identify outliers. Data points are considered potential outliers if they fall more than 1.5 times the IQR below Q1 or above Q3. For example, if the IQR is 8, the lower boundary is Q1 - (1.5 × IQR) = 14 - 12 = 2, and the upper boundary is Q3 + (1.5 × IQR) = 22 + 12 = 34. Any values below 2 or above 34 are potential outliers. In the dataset 10, 12, 14, 16, 18, 20, 22, 24, and 1000, the value 1000 is an outlier because it exceeds the upper boundary.

The IQR is commonly visualized using a box plot, where the box represents the IQR, the line inside the box marks the median, and whiskers extend to the smallest and largest non-outlier values. Outliers are plotted as individual points outside the whiskers. This visualization provides a concise summary of the data distribution, highlighting the central tendency, variability, and potential anomalies.

Percentiles and the IQR are particularly useful in skewed distributions. For example, in income data, the mean is often inflated by high earners, while the IQR accurately captures the spread of typical incomes. Similarly, in real estate, the IQR highlights the range of house prices in the middle market, excluding luxury and distressed properties.

These measures also aid in comparing distributions across groups. For instance, in a study comparing test scores between two schools, the IQR can reveal differences in variability, while the percentiles show how students in each school rank relative to each other. If one school has a narrower IQR, it indicates more consistent performance.

While percentiles and the IQR are robust and informative, they have limitations. Percentiles are affected by sample size, as smaller datasets may lead to less precise percentile calculations. Interpolation methods help mitigate this issue but may still introduce approximation errors. Additionally, the IQR, while resistant to outliers, provides no information about the tails of the distribution.

Modern tools simplify the calculation of percentiles and the IQR. Software like Excel, R, and Python automates these processes. In Python, the `numpy` library includes a `percentile()` function, and the `iqr()` function in the `scipy.stats` module calculates the IQR directly. These tools handle large datasets efficiently, making advanced statistical analysis more accessible.

Percentiles and the IQR are versatile measures of dispersion that provide detailed insights into data distribution. They emphasize relative positions and focus on the central range, making them ideal for identifying variability and outliers, especially in skewed or complex datasets.

Chapter 5: Probability Basics

Definitions: Experimental vs. Theoretical Probability

Probability quantifies the likelihood of an event occurring, expressed as a value between 0 and 1. A probability of 0 means the event will not happen, while a probability of 1 means it will certainly happen. Understanding probability is essential in statistics, where it is used to model uncertainty and predict outcomes. Two fundamental approaches to probability are **experimental probability** and **theoretical probability**. Each has distinct methods and applications.

Theoretical probability is based on reasoning and assumes all outcomes are equally likely. It uses a formula:

Probability of an event = (Number of favorable outcomes) ÷ (Total number of possible outcomes)

For example, when rolling a fair six-sided die, each face (1, 2, 3, 4, 5, 6) has an equal chance of appearing. To find the probability of rolling a 4, count the favorable outcomes (1) and divide by the total outcomes (6). The probability is 1 ÷ 6 ≈ 0.167, or 16.7%.

Theoretical probability relies on idealized scenarios, making it most useful when the system is well-defined and controlled. Examples include card games, coin tosses, or rolling dice. For instance, the probability of drawing a red card from a standard deck is 26 ÷ 52 = 0.5, or 50%, assuming the deck is well-shuffled and complete.

Experimental probability, on the other hand, is determined through observation and experimentation. It calculates probability based on actual results from trials. The formula is:

Probability of an event = (Number of times the event occurs) ÷ (Total number of trials)

For example, if you roll a die 100 times and observe that the number 4 appears 18 times, the experimental probability of rolling a 4 is 18 ÷ 100 = 0.18, or 18%. Unlike theoretical probability, experimental probability may not perfectly match expected values due to random variation and sample size limitations.

Experimental probability becomes more accurate as the number of trials increases. This concept, known as the **law of large numbers**, states that as the number of trials grows, the experimental probability approaches the theoretical probability. For instance, if you flip a coin 10 times, you might get heads 7 times (70%), but flipping it 1,000 times should yield closer to 50% heads.

Comparing experimental and theoretical probability highlights their respective strengths. Theoretical probability is precise and relies on logic, making it ideal for situations where all outcomes are well-defined and equally likely. However, it may not account for real-world complexities, like biased dice or human error. Experimental probability, while less exact for small samples, reflects actual conditions and can capture irregularities, such as manufacturing defects or environmental influences.

Consider a practical example: the probability of a light bulb failing within a year. The theoretical probability might assume perfect manufacturing and calculate failure rates based on ideal conditions. Experimental probability, by contrast, would involve testing a batch of light bulbs under real-world conditions and recording how many fail. The experimental result may reveal deviations from the theoretical model, providing a more accurate reflection of actual performance.

Key Differences Between Theoretical and Experimental Probability

One significant difference is that theoretical probability requires no physical trials. Instead, it is derived from mathematical models. For instance, in a lottery where players pick six numbers from a set of 49, theoretical probability calculates the likelihood of winning as 1 ÷ (49 choose 6), without conducting any actual lottery draws.

Experimental probability, in contrast, depends entirely on trials and observations. For example, if you study traffic patterns at an intersection, the probability of a red light lasting more than 30 seconds must be determined by timing actual light cycles. This real-world dependency makes experimental probability more context-specific.

Another distinction is that theoretical probability assumes equal likelihood of outcomes, which is not always true in practice. For example, theoretical models assume a coin is fair, with a 50% chance of heads or tails. However, in reality, factors like weight distribution or flipping technique can create a slight bias, which experimental probability can detect.

Applications of Theoretical Probability

Theoretical probability is foundational in games of chance, cryptography, and statistical modeling. In card games, players use theoretical probability to calculate the likelihood of drawing specific hands. For instance, the probability of being dealt a full house in poker is based on the number of possible combinations.

In cryptography, theoretical probability assesses the strength of encryption methods. By analyzing possible combinations of keys, cryptographers calculate the probability of successfully breaking an encryption using brute force. This helps evaluate security systems and guide improvements.

Applications of Experimental Probability

Experimental probability is common in scientific research, engineering, and quality control. In scientific experiments, researchers collect data through repeated trials to estimate probabilities. For example, a drug trial might calculate the probability of side effects occurring in patients by testing the drug on a sample population.

In engineering, experimental probability helps assess product reliability. For example, if 1,000 car engines are tested and 5 fail, the experimental probability of failure is 5 ÷ 1,000 = 0.005, or 0.5%. This information guides design improvements and risk assessments.

In marketing, companies use experimental probability to predict customer behavior. For instance, an online retailer might calculate the probability of a customer clicking on an advertisement by observing click rates over thousands of impressions. These probabilities inform targeting strategies and ad placement.

Limitations and Challenges

Both theoretical and experimental probability have limitations. Theoretical probability assumes perfect conditions, which are rarely present in real-world scenarios. For instance, calculating the probability of rain theoretically would require knowledge of every atmospheric variable, which is impractical.

Experimental probability, while grounded in reality, is limited by sample size and potential bias. A small sample may not accurately represent the population, leading to unreliable results. For example, testing 10 coins for fairness may yield 7 heads and 3 tails, suggesting a 70% probability of heads. This result is likely due to random variation rather than a genuine bias.

Combining Theoretical and Experimental Probability

In practice, combining both approaches often yields the best results. For example, a manufacturer may use theoretical models to predict failure rates under ideal conditions and experimental data to validate those predictions in real-world settings. Comparing the two can reveal discrepancies and guide adjustments.

Rules of Probability: Addition and Multiplication

Probability is governed by fundamental rules that determine how the likelihood of events is calculated. The **addition rule** and the **multiplication rule** are two of the most important principles. These rules help calculate probabilities for single events, combined events, and sequences of events, allowing for a structured approach to solving complex problems.

The Addition Rule

The addition rule calculates the probability of one event or another occurring. The rule differs based on whether the events are **mutually exclusive** or **not mutually exclusive**.

For **mutually exclusive events**, where two events cannot occur simultaneously, the probability of either event occurring is the sum of their individual probabilities. Mathematically:

$$P(A \text{ or } B) = P(A) + P(B)$$

For example, consider rolling a six-sided die. The probability of rolling a 2 (P(A)) is 1/6, and the probability of rolling a 5 (P(B)) is also 1/6. Since these events are mutually exclusive (you cannot roll both a 2 and a 5 in the same roll), the probability of rolling a 2 or a 5 is:

$$P(A \text{ or } B) = 1/6 + 1/6 = 2/6 = 1/3$$

For **not mutually exclusive events**, where two events can occur at the same time, the formula adjusts to account for overlap:

$$P(A \text{ or } B) = P(A) + P(B) - P(A \text{ and } B)$$

This adjustment avoids double-counting the overlap. For example, in a card deck, the probability of drawing a heart (P(A)) is 13/52, and the probability of drawing a face card (P(B)) is 12/52. However, some face cards are hearts (3 out of 52 cards), so we subtract the overlap:

$$P(A \text{ or } B) = 13/52 + 12/52 - 3/52 = 22/52 \approx 0.423$$

The addition rule applies to **discrete outcomes** and simplifies calculations for probabilities involving "or" statements. By accounting for whether events are mutually exclusive or not, it ensures accuracy across a range of scenarios.

The Multiplication Rule

The multiplication rule determines the probability of two events occurring together, expressed as **P(A and B)**. The formula depends on whether the events are **independent** or **dependent**.

For **independent events**, where one event does not influence the other, the rule is:

$$P(A \text{ and } B) = P(A) \times P(B)$$

For instance, consider flipping a coin and rolling a die. The probability of getting heads on the coin (P(A)) is 1/2, and the probability of rolling a 4 on the die (P(B)) is 1/6. Since the outcome of the coin flip does not affect the die roll, these events are independent. The probability of getting heads and rolling a 4 is:

$$P(A \text{ and } B) = 1/2 \times 1/6 = 1/12 \approx 0.083$$

For **dependent events**, where the outcome of one event influences the probability of the other, the rule incorporates conditional probability:

$$P(A \text{ and } B) = P(A) \times P(B|A)$$

Here, **P(B|A)** represents the probability of event B occurring given that event A has already occurred. For example, suppose a bag contains 5 red balls and 3 blue balls. If you draw one ball without replacement, the events are dependent. The probability of drawing a red ball first (P(A)) is 5/8. If this happens, only 7 balls remain, and the probability of drawing another red ball (P(B|A)) becomes 4/7. The probability of drawing two red balls is:

$$P(A \text{ and } B) = P(A) \times P(B|A) = 5/8 \times 4/7 = 20/56 = 5/14 \approx 0.357$$

The multiplication rule is essential for calculating probabilities in sequences or combinations of events, whether they are independent or dependent.

Combining the Rules

In many scenarios, the addition and multiplication rules work together to calculate probabilities for complex problems. For example, consider the problem of finding the probability of drawing at least one ace in two draws from a standard deck without replacement. This involves both the addition and multiplication rules.

First, calculate the probability of drawing an ace on the first draw (P(A)):

$$P(A) = 4/52 = 1/13$$

If an ace is drawn, the probability of drawing another ace (P(B|A)) becomes:

$$P(B|A) = 3/51 = 1/17$$

Using the multiplication rule, the probability of drawing two aces is:

$$P(A \text{ and } B) = P(A) \times P(B|A) = 1/13 \times 1/17 \approx 0.0045$$

Now consider the probability of drawing at least one ace in two draws. This requires using the complement rule, which states that the probability of at least one ace is:

$$P(\text{at least one ace}) = 1 - P(\text{no aces})$$

The probability of not drawing an ace on the first draw is:

$$P(\text{not } A) = 48/52 = 12/13$$

The probability of not drawing an ace on the second draw, given that the first card was not an ace, is:

$$P(\text{not } B|\text{not } A) = 47/51$$

Using the multiplication rule:

$$P(\text{no aces}) = P(\text{not A}) \times P(\text{not B}|\text{not A}) = 12/13 \times 47/51 \approx 0.846$$

Thus, the probability of at least one ace is:

$$P(\text{at least one ace}) = 1 - 0.846 = 0.154$$

This example demonstrates how the addition and multiplication rules, along with complementary reasoning, can solve layered probability problems.

Applications of the Rules

The addition and multiplication rules are widely used in real-world contexts. In healthcare, the addition rule calculates the probability of patients having either one condition or another, accounting for overlaps like co-occurring diseases. In reliability engineering, the multiplication rule assesses the likelihood of systems functioning together, such as components in a machine.

In genetics, these rules predict the probability of inheriting certain traits. For example, if a child's probability of inheriting a dominant gene from one parent is 1/2 and from the other parent is also 1/2, the multiplication rule calculates the likelihood of inheriting the gene from both:

$$P(A \text{ and } B) = 1/2 \times 1/2 = 1/4$$

In marketing, the rules estimate campaign success. If a marketing team predicts a 30% chance of customers opening an email (P(A)) and a 10% chance of clicking a link given they opened it (P(B|A)), the multiplication rule calculates the probability of both events:

$$P(A \text{ and } B) = 0.3 \times 0.1 = 0.03, \text{ or } 3\%$$

Limitations and Challenges

The addition and multiplication rules require accurate assumptions about mutual exclusivity and independence. Misjudging these conditions can lead to incorrect probabilities. For example, assuming events are independent when they are not will produce inaccurate results. Additionally, for large datasets or complex scenarios, manually applying these rules becomes cumbersome, requiring computational tools.

Independent and Dependent Events

Understanding the distinction between **independent** and **dependent events** is critical in probability theory. These concepts influence how probabilities are calculated for combined events, whether they occur in sequence or simultaneously. Correctly identifying event relationships ensures accurate application of probability rules.

Independent Events

Independent events are those whose outcomes do not affect each other. The probability of one event occurring is not influenced by whether another event has happened. Mathematically, two events A and B are independent if:

$$P(A \text{ and } B) = P(A) \times P(B)$$

For example, consider flipping a coin and rolling a six-sided die. The result of the coin flip (heads or tails) does not influence the outcome of the die roll (1 through 6). If the probability of heads is 1/2 and the probability of rolling a 4 is 1/6, the probability of getting heads and rolling a 4 is:

$$P(A \text{ and } B) = P(A) \times P(B) = 1/2 \times 1/6 = 1/12 \approx 0.083$$

The key feature of independent events is that their joint probability is simply the product of their individual probabilities.

Real-World Examples of Independence

Independent events are common in controlled or random scenarios. For example:

1. **Card Games:** If a card is drawn, recorded, and replaced back into the deck before drawing again, the two draws are independent. The probability of drawing an ace on the first draw is 4/52, and the probability on the second draw remains 4/52 because the deck is restored to its original state.

2. **Manufacturing:** In quality control, the failure of one product on an assembly line is often independent of another's failure, assuming no systemic issues.

3. **Weather Events:** The probability of rain today may be independent of rain a week from now, assuming no overlapping weather systems.

Dependent Events

Dependent events occur when the outcome of one event influences the probability of another. In such cases, the probability of the second event changes depending on the outcome of the first. Mathematically, for dependent events A and B:

$$P(A \text{ and } B) = P(A) \times P(B|A)$$

Here, $P(B|A)$ represents the conditional probability of event B occurring given that event A has already occurred.

For example, consider drawing two cards from a standard deck without replacement. If the first card drawn is an ace ($P(A) = 4/52$), there are now 51 cards left, including 3 aces. The probability of drawing another ace ($P(B|A)$) is:

$$P(B|A) = 3/51$$

The joint probability of drawing two aces is:

$$P(A \text{ and } B) = P(A) \times P(B|A) = (4/52) \times (3/51) = 12/2652 \approx 0.0045, \text{ or } 0.45\%$$

Real-World Examples of Dependence

Dependent events are common when outcomes are interconnected or when sampling occurs without replacement. Examples include:

1. **Epidemiology:** The probability of a person contracting an illness may depend on their exposure to another infected individual.

2. **Finance:** The likelihood of a stock market decline may depend on prior events, such as economic reports or geopolitical tensions.

3. **Genetics:** The probability of inheriting a genetic trait depends on the combination of alleles inherited from each parent.

4. **Resource Allocation:** In a raffle, the probability of winning decreases for others after each winner is drawn, as the pool of remaining participants shrinks.

Identifying Independent vs. Dependent Events

Determining whether events are independent or dependent requires examining their relationship. Consider the following scenarios:

1. **Scenario 1:** A company surveys employees about job satisfaction and attendance. If the probability of satisfaction does not change based on attendance, the events are independent. If employees who attend regularly are more satisfied, the events are dependent.

2. **Scenario 2:** A factory produces widgets, and 10% are defective. If you select one widget and then another without replacement, the events are dependent because the first selection changes the pool of remaining widgets.

3. **Scenario 3:** Tossing two coins is independent, as the result of one toss does not influence the other.

Calculations with Dependent Events

Dependent events require conditional probabilities to calculate joint probabilities. For example, consider a jar with 3 red balls and 2 blue balls. If two balls are drawn without replacement, the probabilities change dynamically:

1. Probability of drawing a red ball first ($P(A)$) is:

$$P(A) = 3/5$$

2. After one red ball is removed, only 4 balls remain. The probability of drawing a blue ball next ($P(B|A)$) is:

$$P(B|A) = 2/4 = 1/2$$

3. The probability of drawing a red ball and then a blue ball is:

$$P(A \text{ and } B) = P(A) \times P(B|A) = (3/5) \times (1/2) = 3/10 = 0.3, \text{ or } 30\%$$

These conditional adjustments are necessary whenever events are dependent.

Common Errors in Identifying Event Relationships

A frequent mistake is assuming events are independent when they are not. For instance, in a lottery where numbers are drawn without replacement, many people mistakenly calculate probabilities as if numbers are replaced. This error leads to overestimated probabilities.

Another misconception is failing to recognize conditional relationships. For example, if a person draws a red marble from a bag and does not replace it, the probabilities for subsequent draws are often calculated as if the total remains constant, which is incorrect.

Applications in Real-World Scenarios

1. **Medical Testing:** In diagnostic tests, the probability of a positive test result depends on the presence of the condition (dependent events). Sensitivity and specificity metrics are examples of conditional probabilities in this context.

2. **Supply Chain:** The probability of a delay in one segment of a supply chain may depend on delays in preceding segments, reflecting dependence.

3. **Sports:** In basketball, the probability of a player scoring a second free throw may depend on whether they scored the first, influenced by confidence or fatigue.

4. **Risk Assessment:** In insurance, the probability of a car accident may depend on factors such as weather, road conditions, or driver history, illustrating dependence.

Simulating Independent and Dependent Events

Simulations help visualize and understand independent and dependent events. For example, in Python, you could simulate rolling two dice (independent events) and compare this with drawing cards without replacement (dependent events). These exercises reinforce the differences in probability calculations.

Why This Distinction Matters

The distinction between independent and dependent events is essential for applying probability rules correctly. Independent events use straightforward multiplication, while dependent events require adjustments based on conditional probabilities. Misidentifying event relationships leads to incorrect probabilities and flawed analyses.

Conditional Probability and Bayes' Theorem

Conditional probability quantifies the likelihood of an event occurring given that another event has already happened. It is a foundational concept in probability theory, essential for understanding how events relate to one another. Bayes' Theorem builds on conditional probability, providing a structured way to revise probabilities in light of new evidence.

Conditional Probability: Definition and Formula

The conditional probability of an event B occurring given that event A has occurred is denoted as P(B|A). The formula is:

$$P(B|A) = P(A \text{ and } B) \div P(A), \text{ provided } P(A) > 0$$

This formula calculates the probability of B within the subset of outcomes where A has already occurred. For example, consider a deck of 52 playing cards. If one card is drawn and it's known to be a heart (A), the conditional probability of it being the Ace of Hearts (B) is:

$$P(B|A) = P(A \text{ and } B) \div P(A)$$
$$P(A \text{ and } B) = \text{Probability of Ace of Hearts} = 1/52$$
$$P(A) = \text{Probability of any heart} = 13/52$$

$$P(B|A) = (1/52) \div (13/52) = 1/13$$

This shows that given the first condition (the card is a heart), the probability of the second condition (it's the Ace of Hearts) adjusts accordingly.

Applications of Conditional Probability

Conditional probability is widely applicable in real-world scenarios. For example:

1. **Healthcare:** In diagnostic testing, the probability of having a disease given a positive test result is a conditional probability. This depends on the test's sensitivity (true positive rate), specificity (true negative rate), and the disease's prevalence in the population.

2. **Sports:** The probability of a team winning a game given that they are leading at halftime reflects conditional relationships. Historical data on halftime leads and game outcomes can calculate this.

3. **Weather Forecasting:** The likelihood of rain given cloudy conditions uses conditional probabilities, as cloud cover influences precipitation likelihood.

Bayes' Theorem: Revising Probabilities

Bayes' Theorem builds on conditional probability, enabling the calculation of P(A|B) (the probability of A given B) using known probabilities like P(B|A) and P(A). The formula is:

$$P(A|B) = [P(B|A) \times P(A)] \div P(B)$$

This formula is particularly useful for updating probabilities as new information becomes available. For example, in medical diagnosis:

- Let A represent having a disease.
- Let B represent a positive test result.

P(A|B) calculates the probability of having the disease given the positive result, considering:

1. P(A): The prior probability of having the disease (prevalence).
2. P(B|A): The likelihood of testing positive if the person has the disease (sensitivity).
3. P(B): The overall probability of a positive test result, considering all possible causes.

Example: Medical Diagnosis

Suppose a disease affects 1% of the population (P(A) = 0.01). A test has a 95% sensitivity (P(B|A) = 0.95) and a 90% specificity, meaning a 10% false positive rate. Calculate the probability of having the disease given a positive test result (P(A|B)).

First, calculate P(B), the overall probability of a positive test result:

$$P(B) = P(B|A) \times P(A) + P(B|\text{not } A) \times P(\text{not } A)$$
$$P(B) = (0.95 \times 0.01) + (0.10 \times 0.99)$$
$$P(B) = 0.0095 + 0.099 = 0.1085$$

Now use Bayes' Theorem:

$$P(A|B) = [P(B|A) \times P(A)] \div P(B)$$
$$P(A|B) = (0.95 \times 0.01) \div 0.1085 \approx 0.0876, \text{ or } 8.76\%$$

This result highlights an important concept: even with a positive test result, the probability of having the disease is relatively low because the disease is rare.

Intuition Behind Bayes' Theorem

Bayes' Theorem combines prior knowledge (P(A)) with new evidence (P(B|A)) to produce an updated probability (P(A|B)). In the example above, the rarity of the disease (low prior probability) heavily influences the final result. This relationship between prior and conditional probabilities ensures that new evidence is interpreted in context.

Real-World Applications of Bayes' Theorem

1. **Spam Filtering:** Email filters use Bayes' Theorem to classify messages. For example, the probability of an email being spam (A) given specific words in the subject line (B) is calculated by combining prior probabilities (spam frequency) with word likelihoods in spam emails.

2. **Medical Research:** In clinical trials, Bayes' Theorem helps evaluate the effectiveness of treatments by combining prior knowledge about success rates with observed trial outcomes.

3. **Finance:** Investors use Bayes' Theorem to update probabilities of market trends based on new economic data or market indicators.

4. **Machine Learning:** Bayesian models in artificial intelligence rely on Bayes' Theorem for tasks like image recognition, where prior probabilities of object categories are updated with pixel data.

Bayes' Theorem for Multiple Events

Bayes' Theorem extends to multiple events, allowing complex scenarios to be analyzed. For example, in genetics, calculating the probability of inheriting a specific trait given multiple genetic markers involves conditional probabilities across several events. Similarly, in weather forecasting, the likelihood of a hurricane given wind speed, temperature, and pressure data requires Bayesian calculations.

Challenges and Misconceptions

While powerful, conditional probability and Bayes' Theorem are prone to misinterpretation. Common challenges include:

1. **Ignoring Base Rates:** The base rate, or prior probability, is often overlooked. For example, if a test has high sensitivity, people may overestimate its accuracy without considering the prevalence of the condition.

2. **Misjudging Independence:** Conditional probabilities assume specific dependencies. Incorrectly assuming independence between events can lead to flawed calculations.

3. **Complex Calculations:** Real-world problems often involve multiple overlapping conditions, making manual Bayesian calculations impractical. However, modern software tools simplify these analyses.

Tools for Conditional Probability and Bayesian Analysis

Statistical software like R, Python, and specialized Bayesian tools such as JAGS and Stan facilitate complex calculations. Python libraries like `pandas` and `numpy` handle conditional probabilities, while `scipy.stats` supports Bayesian analysis. For example, in Python, you can simulate conditional probabilities with `numpy.random` or apply Bayesian models with the `pymc3` library.

Chapter 6: Probability Distributions

Discrete vs. Continuous Distributions

Probability distributions describe how values of a random variable are distributed. They serve as mathematical models for understanding randomness and variability in data. Random variables are classified into two main types: discrete and continuous. The distinction between these types defines the nature of their respective probability distributions.

Discrete Distributions

Discrete random variables take on a countable number of distinct values. These values are often whole numbers, such as the number of cars in a parking lot, the outcome of rolling a die, or the number of defective items in a batch. A **discrete probability distribution** assigns probabilities to each possible value of the random variable.

The probabilities of a discrete random variable must satisfy two conditions:

1. The probability of each value must be between 0 and 1.
2. The sum of the probabilities for all possible values must equal 1.

For example, consider the roll of a fair six-sided die. The random variable X represents the result of the roll, and its possible values are 1, 2, 3, 4, 5, and 6. The probability distribution is:

$$P(X = 1) = 1/6$$
$$P(X = 2) = 1/6$$
$$...$$
$$P(X = 6) = 1/6$$

The sum of these probabilities is 1, satisfying the conditions of a valid distribution.

Discrete distributions are commonly visualized using probability mass functions (PMFs), which display the probability of each possible value. In the die example, the PMF would show six bars, each representing a probability of 1/6.

Several well-known discrete distributions include:

- **Binomial Distribution**: Models the number of successes in a fixed number of trials, such as flipping a coin multiple times.
- **Poisson Distribution**: Models the count of events occurring in a fixed interval of time or space, like the number of emails received per hour.

Continuous Distributions

Continuous random variables can take on an infinite number of possible values within a given range. Examples include the height of individuals, the time it takes to complete a task, or the temperature on a particular day. A **continuous probability distribution** describes the likelihood of the variable falling within certain intervals.

Unlike discrete distributions, the probability of a continuous random variable taking on an exact value is always zero. Instead, probabilities are defined over intervals. For instance, in a temperature distribution, we might calculate the probability that the temperature lies between 20°C and 25°C.

The total area under the curve of a continuous probability distribution equals 1, ensuring that all probabilities within the range add up correctly. The **probability density function** (PDF) describes the shape of the distribution, with higher regions indicating greater likelihood. For example, a normal distribution's PDF is a bell-shaped curve, symmetric around the mean.

Key continuous distributions include:

- **Normal Distribution**: Commonly used to model phenomena like test scores, heights, and measurement errors.
- **Exponential Distribution**: Models the time between events, such as the time until the next customer arrives at a service counter.
- **Uniform Distribution**: Assumes all intervals of equal length within the range have the same probability.

Differences Between Discrete and Continuous Distributions

1. **Number of Values**: Discrete distributions deal with countable outcomes, while continuous distributions involve an infinite number of possible values within a range.

2. **Representation**: Discrete distributions use PMFs to assign probabilities to specific values. Continuous distributions use PDFs to represent probabilities across intervals.

3. **Probability Calculation**: In discrete distributions, probabilities are assigned to individual values. For continuous distributions, probabilities are determined by calculating the area under the curve of the PDF within an interval.

4. **Visualization**: Discrete distributions are typically visualized with bar charts, while continuous distributions use smooth curves.

Examples of Discrete and Continuous Scenarios

1. **Discrete Example**: A company produces light bulbs, and a random variable X represents the number of defective bulbs in a batch of 100. Since X can only take integer values from 0 to 100, it is a discrete variable. The binomial distribution is a suitable model here.

2. **Continuous Example**: In the same company, a random variable Y represents the lifespan of a bulb in hours. Since Y can take any positive real number (e.g., 120.4 hours or 150.8 hours), it is a continuous variable. The normal or exponential distribution might model this scenario, depending on the data's characteristics.

Similarities and Connections

Although discrete and continuous distributions differ fundamentally, they share some common properties:

- Both describe random variables and their probabilities.
- Both have expectations (means) and variances, which summarize the central tendency and variability of the data.
- Both can be used to compute cumulative probabilities. The cumulative distribution function (CDF) applies to both types, providing the probability that a random variable is less than or equal to a given value.

Discrete and continuous distributions can also approximate each other in specific cases. For instance, as the number of trials in a binomial distribution increases, it approaches a normal distribution if the probability of success is not too close to 0 or 1. This is the basis for the **normal approximation to the binomial**.

Applications of Discrete and Continuous Distributions

Both types of distributions are used across various fields:

1. **In Quality Control**: A factory might use a discrete distribution (e.g., Poisson) to model the number of defects per hour, while a continuous distribution (e.g., normal) might model the variability in product dimensions.

2. **In Medicine**: Discrete distributions can model the count of patients responding to a treatment, while continuous distributions analyze measurements like blood pressure or cholesterol levels.

3. **In Finance**: Discrete distributions model the number of days a stock closes above a target price, while continuous distributions model returns on investments.

4. **In Environmental Science**: Discrete distributions predict the number of rainy days in a month, while continuous distributions estimate daily rainfall amounts.

Limitations and Considerations

Choosing the appropriate distribution depends on the nature of the random variable and the context. Misidentifying a variable as discrete or continuous can lead to incorrect models and invalid conclusions. For example, using a normal distribution for count data may produce nonsensical negative values.

Another consideration is sample size. Small datasets may not clearly reveal the underlying distribution, requiring more data or alternative modeling techniques.

The Binomial Distribution: Success/Failure Scenarios

The binomial distribution is a discrete probability distribution that models the number of successes in a fixed number of independent trials, where each trial has two possible outcomes: success or failure. It is widely used to analyze scenarios involving repeated experiments, such as flipping a coin, conducting surveys, or testing products for defects.

To define the binomial distribution, consider a random variable X that represents the number of successes in n trials. Each trial has a probability of success denoted by p and a probability of failure denoted by q, where q = 1 - p. The probability of observing exactly k successes is given by the formula:

$$P(X = k) = (n \text{ choose } k) \times p^k \times q^{(n-k)}$$

Here, (n choose k) is the number of ways to choose k successes from n trials, calculated as:

$$(n \text{ choose } k) = n! \div [k!(n - k)!]$$

For example, consider flipping a fair coin 4 times. Each flip has a 50% chance of landing heads (success), so p = 0.5 and q = 0.5. If X represents the number of heads in 4 flips, the probability of getting exactly 2 heads (k = 2) is:

$$P(X = 2) = (4 \text{ choose } 2) \times 0.5^2 \times 0.5^2$$
$$(4 \text{ choose } 2) = 4! \div [2!(4 - 2)!] = 6$$
$$P(X = 2) = 6 \times 0.25 \times 0.25 = 6 \times 0.0625 = 0.375$$

Thus, there is a 37.5% chance of flipping exactly 2 heads in 4 coin flips.

The binomial distribution has several key properties. The mean (expected value) of the distribution is given by:

$$\text{Mean} = n \times p$$

This represents the average number of successes in n trials. For example, in the coin-flipping scenario with 4 flips and p = 0.5, the mean is:

$$\text{Mean} = 4 \times 0.5 = 2$$

This means that, on average, you would expect 2 heads in 4 flips.

The variance, which measures the spread of the distribution, is calculated as:

$$\text{Variance} = n \times p \times q$$

For the same example, the variance is:

$$\text{Variance} = 4 \times 0.5 \times 0.5 = 1$$

The standard deviation is the square root of the variance, providing a measure of variability in the same units as the random variable.

The shape of the binomial distribution depends on the values of n and p. When $p = 0.5$, the distribution is symmetric, with its peak at the mean. For example, in a scenario with 10 trials and $p = 0.5$, the probability distribution is evenly distributed around 5 successes. As p moves away from 0.5, the distribution becomes skewed. For instance, when $p = 0.8$, the distribution is skewed to the left, with most probabilities concentrated near the maximum number of successes.

One of the practical applications of the binomial distribution is in quality control. For example, a factory may produce items with a defect rate of 5% ($p = 0.05$). If a sample of 20 items is inspected, the binomial distribution can calculate the probability of finding exactly 2 defective items:

$$P(X = 2) = (20 \text{ choose } 2) \times 0.05^2 \times 0.95^{18}$$
$$(20 \text{ choose } 2) = 20! \div [2!(20 - 2)!] = 190$$
$$P(X = 2) = 190 \times (0.05^2) \times (0.95^{18})$$
$$P(X = 2) \approx 0.285$$

This means there is approximately a 28.5% chance of finding exactly 2 defective items in the sample.

The binomial distribution is also used in surveys to model the number of respondents who provide a specific answer. For example, if 60% of people prefer a particular brand ($p = 0.6$), and a survey of 10 people is conducted, the probability of exactly 7 people choosing the brand is:

$$P(X = 7) = (10 \text{ choose } 7) \times 0.6^7 \times 0.4^3$$
$$(10 \text{ choose } 7) = 10! \div [7!(10 - 7)!] = 120$$
$$P(X = 7) = 120 \times (0.6^7) \times (0.4^3)$$
$$P(X = 7) \approx 0.215$$

This result indicates a 21.5% probability that 7 out of 10 respondents will prefer the brand.

While the binomial distribution is powerful, it has certain limitations. It assumes that trials are independent, which may not always be realistic in real-world situations. For example, in a manufacturing process, if one defective item increases the likelihood of another defect, the trials are not independent. Similarly, the binomial distribution requires a fixed probability of success (p) across all trials, which may not hold in variable conditions.

For large values of n, the calculations for the binomial distribution can become computationally intensive. In such cases, the **normal approximation to the binomial** can simplify calculations. If n is large and p is not too close to 0 or 1, the binomial distribution can be approximated by a normal distribution with mean $\mu = n \times p$ and standard deviation $\sigma = \sqrt{(n \times p \times q)}$. For example, in a scenario with n = 100 and p = 0.5, the binomial distribution is approximated by a normal distribution with $\mu = 50$ and $\sigma = \sqrt{(100 \times 0.5 \times 0.5)} = 5$.

The Normal Distribution: Properties and Applications

The normal distribution, often called the bell curve or Gaussian distribution, is one of the most important and widely used probability distributions in statistics. Its symmetric, bell-shaped curve describes how values of a random variable are distributed around the mean. The normal distribution appears naturally in many fields, from natural and social sciences to business and engineering, due to the Central Limit Theorem.

Defining Characteristics

A normal distribution is defined by two parameters: the mean (μ) and the standard deviation (σ). The mean determines the center of the distribution, while the standard deviation controls the spread or width of the curve. Larger standard deviations result in wider, flatter curves, while smaller ones produce narrower, taller curves.

The probability density function (PDF) of the normal distribution is expressed as:

$$f(x) = (1 / (\sigma\sqrt{(2\pi)})) \times e^{\wedge}(-(x - \mu)^2 / (2\sigma^2))$$

Here:

- x represents the random variable,
- μ is the mean,
- σ is the standard deviation,
- π is the mathematical constant pi, and
- e is Euler's number.

The curve is symmetric about the mean, with 50% of the data falling on either side. It decreases as x moves away from the mean, approaching but never touching the x-axis.

Key Properties

1. **Symmetry**: The normal distribution is perfectly symmetric around the mean. The mean, median, and mode are identical and located at the center of the curve.

2. **Empirical Rule**: Approximately 68% of data falls within one standard deviation of the mean ($\mu \pm \sigma$), 95% within two standard deviations ($\mu \pm 2\sigma$), and 99.7% within three standard deviations ($\mu \pm 3\sigma$). This is often called the **68-95-99.7 rule**.

3. **Tails**: The tails of the normal distribution extend infinitely in both directions, though they approach zero as they move further from the mean.

4. **Standardization**: Any normal distribution can be converted into a standard normal distribution, which has a mean of 0 and a standard deviation of 1. Standardization involves calculating the z-score for each data point using the formula: $\mathbf{z = (x - \mu) / \sigma}$
The z-score represents the number of standard deviations a data point is from the mean, enabling comparisons across different datasets.

Applications of the Normal Distribution

1. **Natural Phenomena**: Many natural and biological processes follow a normal distribution. For instance, heights of adults, weights of newborns, and measurement errors in experiments tend to exhibit normality.

2. **Quality Control**: In manufacturing, the normal distribution helps monitor process consistency. For example, the diameter of produced bolts might be expected to follow a normal distribution centered around the target diameter.

3. **Finance**: The normal distribution models returns on investments, assuming market conditions are stable. For example, the daily returns of a stock often approximate a normal distribution over short periods.

4. **Standardized Testing**: Test scores, such as IQ tests or SAT results, are often designed to follow a normal distribution with a specific mean and standard deviation, enabling comparisons between test-takers.

Central Limit Theorem

The ubiquity of the normal distribution stems from the Central Limit Theorem (CLT). The CLT states that the sampling distribution of the sample mean approaches a normal distribution as the sample size increases, regardless of the population's original distribution. This property enables statisticians to make inferences about population parameters using sample data.

For example, suppose the weights of apples in an orchard are not normally distributed but skewed. If you take repeated samples of 30 apples and calculate their means, the distribution of these sample means will approximate normality, provided the sample size is sufficiently large.

Z-Scores and Probabilities

The z-score is a framework for working with normal distributions, allowing the calculation of probabilities and comparisons between values. For example, consider a dataset of exam scores with $\mu = 75$ and $\sigma = 10$. To find the probability of a student scoring above 85:

1. Calculate the z-score: $z = (85 - 75) / 10 = 1$

2. Use a z-table or statistical software to find the cumulative probability up to $z = 1$, which is approximately 0.8413.

3. Subtract this from 1 to find the probability of scoring above 85: $P(X > 85) = 1 - 0.8413 = 0.1587$, or 15.87%.

This method extends to finding probabilities for any interval, such as $P(70 < X < 90)$, by calculating z-scores for both bounds and subtracting their cumulative probabilities.

Normal Approximation to the Binomial

For large sample sizes, the binomial distribution can be approximated by a normal distribution if np and nq (where $q = 1 - p$) are both greater than 5. This simplifies calculations for binomial probabilities.

For example, consider a coin flipped 100 times, with $p = 0.5$ (probability of heads). The mean and standard deviation of the binomial distribution are:

$$\mu = n \times p = 100 \times 0.5 = 50$$
$$\sigma = \sqrt{(n \times p \times q)} = \sqrt{(100 \times 0.5 \times 0.5)} = \sqrt{25} = 5$$

To find the probability of getting between 45 and 55 heads (inclusive), standardize the range:

$$z1 = (45 - 50) / 5 = -1$$
$$z2 = (55 - 50) / 5 = 1$$

Using a z-table, the cumulative probability for $z = -1$ is 0.1587, and for $z = 1$, it is 0.8413. The probability of getting between 45 and 55 heads is:

$$P(45 \leq X \leq 55) = 0.8413 - 0.1587 = 0.6826, \text{ or } 68.26\%.$$

Limitations of the Normal Distribution

Despite its wide applicability, the normal distribution has limitations. Many datasets are not normally distributed, especially those with significant skewness or kurtosis. For example, income distributions are often skewed right, with a long tail of high earners.

Additionally, real-world data may have outliers or heavy tails that deviate from the normal curve. In such cases, alternative distributions, such as the log-normal or exponential, may provide better models.

Another limitation is the assumption of independence and identical distribution, which underpins the CLT. If data points are highly correlated or non-identical, normality may not apply.

Technology and the Normal Distribution

Modern tools make working with the normal distribution more accessible. Software like Excel, R, Python, and statistical calculators provide built-in functions for calculating probabilities, generating random normal variables, and creating visualizations.

In Python, the `scipy.stats` module includes functions like `norm.pdf` (probability density function), `norm.cdf` (cumulative distribution function), and `norm.ppf` (percent-point function for inverse calculations). For example, to find $P(X > 85)$ in Python:

```
from scipy.stats import norm
probability = 1 - norm.cdf(85, loc=75, scale=10)
```

This simplifies calculations, especially for large datasets or complex intervals.

Applications in Hypothesis Testing

The normal distribution is central to hypothesis testing and confidence intervals. For example, in a one-sample z-test, the z-score determines whether the sample mean significantly differs from the population mean. Similarly, confidence intervals for the mean assume normality when sample sizes are large or the population is normally distributed.

The Poisson Distribution: Modeling Rare Events

The Poisson distribution is a discrete probability distribution that models the likelihood of a given number of events occurring in a fixed interval of time, space, or other measures, provided these events occur independently and at a constant average rate. It is especially useful for modeling rare or infrequent events, such as the number of customer arrivals at a store per hour, system failures in a day, or traffic accidents in a given region.

Defining the Poisson Distribution

The Poisson distribution is characterized by a single parameter, λ (lambda), which represents both the mean and variance of the distribution. The probability of observing exactly k events in a fixed interval is given by the formula:

$$P(X = k) = (\lambda^k \times e^{(-\lambda)}) \div k!$$

Here:

- X is the random variable representing the number of events,
- k is the specific number of events,
- λ is the average rate of events per interval,
- e is Euler's number (approximately 2.718).

For example, if a bookstore averages 4 customers per hour (λ = 4), the probability of exactly 3 customers arriving in the next hour (k = 3) is:

$$P(X = 3) = (4^3 \times e^{(-4)}) \div 3!$$
$$P(X = 3) = (64 \times 0.0183) \div 6 \approx 0.195$$

This means there is roughly a 19.5% chance that 3 customers will arrive in the next hour.

Key Properties

1. **Single Parameter**: The Poisson distribution is defined entirely by λ, simplifying its application. Unlike other distributions, it does not require additional parameters like standard deviation or shape.

2. **Mean and Variance**: Both the mean (expected value) and variance of the Poisson distribution are equal to λ. This unique property is critical when using the Poisson model to analyze data.

3. **Independence**: Events modeled by the Poisson distribution must occur independently. For example, the number of calls received at a call center in one hour should not influence the number received in the next.

4. **Non-Negativity**: The random variable X can only take non-negative integer values (0, 1, 2, etc.), as it counts occurrences.

Applications of the Poisson Distribution

1. **Queueing Systems**: The Poisson distribution is commonly used to model arrival rates in queueing systems, such as customers arriving at a bank or cars at a toll booth.

2. **Reliability Engineering**: It estimates the number of system failures or breakdowns over a specific period. For instance, if a machine averages 2 failures per month, the distribution predicts the likelihood of observing different numbers of failures.

3. **Healthcare**: Poisson models help analyze rare events like the occurrence of diseases, emergency room visits, or the number of surgeries performed daily.

4. **Traffic and Accidents**: Traffic engineers use the Poisson distribution to model the number of accidents at an intersection or the number of cars passing through a checkpoint.

Poisson Distribution in Action

Consider a scenario where a hospital emergency department averages 6 patient arrivals per hour. Using the Poisson distribution, you can calculate the probability of various arrival scenarios:

1. **Probability of Exactly 4 Arrivals (k = 4)**: $\lambda = 6, k = 4$
   $P(X = 4) = (6^4 \times e^{(-6)}) \div 4!$
   $P(X = 4) = (1296 \times 0.002478) \div 24 \approx 0.133$
   There is about a 13.3% chance of exactly 4 arrivals in an hour.

2. **Probability of 0 Arrivals (k = 0)**: $P(X = 0) = (6^0 \times e^{(-6)}) \div 0!$
   $P(X = 0) = (1 \times 0.002478) \div 1 \approx 0.0025$
   There is approximately a 0.25% chance that no patients will arrive in an hour.

3. **Probability of 10 or More Arrivals**: To find this, calculate $1 - P(X \leq 9)$, where $P(X \leq 9)$ is the cumulative probability up to 9 arrivals. Using computational tools or a cumulative Poisson table simplifies this process.

Approximation to the Binomial Distribution

The Poisson distribution is often used as an approximation to the binomial distribution when the number of trials (n) is large, the probability of success (p) is small, and $np = \lambda$ is moderate. For instance, if a company produces 10,000 items daily and each has a 0.0002 probability of being defective, the number of defective items (X) can be approximated using a Poisson distribution with $\lambda = 10{,}000 \times 0.0002 = 2$.

This approximation is particularly valuable for large datasets, where direct binomial calculations are computationally intensive.

Relationship to the Exponential Distribution

The Poisson and exponential distributions are closely related. While the Poisson models the number of events in a fixed interval, the exponential distribution models the time between these events. For example, if customer arrivals at a store follow a Poisson process with $\lambda = 5$ per hour, the time between arrivals follows an exponential distribution with a mean of $1/\lambda = 1/5 = 0.2$ hours (12 minutes).

Fitting the Poisson Distribution

To determine whether data follows a Poisson distribution, compare the sample mean and variance. If they are approximately equal, the data may fit a Poisson model. Statistical tests, such as the chi-squared goodness-of-fit test, can provide further confirmation.

Limitations and Assumptions

1. **Independence**: The Poisson distribution assumes that events occur independently. Violations of this assumption, such as clustering of events, can distort the model.

2. **Constant Rate**: The event rate λ must remain constant over time or space. For example, if customer arrival rates vary throughout the day, the Poisson distribution may not be appropriate.

3. **Rare Events**: The Poisson distribution is best suited for rare or infrequent events. When λ is large, the distribution becomes less skewed and approaches a normal distribution.

Technology and the Poisson Distribution

Modern tools make working with the Poisson distribution more efficient. Statistical software like R, Python, and Excel can compute probabilities, simulate data, and visualize distributions. For example, in Python, the `scipy.stats` module includes functions like `poisson.pmf` (probability mass function) and `poisson.cdf` (cumulative distribution function). To calculate $P(X = 4)$ for $\lambda = 6$:

```
from scipy.stats import poisson
probability = poisson.pmf(4, 6)
```

These tools streamline calculations, especially for complex or cumulative probabilities.

Applications in Predictive Modeling

In predictive analytics, the Poisson distribution is used to model count data. For example, it predicts the number of website visits, call center inquiries, or sales transactions. Regression models, such as Poisson regression, extend the distribution to incorporate multiple predictors, allowing for more detailed analyses.

Summary

The Poisson distribution (below left) models the frequency of rare events with a skewed yet discrete spread, the Binomial distribution (center) represents the probabilities of a fixed number of successes with symmetric peaks near the mean for moderate probabilities, and the Normal distribution (right) is a continuous, bell-shaped curve symmetric about the mean, commonly used for naturally occurring data.

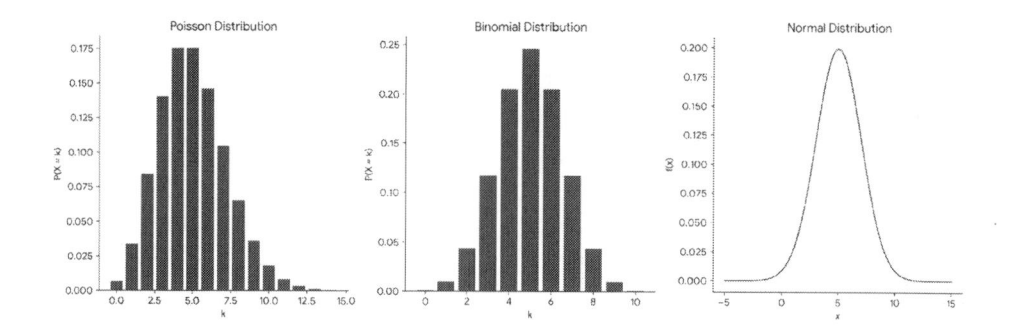

Nonparametric Distributions

Nonparametric distributions represent a class of statistical models that do not assume a specific functional form for the distribution of the data. Unlike parametric models, which are based on predefined distributions such as normal, binomial, or Poisson, nonparametric approaches allow the data to speak for itself. This flexibility makes nonparametric distributions particularly useful when the underlying distribution is unknown, irregular, or when data violates assumptions of traditional parametric methods.

What are Nonparametric Distributions?

Nonparametric distributions focus on the structure and pattern of the data rather than fitting it to a predefined mathematical equation. For example, instead of assuming that data follows a normal distribution, a nonparametric approach might use the actual data points to construct a probability density function or cumulative distribution function. This flexibility ensures that nonparametric methods are adaptive to the data's true characteristics, capturing subtleties that parametric models might miss.

The term "nonparametric" does not imply that these methods lack parameters altogether. Instead, it means that the number or nature of the parameters is not fixed in advance. Nonparametric methods often rely on the data size or distribution to determine their complexity, making them highly adaptive to varying datasets.

Key Features of Nonparametric Distributions

1. **Flexibility**: Nonparametric distributions are not restricted to specific shapes. This is particularly advantageous when dealing with multimodal, skewed, or irregular distributions that deviate from standard models like the normal distribution.

2. **No Assumptions**: Nonparametric approaches do not assume that the data is normally distributed or follows any other predefined form. This makes them robust to outliers, nonlinearity, and heteroscedasticity (unequal variances).

3. **Data-Driven**: These methods directly use the data to estimate distributions, probabilities, or relationships. Techniques like kernel density estimation or empirical cumulative distribution functions rely entirely on observed values.

4. **Scalability**: Nonparametric methods adapt as more data becomes available, refining their estimates to better reflect the true underlying distribution.

Types of Nonparametric Distributions

Several techniques and methods fall under the umbrella of nonparametric distributions. Below are some of the most widely used approaches:

1. **Empirical Cumulative Distribution Function (ECDF)**: The ECDF is a step function that estimates the cumulative distribution of a dataset. It calculates the proportion of data points less than or equal to a given value. For example, if a dataset consists of the numbers 2, 4, 6, and 8, the ECDF at x = 6 is 0.75, as 75% of the data points are less than or equal to 6. The ECDF provides a visual and mathematical representation of the data without assuming any specific underlying distribution.

2. **Kernel Density Estimation (KDE)**: KDE is a popular technique for estimating the probability density function (PDF) of a random variable. It smooths the data by placing a kernel (e.g., a Gaussian bell curve) over each data point and summing the contributions to create a continuous curve. KDE is particularly useful for visualizing the distribution of data when the histogram is too rough or when the true underlying distribution is unknown. The bandwidth of the kernel determines the level of smoothing, with smaller bandwidths capturing more detail and larger bandwidths providing smoother curves.
For example, in a dataset of daily rainfall measurements, KDE can create a smooth curve representing the likelihood of specific rainfall amounts, highlighting peaks and spread without assuming normality.

3. **Histogram-Based Methods**: While histograms are technically parametric (since bin widths and intervals are set by the user), they can function as nonparametric estimates when used to describe data without reference to a theoretical distribution. Histograms divide data into bins and count the frequency of values in each bin, offering a simple and intuitive visualization of the distribution.

4. **Rank-Based Methods**: Many nonparametric approaches rely on data ranks rather than raw values. This eliminates the influence of extreme values or outliers. For example, the Wilcoxon signed-rank test and the Mann-Whitney U test compare groups based on their ranks, making them robust alternatives to parametric t-tests when data does not meet normality assumptions.

5. **Bootstrap Distributions**: Bootstrapping is a resampling technique that generates an empirical distribution by repeatedly sampling with replacement from the original dataset. This approach is used to estimate parameters such as

means, medians, or variances without assuming a specific distribution. For example, bootstrapping can estimate the confidence interval of a sample mean by simulating thousands of new datasets from the original data and observing the variation in the sample means.

6. **Spline-Based and Local Regression Methods**: These methods, such as LOESS (locally estimated scatterplot smoothing), use nonparametric techniques to model data relationships. While primarily used for regression, they can also estimate densities and trends by focusing on local patterns in the data.

Applications of Nonparametric Distributions

Nonparametric distributions are used across various fields and disciplines. Their versatility makes them invaluable in situations where assumptions of parametric models are inappropriate or unverifiable.

1. **Medicine and Biology**: In medical research, nonparametric methods analyze data such as survival times or disease prevalence, where distributions are often skewed or contain censored observations. For instance, the Kaplan-Meier estimator uses nonparametric techniques to estimate survival functions, helping researchers understand patient survival probabilities over time.

2. **Finance and Economics**: Nonparametric approaches are applied to model market returns, risk distributions, and consumer behavior. For example, kernel density estimation can visualize the distribution of stock price changes, highlighting areas of high volatility without assuming normality.

3. **Environmental Science**: In climate studies, nonparametric methods analyze irregular or heavy-tailed data, such as daily temperature or rainfall extremes. Rank-based tests are commonly used to compare environmental conditions across regions or time periods.

4. **Social Sciences**: Surveys and questionnaires often generate ordinal or categorical data that do not conform to standard parametric assumptions. Nonparametric methods allow researchers to analyze this data accurately, even with small sample sizes or skewed distributions.

5. **Machine Learning**: Nonparametric distributions underpin algorithms like k-nearest neighbors (KNN) and decision trees. These methods adapt to data patterns without imposing rigid assumptions, making them ideal for complex, high-dimensional datasets.

Advantages of Nonparametric Distributions

1. **Robustness**: Nonparametric methods handle outliers, skewness, and irregularities effectively, providing reliable results even when assumptions of parametric models are violated.

2. **Flexibility**: By not imposing a fixed form, nonparametric distributions can capture diverse patterns and relationships in data.

3. **Interpretability**: Methods like ECDFs and histograms offer intuitive visual representations, making them accessible to non-specialists.

4. **Scalability**: Nonparametric techniques improve with larger datasets, refining their estimates as more data becomes available.

Challenges and Limitations

Despite their advantages, nonparametric methods are not without challenges:

1. **Computational Intensity**: Many nonparametric methods, such as KDE and bootstrapping, require significant computational resources, especially for large datasets.

2. **Overfitting**: The flexibility of nonparametric methods can lead to overfitting, particularly with small sample sizes. Careful parameter selection, such as bandwidth in KDE, is crucial to balance detail and generalization.

3. **Lack of Theoretical Framework**: Nonparametric approaches may lack the predictive power or mathematical rigor of parametric models, making them less suitable for certain inferential tasks.

4. **Data-Dependence**: Nonparametric methods heavily rely on the quality and quantity of the available data. Sparse or noisy data can lead to unreliable results.

Choosing Between Parametric and Nonparametric Approaches

The choice between parametric and nonparametric methods depends on the nature of the data and the research question. When data meets the assumptions of parametric models, such as normality, parametric methods are often preferred for their simplicity and efficiency. However, when assumptions are violated or the underlying distribution is unknown, nonparametric approaches provide a reliable alternative.

For example, in analyzing customer satisfaction scores that are highly skewed, a nonparametric approach like the Mann-Whitney U test would be more appropriate than a parametric t-test. Similarly, in estimating income distributions with heavy tails, KDE provides a more accurate representation than fitting a normal distribution.

Chapter 7: Sampling Distributions and the Central Limit Theorem

Sampling Distribution of the Mean

The sampling distribution of the mean is a fundamental concept in statistics. It represents the probability distribution of sample means drawn from a population. When you repeatedly take random samples of the same size from a population, calculate the mean of each sample, and plot these means, the resulting distribution is the sampling distribution of the mean. This distribution is essential for understanding how sample statistics relate to population parameters and serves as the foundation for inferential statistics.

Imagine a population with a mean μ and a standard deviation σ. If you take a random sample of size n from this population and calculate the sample mean ($\bar{x}$), the value of $\bar{x}$ will vary from sample to sample. This variability arises because each sample captures a different subset of the population. However, the distribution of these sample means has distinct properties that make it predictable and useful.

Key Properties of the Sampling Distribution of the Mean

1. **Mean of the Sampling Distribution**: The mean of the sampling distribution of the mean is equal to the population mean (μ). This property ensures that the sampling distribution is unbiased, meaning that the average of all sample means is an accurate estimate of the population mean.
   For example, if the population mean is $\mu = 50$, then the mean of the sampling distribution of the mean is also 50, regardless of sample size.

2. **Standard Error of the Mean**: The standard deviation of the sampling distribution is called the standard error of the mean (SE). It measures the spread of sample means around the population mean and is calculated as:
   $SE = \sigma \div \sqrt{n}$
   Here, σ is the population standard deviation, and n is the sample size. The formula shows that larger sample sizes result in smaller standard errors, meaning sample means cluster more tightly around the population mean.
   For instance, if the population standard deviation is $\sigma = 10$ and the sample size is $n = 25$, the standard error is:
   $SE = 10 \div \sqrt{25} = 10 \div 5 = 2$
   This indicates that the variability of sample means decreases as the sample size increases, making larger samples more reliable for estimating the population mean.

3. **Shape of the Sampling Distribution**: The shape of the sampling distribution depends on the shape of the population distribution and the sample size. If the population distribution is normal, the sampling distribution of the mean is also normal, regardless of sample size. However, if the population distribution is not normal, the shape of the sampling distribution approaches normality as the sample size increases, thanks to the Central Limit Theorem (CLT).

For small sample sizes drawn from a non-normal population, the sampling distribution may retain some of the skewness or kurtosis of the population. As n becomes larger, typically greater than 30, the sampling distribution becomes approximately normal.

Why the Sampling Distribution of the Mean Matters

The sampling distribution of the mean allows statisticians to make inferences about the population mean based on sample data. It provides the foundation for hypothesis testing, confidence intervals, and other inferential techniques. Without it, determining the accuracy and reliability of sample statistics would be impossible.

For example, consider a researcher who wants to estimate the average height of adults in a city. Measuring every adult is impractical, so the researcher takes a random sample of 50 people and calculates the sample mean. The sampling distribution of the mean tells the researcher how much variability to expect if they were to repeat this sampling process many times. Using the standard error, the researcher can construct confidence intervals to estimate the population mean with a known level of certainty.

Illustrative Example

Suppose a population of exam scores has a mean $\mu = 80$ and a standard deviation $\sigma = 12$. A teacher randomly selects 36 students and calculates their average score. What is the probability that the sample mean is between 78 and 82?

First, calculate the standard error:

$SE = \sigma \div \sqrt{n} = 12 \div \sqrt{36} = 12 \div 6 = 2$

Next, convert the sample means (78 and 82) into z-scores:

$z = (\bar{x} - \mu) \div SE$

For $\bar{x} = 78$:

$z = (78 - 80) \div 2 = -2 \div 2 = -1$

For $\bar{x} = 82$:

$z = (82 - 80) \div 2 = 2 \div 2 = 1$

Using a standard normal distribution table, the cumulative probability for z = -1 is approximately 0.1587, and for z = 1, it is approximately 0.8413. The probability that the sample mean is between 78 and 82 is:

$$P(78 \leq \bar{x} \leq 82) = 0.8413 - 0.1587 = 0.6826$$

This result shows there is a 68.26% chance that the sample mean falls within one standard error of the population mean, consistent with the Empirical Rule for normal distributions.

Factors Affecting the Sampling Distribution

1. **Sample Size**: The sample size directly affects the standard error. Larger samples reduce the variability of sample means, making them more reliable. A small sample size increases variability, making the sampling distribution wider and less precise.

2. **Population Variability**: Higher variability in the population (larger σ) leads to greater variability in sample means, increasing the standard error. In contrast, a more homogeneous population (smaller σ) produces a narrower sampling distribution.

3. **Random Sampling**: The sampling distribution assumes that samples are randomly drawn from the population. Non-random samples can introduce bias, distorting the distribution and making inferences invalid.

Applications in Real-World Scenarios

1. **Manufacturing**: In quality control, sampling distributions help monitor product consistency. For example, a factory producing light bulbs might take random samples of 50 bulbs each day and measure their average lifespan. The sampling distribution allows the factory to detect deviations from the target lifespan, indicating potential production issues.

2. **Medicine**: Researchers use sampling distributions to estimate population parameters like average blood pressure or cholesterol levels. For instance, a clinical trial might involve taking random samples of patients and calculating the average reduction in symptoms after treatment. The sampling distribution provides a basis for testing whether the treatment effect is statistically significant.

3. **Market Research**: Businesses rely on sampling distributions to analyze consumer preferences. For example, a company surveying customer satisfaction might use the sampling distribution of the mean to estimate the average satisfaction level across the entire customer base.

Challenges and Limitations

While the sampling distribution of the mean is useful, it has limitations. Small sample sizes can produce sampling distributions that are not representative of the population, especially when the population distribution is highly skewed. In such cases, the Central Limit Theorem may not apply, and additional caution is required when making inferences.

Another challenge is ensuring random sampling. Bias in the sampling process can lead to inaccurate results, undermining the validity of the sampling distribution. Proper design and execution of sampling procedures are critical for reliable outcomes.

The Role of the Central Limit Theorem

The Central Limit Theorem (CLT) is one of the most important principles in statistics, forming the backbone of many inferential techniques. It describes how the sampling distribution of the sample mean becomes approximately normal, regardless of the shape of the population distribution, as the sample size increases. This property allows statisticians to make valid inferences about population parameters even when the population itself is not normally distributed.

What Does the Central Limit Theorem State?

The CLT states that if you take random samples of size n from a population with any distribution, the sampling distribution of the sample mean will approach a normal distribution as n becomes sufficiently large. The key points are:

1. **Mean of the Sampling Distribution**: The mean of the sampling distribution of the sample mean is equal to the population mean (μ).

2. **Standard Error**: The standard deviation of the sampling distribution, known as the standard error (SE), is given by:
   $SE = \sigma \div \sqrt{n}$
   Here, σ is the population standard deviation, and n is the sample size.

3. **Normality**: As n increases, the shape of the sampling distribution approaches normality, regardless of the population's original shape. For most practical purposes, a sample size of $n \geq 30$ is considered sufficient for the CLT to hold, though smaller sizes may suffice if the population is not highly skewed.

Why is the CLT Important?

The CLT is critical because it enables the use of normal distribution-based methods to analyze data from populations that do not follow a normal distribution. In practice, many real-world populations—such as income, wait times, or biological measurements—are skewed, multimodal, or irregular. The CLT allows statisticians to overcome these challenges by focusing on the sampling distribution of the mean, which becomes normal as sample size increases.

For example, suppose you want to estimate the average time customers spend in a store. The population distribution of customer times might be skewed, with many customers spending only a few minutes and a few spending hours. Despite this skewness, the CLT ensures that the sampling distribution of the mean will be approximately normal if the sample size is large enough. This normality allows for accurate calculation of confidence intervals and hypothesis tests.

Demonstration of the CLT

Consider a population with a uniform distribution, where every value between 0 and 10 is equally likely. This distribution is not normal; it is flat and rectangular in shape. If you randomly sample n = 2 values and calculate the mean of each sample, the sampling distribution of the mean begins to take shape. With n = 2, it might retain some uniform characteristics. However, as n increases to 10, 20, or more, the sampling distribution becomes smoother and more bell-shaped, closely resembling a normal distribution.

Similarly, if the population is highly skewed—such as an exponential distribution with a long right tail—the sampling distribution of the mean may initially retain the skewness. However, as n grows larger, the central limit theorem ensures that the sampling distribution approaches normality, even if the original population remains skewed.

Applications of the Central Limit Theorem

1. **Confidence Intervals**: The CLT enables the calculation of confidence intervals for population means. By assuming the sampling distribution of the mean is normal, statisticians can estimate the range within which the true population mean likely lies. For example, if the sample mean of exam scores is 75 with a standard error of 2, a 95% confidence interval for the population mean is:
Mean ± (z × SE) = 75 ± (1.96 × 2) = 75 ± 3.92 = (71.08, 78.92)
The CLT ensures the validity of this interval, even if the population distribution is non-normal.

2. **Hypothesis Testing**: Many statistical tests, such as the t-test and z-test, rely on the assumption that the sampling distribution of the test statistic is normal. The CLT justifies this assumption, allowing tests to assess whether observed sample data deviates significantly from a null hypothesis.
For instance, a factory claims its machines produce bolts with an average length of 10 cm. To test this claim, you take a sample of 50 bolts and find a mean length of 9.8 cm with a standard deviation of 0.5 cm. Using the CLT, you calculate the z-score:
$z = (\bar{x} - \mu) \div (\sigma \div \sqrt{n}) = (9.8 - 10) \div (0.5 \div \sqrt{50}) \approx -2.83$
This z-score corresponds to a very low probability under the null hypothesis, suggesting the claim may be incorrect.

3. **Sampling in Non-Normal Populations**: The CLT is particularly valuable when dealing with non-normal populations. For example, income data is often right-skewed due to high earners. If you sample 100 individuals and calculate the mean income, the sampling distribution of this mean will be approximately normal, allowing valid inferences about the population mean.

4. **Predictive Analytics**: In predictive modeling, the CLT supports the assumption of normality in residuals (differences between observed and predicted values). This assumption underpins many machine learning algorithms and regression techniques, ensuring reliable model performance.

5. **Polling and Surveys**: Pollsters rely on the CLT to estimate public opinion. For example, if a random sample of 1,000 voters shows 52% favor a candidate with a standard deviation of 4%, the CLT ensures the sampling distribution of the proportion is normal. This allows the calculation of confidence intervals and the prediction of election outcomes.

Practical Considerations

While the CLT is powerful, it has limitations and conditions:

1. **Sample Size**: The sample size must be large enough for the CLT to apply. While $n \geq 30$ is a common rule of thumb, skewed or heavy-tailed populations may require larger samples.

2. **Independence**: The CLT assumes that samples are independent. Correlated data can distort the sampling distribution, violating normality.

3. **Random Sampling**: Random sampling is crucial for the CLT to hold. Biased or non-random samples can lead to incorrect inferences.

4. **Finite Population Correction**: When sampling without replacement from a finite population, the sampling distribution changes slightly. The standard error must be adjusted using the finite population correction factor:
Adjusted SE = $(\sigma \div \sqrt{n}) \times \sqrt{((N - n) \div (N - 1))}$
Here, N is the population size, and n is the sample size.

Illustrative Example

Suppose a call center tracks the number of calls received per hour, with a mean of 50 and a standard deviation of 10. If you take random samples of 36 hours and calculate the mean calls per sample, the sampling distribution of the mean will have:

Mean = 50
Standard Error = $\sigma \div \sqrt{n} = 10 \div \sqrt{36} = 10 \div 6 = 1.67$

If you want to find the probability of observing a sample mean between 48 and 52, calculate the z-scores for these values:

$$z = (\bar{x} - \mu) \div SE$$

For $\bar{x} = 48$:

$$z = (48 - 50) \div 1.67 \approx -1.2$$

For $\bar{x} = 52$:

$$z = (52 - 50) \div 1.67 \approx 1.2$$

Using a z-table, the cumulative probability for $z = -1.2$ is approximately 0.1151, and for $z = 1.2$, it is approximately 0.8849. The probability of observing a sample mean between 48 and 52 is:

$$P(48 \leq \bar{x} \leq 52) = 0.8849 - 0.1151 = 0.7698, \text{ or } 76.98\%.$$

This example demonstrates how the CLT enables the calculation of probabilities and inferences using the normal distribution.

Practical Applications of Sampling Distributions

Sampling distributions are an essential concept in statistics, enabling researchers and analysts to make inferences about populations based on sample data. The real-world applications of sampling distributions span across industries and fields, as they provide a framework for hypothesis testing, estimation, and decision-making under uncertainty. By understanding how sample statistics behave, we can gain insights about population parameters without examining the entire population.

1. Estimating Population Parameters

One of the most common applications of sampling distributions is estimating population parameters, such as the mean, proportion, or variance. By taking a sample from a population, we calculate a statistic (e.g., sample mean or sample proportion) and use it to infer the corresponding population parameter. Sampling distributions help quantify the accuracy of these estimates.

For instance, in public health, researchers might estimate the average blood pressure of adults in a city. Measuring every individual's blood pressure is impractical, so they take a random sample of 200 adults. The sample mean provides an estimate of the population mean, while the standard error (derived from the sampling distribution) indicates how much the sample mean is likely to vary from the true mean. This information allows researchers to construct confidence intervals, providing a range of plausible values for the population mean.

2. Confidence Intervals

Sampling distributions are the foundation for constructing confidence intervals, which are widely used to estimate population parameters with a specific level of certainty. For example, a political poll might report that 60% of voters favor a candidate, with a 95% confidence interval of ±3%. This means the true proportion of voters who favor the candidate is likely between 57% and 63%.

The width of a confidence interval depends on the standard error, which is derived from the sampling distribution. Larger sample sizes reduce the standard error, resulting in narrower confidence intervals and more precise estimates. This relationship emphasizes the importance of sample size in achieving reliable results.

Consider a survey estimating the average monthly spending of households. If the sample mean is $2,500, the standard error is $100, and the confidence level is 95%, the confidence interval is:

$$\text{Mean} \pm (z \times \text{SE}) = 2500 \pm (1.96 \times 100) = 2500 \pm 196 = (2304, 2696)$$

The confidence interval indicates that the true mean spending likely falls between $2,304 and $2,696, assuming the sampling distribution is approximately normal.

3. Hypothesis Testing

Sampling distributions are critical in hypothesis testing, where we assess whether observed data supports a specific claim or hypothesis about a population. For example, a manufacturer might claim that the mean weight of a product is 500 grams. To verify this claim, quality control engineers take a random sample of 50 products and calculate the sample mean. The sampling distribution of the mean allows them to determine whether the observed sample mean deviates significantly from the claimed value.

In hypothesis testing, we calculate a test statistic (e.g., z-score or t-score) based on the sample data and compare it to the expected sampling distribution under the null hypothesis. If the test statistic falls within the critical region (extreme values of the sampling distribution), we reject the null hypothesis.

For instance, if the sample mean is 495 grams with a standard error of 2 grams, the z-score is:

$$z = (\bar{x} - \mu) \div \text{SE} = (495 - 500) \div 2 = -2.5$$

Using a standard normal distribution table, a z-score of -2.5 corresponds to a cumulative probability of 0.0062. If the significance level is 0.05, the p-value (0.0062) is smaller, leading to the rejection of the null hypothesis. This suggests that the manufacturer's claim may be inaccurate.

4. Quality Control and Manufacturing

In industrial settings, sampling distributions are used to monitor and improve product quality. Quality control processes rely on samples taken from production lines to ensure products meet specifications. For example, a factory producing lightbulbs might test the average lifespan of bulbs in random batches. If the sampling distribution of the mean lifespan deviates significantly from the target, this indicates potential issues in the production process.

Control charts, a tool in statistical process control (SPC), use sampling distributions to detect variability in manufacturing. The control limits on these charts are based on the sampling distribution, helping identify when a process is out of control. For example, if the mean weight of a packaged product falls outside the control limits, it signals the need for adjustments.

5. Medical Research and Clinical Trials

In medical research, sampling distributions help evaluate the effectiveness of treatments and interventions. Clinical trials often compare treatment groups using sample data to infer differences in population outcomes. For example, a trial might test a new drug's ability to reduce blood pressure compared to a placebo. Researchers calculate the mean reduction in blood pressure for each group and use the sampling distribution of the difference between means to assess statistical significance.

If the sample size is large enough, the difference in means follows a normal distribution. Using this distribution, researchers calculate confidence intervals and p-values to determine whether the observed difference is likely due to chance or reflects a true effect.

6. Survey Sampling and Polling

Sampling distributions are important in survey research and polling. Political polls, customer satisfaction surveys, and market research studies rely on random samples to infer population preferences or opinions. For example, a polling organization might survey 1,000 voters to estimate the proportion who favor a specific policy. The sampling distribution of the sample proportion allows pollsters to calculate margins of error and confidence intervals.

If 600 out of 1,000 voters support the policy, the sample proportion is 0.6. The standard error for the proportion is:

$$SE = \sqrt{p \times (1 - p) \div n} = \sqrt{0.6 \times 0.4 \div 1000} \approx 0.0155$$

A 95% confidence interval is:

$$p \pm (z \times SE) = 0.6 \pm (1.96 \times 0.0155) = 0.6 \pm 0.0304 = (0.57, 0.63)$$

This indicates that the true proportion of voters who support the policy likely falls between 57% and 63%.

7. Financial Analysis

In finance, sampling distributions are used to model risk and uncertainty. For example, portfolio managers analyze the sampling distribution of returns to estimate the expected return and volatility of investments. Sampling distributions also underlie techniques like bootstrapping, which resamples data to estimate the confidence intervals of financial metrics, such as the Sharpe ratio or beta coefficients.

8. Environmental Science

Environmental scientists use sampling distributions to monitor and assess ecological conditions. For example, water quality tests involve taking samples from rivers or lakes to estimate pollution levels. The sampling distribution of the mean concentration of pollutants helps determine whether observed levels exceed regulatory limits.

Challenges and Limitations

Sampling distributions are subject to certain limitations:

1. **Sample Size**: Small sample sizes lead to greater variability in sample statistics, making the sampling distribution less reliable. Larger samples produce more precise estimates.

2. **Bias in Sampling**: Non-random samples or sampling bias can distort the sampling distribution, leading to invalid conclusions. Proper random sampling is essential.

3. **Assumptions**: Many applications assume the sampling distribution is approximately normal, which may not hold for small samples or highly skewed populations.

4. **Finite Populations**: When sampling without replacement from finite populations, the standard error must be adjusted using the finite population correction factor.

Sampling Distribution of Proportions

The sampling distribution of proportions describes the distribution of sample proportions obtained from repeated random samples of the same size drawn from a population. It is a cornerstone of inferential statistics, enabling statisticians to estimate population proportions, construct confidence intervals, and perform hypothesis tests. This distribution is particularly useful when analyzing binary outcomes, such as success or failure, yes or no, or present or absent.

What is a Sample Proportion?

A sample proportion (denoted as p̂) is the fraction or percentage of a sample with a particular characteristic of interest. It is calculated as:

$$\hat{p} = x \div n$$

Here:

- x is the number of successes (or observations with the characteristic),
- n is the sample size.

For example, if a survey of 100 voters finds that 60 support a particular candidate, the sample proportion is:

$$\hat{p} = 60 \div 100 = 0.6 \text{ (or 60\%)}$$

The sample proportion varies across different samples, and the distribution of these sample proportions is the **sampling distribution of proportions**.

Key Properties of the Sampling Distribution of Proportions

1. **Mean of the Sampling Distribution**: The mean of the sampling distribution of proportions is equal to the population proportion (p). This means the average of all sample proportions across repeated samples is an unbiased estimate of the true population proportion.
   If the population proportion is p = 0.5, then the mean of the sampling distribution is also 0.5.

2. **Standard Error of the Proportion**: The variability of sample proportions is measured by the standard error (SE). The standard error of the proportion is given by: **SE = √[p × (1 - p) ÷ n]**
   This formula shows that the standard error decreases as the sample size (n) increases. Larger samples lead to more precise estimates of the population proportion. For instance, if p = 0.6 and n = 100, the standard error is:
   SE = √[0.6 × 0.4 ÷ 100] = √[0.24 ÷ 100] = √0.0024 ≈ 0.049

3. **Shape of the Sampling Distribution**: The shape of the sampling distribution of proportions depends on the sample size and the population proportion. According to the Central Limit Theorem, the sampling distribution is approximately normal if:

    ○ The sample size is large enough, and
    ○ np ≥ 10 and n(1 - p) ≥ 10.

4. If these conditions are met, the sampling distribution can be treated as normal, even if the population itself is not.

Constructing Confidence Intervals

One of the primary uses of the sampling distribution of proportions is constructing confidence intervals to estimate the population proportion. A confidence interval provides a range of plausible values for the true population proportion, with a specified level of confidence.

The formula for a confidence interval is:

$$\hat{p} \pm (z \times SE)$$

Here:

- $\hat{p}$ is the sample proportion,
- z is the z-score corresponding to the desired confidence level,
- SE is the standard error of the proportion.

For example, suppose a poll finds that 55% of respondents favor a new policy ($\hat{p} = 0.55$) based on a sample of 400 people (n = 400). The standard error is:

$$SE = \sqrt{[\hat{p} \times (1 - \hat{p}) \div n]} = \sqrt{[0.55 \times 0.45 \div 400]} = \sqrt{[0.2475 \div 400]} = \sqrt{0.00061875} \approx 0.025$$

For a 95% confidence level (z ≈ 1.96), the confidence interval is:

$$0.55 \pm (1.96 \times 0.025) = 0.55 \pm 0.049 = (0.501, 0.599)$$

This indicates that the true proportion of people who favor the policy is likely between 50.1% and 59.9%, with 95% confidence.

Hypothesis Testing with Proportions

The sampling distribution of proportions also underpins hypothesis testing, where we evaluate claims about a population proportion. For instance, a company may claim that 80% of customers are satisfied with their service. To test this claim, we take a sample and calculate the sample proportion.

The test statistic (z) is calculated as:

$$z = (\hat{p} - p) \div SE$$

For example, if the sample proportion is $\hat{p} = 0.75$, the claimed population proportion is p = 0.8, and the sample size is n = 200, the standard error is:

$$SE = \sqrt{[p \times (1 - p) \div n]} = \sqrt{[0.8 \times 0.2 \div 200]} = \sqrt{[0.16 \div 200]} = \sqrt{0.0008} \approx 0.028$$

The z-score is:

$$z = (\hat{p} - p) \div SE = (0.75 - 0.8) \div 0.028 \approx -1.79$$

Using a standard normal distribution table, a z-score of -1.79 corresponds to a p-value of approximately 0.073. If the significance level is 0.05, we fail to reject the null hypothesis, as the p-value is greater than 0.05. This suggests there is insufficient evidence to conclude that customer satisfaction differs from the claimed 80%.

Applications of Sampling Distribution of Proportions

1. **Polling and Election Forecasting**: Political polls frequently estimate the proportion of voters supporting a candidate or policy. For example, a polling agency might survey 1,000 voters to estimate the proportion supporting a candidate. The sampling distribution allows pollsters to calculate margins of error and predict outcomes.

2. **Quality Control**: In manufacturing, sampling distributions are used to monitor product quality. For instance, a factory may test a sample of 500 items to estimate the proportion of defective products. The sampling distribution helps determine whether the observed defect rate deviates significantly from acceptable limits.

3. **Medical Research**: Researchers use sampling distributions to analyze proportions in clinical trials. For example, they might estimate the proportion of patients who respond positively to a treatment. The sampling distribution provides a framework for testing whether the observed response rate differs from expectations.

4. **Market Research**: Businesses often estimate the proportion of customers who prefer a product or service. For instance, a company surveying 1,200 customers might find that 65% prefer their new product. The sampling distribution helps determine the reliability of this estimate and guides marketing decisions.

5. **Environmental Studies**: Sampling distributions are used to estimate proportions in ecological data, such as the percentage of polluted water samples in a lake. Researchers can test whether observed proportions meet regulatory standards or differ across regions.

Challenges and Limitations

1. **Small Sample Sizes**: The sampling distribution of proportions may not be approximately normal for small sample sizes, especially when p is close to 0 or 1. In such cases, alternative methods, such as exact binomial tests, are more appropriate.

2. **Sampling Bias**: Non-random samples can distort the sampling distribution, leading to invalid inferences. Ensuring random and representative sampling is critical for accurate results.

3. **Finite Population Correction**: When sampling without replacement from a finite population, the standard error must be adjusted using the finite population correction factor: **Adjusted SE = SE × $\sqrt{((N - n) \div (N - 1))}$**
Here, N is the population size, and n is the sample size.

Chapter 8: Hypothesis Testing Fundamentals

Null and Alternative Hypotheses: Setting the Stage

Hypothesis testing is a statistical method used to make decisions or inferences about a population based on sample data. At the heart of hypothesis testing lies the formulation of two opposing statements: the null hypothesis (H_0) and the alternative hypothesis (H_a). These statements form the basis for evaluating whether observed data provides sufficient evidence to support a particular claim or belief.

What is a Null Hypothesis?

The null hypothesis (H_0) is a statement of no effect, no difference, or no relationship. It represents the default assumption or status quo that the data is assumed to follow unless there is strong evidence to suggest otherwise. The null hypothesis is always written as a specific claim about a population parameter.

For example:

1. In a clinical trial, H_0 might state that a new drug has no effect compared to a placebo.
2. In quality control, H_0 could state that the average weight of a product is equal to the target weight of 500 grams.
3. In an election poll, H_0 may claim that 50% of voters support a candidate.

The null hypothesis provides a baseline for statistical testing. Rejecting H_0 implies that there is evidence to support an alternative explanation.

What is an Alternative Hypothesis?

The alternative hypothesis (H_a) is the statement that contradicts the null hypothesis. It reflects what the researcher aims to support or prove based on the data. The alternative hypothesis suggests that there is an effect, a difference, or a relationship.

For example:

1. In the clinical trial, H_a might state that the new drug is more effective than the placebo.
2. In quality control, H_a could claim that the average weight of the product is not equal to 500 grams.
3. In the election poll, H_a may assert that more than 50% of voters support the candidate.

The alternative hypothesis can take three possible forms:

1. **Two-Tailed Hypothesis**: This states that the parameter is different from the value specified in H_0, without specifying the direction. For example, $H_a: \mu \neq 500$ (the mean is not equal to 500).
2. **Left-Tailed Hypothesis**: This states that the parameter is less than the value specified in H_0. For example, $H_a: \mu < 500$ (the mean is less than 500).
3. **Right-Tailed Hypothesis**: This states that the parameter is greater than the value specified in H_0. For example, $H_a: \mu > 500$ (the mean is greater than 500).

The choice between a one-tailed or two-tailed test depends on the research question. A two-tailed test is used when deviations in both directions are of interest, while a one-tailed test focuses on a specific direction.

Setting Up Hypotheses

Formulating clear and precise hypotheses is the first step in hypothesis testing. This requires understanding the research question and translating it into a testable statement about a population parameter.

1. **Identify the Population Parameter**: Determine what aspect of the population you are testing (e.g., mean, proportion, variance).
2. **Define the Null Hypothesis (H_0)**: Write a statement that assumes no change, effect, or difference.
3. **Define the Alternative Hypothesis (H_a)**: Write a statement that represents the research goal or alternative claim.
4. **Specify the Test Direction**: Decide whether the test is two-tailed, left-tailed, or right-tailed based on the research question.

For example, suppose a company claims that its light bulbs last an average of 1,000 hours. A researcher suspects that the actual lifespan is shorter. The hypotheses would be:

- $H_0: \mu = 1{,}000$ (the mean lifespan is 1,000 hours).
- $H_a: \mu < 1{,}000$ (the mean lifespan is less than 1,000 hours).

Testing the Hypotheses

After formulating the hypotheses, the next step is to test them using sample data. Hypothesis testing involves the following steps:

1. **Collect Data**: Obtain a random sample from the population.
2. **Choose a Test Statistic**: Select the appropriate test statistic (e.g., z-score, t-score) based on the type of data and sample size.
3. **Calculate the Test Statistic**: Use the sample data to calculate the value of the test statistic.
4. **Determine the Critical Region or p-Value**: Identify the threshold for rejecting H_0 based on the chosen significance level (e.g., $\alpha = 0.05$).

5. **Make a Decision**: Compare the test statistic to the critical region or compare the p-value to α. If the test statistic falls in the critical region or the p-value is less than α, reject H_0. Otherwise, fail to reject H_0.

Example of Hypothesis Testing

Suppose a factory claims that the average diameter of its bolts is 10 mm. A quality inspector tests this claim by taking a random sample of 36 bolts, which has a sample mean of 9.8 mm and a standard deviation of 0.3 mm. The inspector wants to know if the mean diameter differs from 10 mm.

1. **Formulate Hypotheses**:

    ○ H_0: $\mu = 10$ (the mean diameter is 10 mm).
    ○ H_a: $\mu \neq 10$ (the mean diameter is not 10 mm).

2. **Choose a Test Statistic**: Since the sample size is large (n ≥ 30), use the z-test.

3. **Calculate the Test Statistic**: $z = (\bar{x} - \mu) \div (\sigma \div \sqrt{n})$ $z = (9.8 - 10) \div (0.3 \div \sqrt{36})$ $z = -0.2 \div 0.05 = -4$

4. **Determine the Critical Region**: For a two-tailed test with $\alpha = 0.05$, the critical z-scores are -1.96 and 1.96. The observed z-score (-4) falls outside this range.

5. **Make a Decision**: Since the z-score is in the critical region, reject H_0. The inspector concludes that the mean diameter is not 10 mm.

Importance of Clear Hypotheses

Well-defined hypotheses are essential for effective hypothesis testing. They ensure that the test aligns with the research question and provides meaningful results. Ambiguous or poorly formulated hypotheses can lead to incorrect conclusions or wasted resources.

For instance, failing to specify whether a test is one-tailed or two-tailed can produce misleading p-values or test statistics. Similarly, choosing inappropriate null or alternative hypotheses can result in invalid inferences.

Common Misconceptions

1. **Failing to Reject H_0 Does Not Prove H_0**: When we fail to reject the null hypothesis, it does not mean that H_0 is true. It simply means there is insufficient evidence to support H_a.
2. **Rejecting H_0 Does Not Confirm H_a**: Rejecting the null hypothesis suggests that the data supports H_a, but it does not definitively prove it. Other explanations or confounding factors may exist.
3. **Hypotheses Are About Populations, Not Samples**: Hypotheses are statements about population parameters, not the sample data itself.

Applications Across Fields

Hypothesis testing is used across various fields, including:

- **Medicine**: Testing the effectiveness of a new drug.
- **Business**: Evaluating the impact of a marketing campaign on sales.
- **Education**: Comparing student performance across teaching methods.
- **Engineering**: Assessing the reliability of new materials or designs.

With clear null and alternative hypotheses, researchers and analysts can systematically evaluate claims, make informed decisions, and advance knowledge in their respective fields.

Types of Errors: Type I and Type II Errors

When conducting hypothesis tests, there are two potential types of errors that can arise due to the inherent uncertainty of working with sample data: Type I errors and Type II errors. Understanding these errors is essential for interpreting the results of hypothesis testing and for making informed decisions about the risks associated with statistical conclusions.

Type I Error (False Positive)

A Type I error occurs when the null hypothesis (H_0) is rejected, even though it is true. In other words, the test concludes that there is an effect, difference, or relationship when none actually exists in the population. This is sometimes referred to as a "false positive."

The probability of making a Type I error is represented by the significance level (α), which is chosen by the researcher before conducting the test. Common choices for α include 0.05, 0.01, and 0.10, corresponding to a 5%, 1%, or 10% probability of rejecting the null hypothesis when it is true.

For example:

1. In a clinical trial, a Type I error might occur if the test incorrectly concludes that a new drug is effective when it is not.
2. In quality control, rejecting the null hypothesis that a production process is functioning properly, when it is actually within acceptable limits, is a Type I error.

The cost of a Type I error depends on the context. In medical research, falsely declaring a treatment effective can lead to wasted resources and harm to patients. In legal contexts, a Type I error might mean convicting an innocent person.

Type II Error (False Negative)

A Type II error occurs when the null hypothesis is not rejected, even though it is false. This means the test fails to detect a real effect, difference, or relationship in the population. A Type II error is often called a "false negative."

The probability of making a Type II error is denoted by β, and its complement $(1 - \beta)$ is called the **power** of the test. Power represents the likelihood of correctly rejecting the null hypothesis when it is false.

For example:

1. In a clinical trial, a Type II error might occur if the test fails to detect the effectiveness of a new drug that actually works.
2. In quality control, failing to detect that a production process is producing defective products is a Type II error.

Type II errors can have serious consequences, especially in situations where missing a real effect leads to negative outcomes. For instance, overlooking the effectiveness of a life-saving drug could delay its availability to patients.

Balancing Type I and Type II Errors

There is a trade-off between Type I and Type II errors. Reducing the probability of one type of error often increases the probability of the other. For instance, lowering the significance level (α) reduces the likelihood of a Type I error but increases the risk of a Type II error, as the test becomes more conservative.

Consider a scenario in which a company tests whether a new marketing campaign increases sales:

- If the company sets $\alpha = 0.01$, it minimizes the chance of concluding that the campaign is effective when it is not (Type I error). However, this stringent threshold may result in failing to detect a real increase in sales (Type II error).
- Conversely, setting $\alpha = 0.10$ increases the chance of detecting an effect, but at the cost of a higher likelihood of making a Type I error.

Researchers must balance these risks based on the context and consequences. In fields like medicine, minimizing Type I errors may be prioritized to avoid approving ineffective treatments. In exploratory research, minimizing Type II errors might take precedence to ensure important discoveries are not overlooked.

Factors Influencing Type I and Type II Errors

Several factors affect the likelihood of Type I and Type II errors:

1. **Significance Level (α):**

- Lowering α reduces the chance of a Type I error but increases the risk of a Type II error.
- Raising α has the opposite effect, making the test more sensitive but increasing the likelihood of false positives.

2. **Sample Size (n)**:
   - Larger sample sizes reduce the variability of the sample statistic, making the test more precise. This decreases both Type I and Type II errors.
   - Small samples increase variability, making it harder to detect true effects and increasing the risk of Type II errors.

3. **Effect Size**:
   - The magnitude of the difference or effect being tested influences the probability of errors. Larger effects are easier to detect, reducing the likelihood of Type II errors.
   - Small effects require larger sample sizes to detect and are more prone to Type II errors.

4. **Test Design**:
   - The choice of test (e.g., z-test, t-test) and its assumptions affect error rates. Using the wrong test or violating assumptions can lead to incorrect conclusions.

5. **Variability in the Data**:
   - Higher variability in the population increases the standard error, making it harder to detect differences and increasing the risk of Type II errors.

Examples of Type I and Type II Errors

1. **Medical Testing**:
   - Null Hypothesis: A patient does not have a disease.
   - Type I Error: Diagnosing the patient with the disease when they do not have it (false positive).
   - Type II Error: Failing to diagnose the disease when the patient actually has it (false negative).

2. In this case, the cost of errors depends on the disease and treatment. A false positive may lead to unnecessary treatments, while a false negative could delay life-saving care.

3. **Quality Control**:

- Null Hypothesis: A batch of products meets quality standards.
- Type I Error: Rejecting a batch that is actually within quality standards.
- Type II Error: Approving a defective batch.

4. In manufacturing, the costs of these errors involve wasted resources (Type I) or customer dissatisfaction and product recalls (Type II).

5. **Legal System**:

    - Null Hypothesis: A defendant is innocent.
    - Type I Error: Convicting an innocent person (false positive).
    - Type II Error: Acquitting a guilty person (false negative).

6. In legal contexts, society must decide whether it is more important to minimize wrongful convictions (Type I) or to ensure that all guilty individuals are convicted (Type II).

Minimizing Errors

1. **Increasing Sample Size**: Larger samples reduce variability, improving the precision of the test and lowering both Type I and Type II error rates.

2. **Adjusting Significance Levels**: The choice of α should reflect the context. For instance, in high-stakes medical research, a lower α (e.g., 0.01) may be chosen to reduce the risk of Type I errors.

3. **Improving Study Design**: Ensuring random sampling, reducing bias, and controlling for confounding variables can enhance the reliability of the test.

4. **Conducting Power Analysis**: Before collecting data, researchers perform a power analysis to determine the required sample size for detecting an effect with a specified probability of avoiding a Type II error.

Significance Levels (p-values) and Decision-Making

Significance levels and p-values are fundamental components of hypothesis testing, providing a framework for deciding whether to reject or fail to reject the null hypothesis (H_0). Together, they quantify the strength of evidence against the null hypothesis and guide statistical decision-making.

What is a Significance Level?

The significance level, denoted as α, is the threshold for determining whether the observed data is unlikely under the null hypothesis. It represents the probability of making a Type I error—rejecting H_0 when it is actually true. Commonly used significance levels include $\alpha = 0.05$, $\alpha = 0.01$, and $\alpha = 0.10$. For example, with $\alpha = 0.05$, there is a 5% risk of rejecting a true null hypothesis.

The choice of α depends on the context and the consequences of making a Type I error:

- In medical research, a smaller α (e.g., 0.01) is often chosen to minimize the risk of approving ineffective treatments.
- In exploratory research, a larger α (e.g., 0.10) might be acceptable to increase sensitivity to potential effects.

What is a p-Value?

The p-value is the probability of observing data as extreme as, or more extreme than, the sample data, assuming that the null hypothesis is true. It measures the compatibility between the observed data and the null hypothesis. Smaller p-values indicate stronger evidence against H_0.

For example:

1. If $p = 0.03$, there is a 3% chance of obtaining the observed results (or more extreme) if H_0 is true.
2. If $p = 0.15$, there is a 15% chance of observing results as extreme as the sample data under H_0.

The p-value is compared to the significance level (α) to make a decision:

- If $p \leq \alpha$, reject H_0. The data provides sufficient evidence to support the alternative hypothesis (H_a).
- If $p > \alpha$, fail to reject H_0. The data does not provide enough evidence to contradict H_0.

Interpreting p-Values

1. **$p \leq \alpha$ (Statistically Significant)**: When the p-value is less than or equal to the significance level, the null hypothesis is rejected. For example, in a drug trial, a p-value of 0.02 with $\alpha = 0.05$ suggests that the drug has a statistically significant effect, as the likelihood of observing the results under H_0 is only 2%.

2. **$p > \alpha$ (Not Statistically Significant)**: When the p-value exceeds α, there is insufficient evidence to reject H_0. For instance, a p-value of 0.08 with $\alpha = 0.05$ implies that the results are not statistically significant, and H_0 cannot be ruled out.

3. **Magnitude of the p-Value**: The size of the p-value indicates the strength of evidence against H_0:

    ◦ Smaller p-values (e.g., 0.001) provide stronger evidence against H_0.

- Larger p-values (e.g., 0.40) suggest that the data is consistent with H_0.

It is important to note that a non-significant p-value does not prove H_0; it merely indicates a lack of strong evidence against it.

Example of Significance Levels and p-Values

Suppose a factory claims that the mean weight of its packaged products is 500 grams. A quality inspector takes a random sample of 30 packages and finds a mean weight of 495 grams with a standard deviation of 10 grams. The inspector tests H_0: $\mu = 500$ against H_a: $\mu \neq 500$ at $\alpha = 0.05$.

1. **Calculate the Test Statistic:** $z = (\bar{x} - \mu) \div (\sigma \div \sqrt{n})$ $z = (495 - 500) \div (10 \div \sqrt{30})$
   $z = -5 \div 1.83 \approx -2.73$

2. **Find the p-Value:** Using a z-table, the cumulative probability for $z = -2.73$ is approximately 0.0032. For a two-tailed test, the p-value is:
   $p = 2 \times 0.0032 = 0.0064$

3. **Compare p with α:** Since $p = 0.0064$ is less than $\alpha = 0.05$, the inspector rejects H_0. This suggests that the mean weight is significantly different from 500 grams.

Choosing the Significance Level

The choice of α depends on the balance between Type I and Type II errors and the context of the study:

1. **Low α (e.g., 0.01):**
   - Used when the cost of a Type I error is high, such as in drug approval or safety testing.
   - Reduces the likelihood of false positives but increases the risk of false negatives.
2. **High α (e.g., 0.10):**
   - Used in exploratory research or when detecting effects is more important than avoiding false positives.
   - Increases the likelihood of detecting true effects but raises the risk of false positives.
3. **Standard α (e.g., 0.05):**
   - Commonly used as a compromise between Type I and Type II errors.
   - Balances sensitivity and specificity.

Common Misinterpretations of p-Values

1. **p is Not the Probability That H_0 is True**: The p-value does not indicate the probability of the null hypothesis being true. It quantifies the probability of observing the data (or more extreme results) under the assumption that H_0 is true.

2. **p is Not the Size of the Effect**: A small p-value indicates strong evidence against H_0 but does not measure the magnitude of the effect. For example, a tiny p-value in a large sample might correspond to a trivial effect size.

3. **Statistical Significance is Not Practical Importance**: Results can be statistically significant but not practically meaningful. For instance, a minor difference in mean weight might not matter in practice, even if it is statistically significant.

Reporting p-Values and Significance Levels

Clear reporting of p-values and significance levels is essential for transparency and reproducibility. Best practices include:

- Reporting the exact p-value rather than simply stating "$p < 0.05$."
- Specifying the significance level used in the analysis (e.g., $\alpha = 0.05$).
- Discussing the practical implications of statistically significant results.

For example, instead of saying, "The result was significant," write, "The test produced a p-value of 0.021, indicating statistical significance at $\alpha = 0.05$. This suggests that the observed effect is unlikely under the null hypothesis."

Applications of Significance Levels and p-Values

1. **Clinical Trials**: In medical research, p-values help determine whether a new treatment is effective compared to a placebo. For example, a p-value of 0.03 might support the claim that a drug reduces blood pressure.

2. **Quality Control**: Manufacturers use p-values to assess whether production processes meet specifications. For instance, a p-value greater than 0.05 might indicate that the defect rate is within acceptable limits.

3. **Market Research**: Businesses analyze customer surveys using p-values to evaluate product preferences. For example, a p-value less than 0.05 might suggest that a new product is favored over competitors.

4. **Environmental Studies**: Researchers use p-values to test hypotheses about pollution levels, climate trends, and ecological patterns. For example, a p-value of 0.01 might indicate significant changes in air quality.

Challenges in Using p-Values

1. **Overemphasis on Statistical Significance**: Solely focusing on p-values can lead to ignoring effect sizes, confidence intervals, and practical relevance. A more comprehensive approach considers all these factors.

2. **Multiple Comparisons**: Conducting multiple hypothesis tests increases the risk of Type I errors. Adjustments, such as the Bonferroni correction, are necessary to maintain the overall significance level.

3. **Misuse in Exploratory Research**: Using p-values to generate hypotheses rather than test them can lead to biased results. Pre-registration of hypotheses and study designs helps mitigate this issue.

Power Analysis: Determining Sample Size Requirements

Power analysis is a statistical method used to determine the sample size required to detect an effect of a given size with a specified level of confidence. It's critical in the planning and design of experiments and studies, ensuring that researchers collect enough data to draw meaningful conclusions without wasting resources. Power analysis balances the probability of detecting true effects (power) against the risks of Type I and Type II errors.

Understanding Statistical Power

Statistical power is the probability of correctly rejecting the null hypothesis (H_0) when it is false. It is calculated as $1 - \beta$, where β is the probability of a Type II error (failing to reject H_0 when it is false). High statistical power indicates a higher likelihood of detecting a true effect.

For example, if a study has a power of 0.80 (or 80%), it means there is an 80% chance of detecting an effect if it exists. The remaining 20% represents the risk of a Type II error. A commonly accepted threshold for power is 0.80, though higher power (e.g., 0.90) is sometimes required in critical research areas such as medicine.

Key Components of Power Analysis

1. **Effect Size**: Effect size is a measure of the magnitude of the difference or relationship being studied. Larger effect sizes are easier to detect, requiring smaller sample sizes, while smaller effect sizes demand larger samples for adequate power. Common metrics for effect size include:

    - Cohen's d for comparing means.
    - Pearson's r for correlations.
    - Odds ratios for categorical data.

2. For example, in a clinical trial, an effect size might represent the difference in blood pressure reduction between a treatment group and a placebo group. A large difference (e.g., 20 mmHg) requires fewer participants to detect, whereas a small difference (e.g., 2 mmHg) requires a much larger sample.

3. **Significance Level (α)**: The significance level is the probability of a Type I error, typically set at 0.05. Lower α values make the test more stringent, increasing the sample size needed to achieve adequate power. For instance, reducing α from 0.05 to 0.01 requires more data to maintain the same power.

4. **Sample Size (n)**: Sample size directly influences power. Larger samples reduce variability, making it easier to detect true effects. Inadequate sample sizes increase the risk of Type II errors, while excessively large samples may waste resources without adding meaningful precision.

5. **Variability in the Data**: The variability or standard deviation of the population affects the required sample size. Higher variability increases the standard error, making it harder to detect differences and requiring larger samples. For example, studying blood pressure in a highly diverse population will demand more participants than studying it in a homogenous group.

6. **Test Type and Design**: The choice of statistical test (e.g., t-test, ANOVA, chi-square test) and study design (e.g., paired vs. independent samples) affects power. Paired designs generally require smaller samples because they control for individual differences, reducing variability.

Steps in Power Analysis

Power analysis typically involves four steps, focusing on any three components to calculate the fourth (e.g., determining sample size given power, effect size, and significance level).

1. **Define the Research Hypothesis**: Clearly specify the null and alternative hypotheses, including whether the test is one-tailed or two-tailed. For example, testing whether a new drug reduces cholesterol compared to a placebo might involve H_0: $\mu = 0$ (no difference) and H_a: $\mu < 0$ (a reduction).

2. **Determine the Effect Size**: Use prior studies, pilot data, or standardized guidelines to estimate the effect size. For instance, Cohen's guidelines suggest small (d = 0.2), medium (d = 0.5), and large (d = 0.8) effects for comparing means.

3. **Set the Desired Power and Significance Level**: Choose a power level (e.g., 0.80) and a significance level (e.g., 0.05). These decisions depend on the context, with stricter thresholds required in high-stakes research.

4. **Calculate the Sample Size**: Use power analysis formulas, software (e.g., G*Power, R, Python), or tables to calculate the required sample size. For

example, in a two-sample t-test with α = 0.05, power = 0.80, and a medium effect size (d = 0.5), the required sample size per group is approximately 64 participants.

Example of Power Analysis

Consider a researcher studying whether a new teaching method improves test scores compared to a traditional method. Based on pilot data, the expected difference in mean scores is 5 points, with a standard deviation of 10 points. The researcher sets α = 0.05 and power = 0.80.

1. **Calculate the Effect Size**: Cohen's d = (Mean1 - Mean2) ÷ SD d = 5 ÷ 10 = 0.5 (medium effect size)

2. **Determine the Sample Size**: Using power analysis software or tables for a two-sample t-test, with d = 0.5, α = 0.05, and power = 0.80, the required sample size is 64 participants per group.

3. **Interpret the Results**: The researcher concludes that a total of 128 participants (64 per group) is needed to detect the effect with 80% power.

Applications of Power Analysis

1. **Clinical Trials**: Power analysis is critical in designing clinical trials to ensure sufficient sample sizes for detecting treatment effects. For instance, testing a new cancer drug may require a high power (e.g., 0.90) due to the serious consequences of Type II errors.

2. **Quality Control**: Manufacturers use power analysis to determine how many products to sample for detecting defects. For example, if a factory produces 10,000 units daily, a power analysis can guide how many units to test for maintaining product quality.

3. **Market Research**: Companies use power analysis to plan surveys and experiments, ensuring enough participants to detect consumer preferences or behavioral changes. For instance, evaluating the impact of a new advertisement might require sampling from thousands of viewers.

4. **Education Research**: Studies comparing teaching methods or interventions rely on power analysis to avoid underpowered conclusions. For example, testing whether small class sizes improve student performance demands a careful balance between sample size and resource availability.

5. **Environmental Studies**: Researchers studying pollution levels or species populations use power analysis to plan fieldwork. For instance, detecting a small reduction in air pollution levels over time may require large samples due to high variability in environmental data.

Challenges and Limitations

1. **Estimating Effect Size**: Effect size estimation can be challenging, especially in new research areas with limited prior data. Overestimating effect sizes leads to underpowered studies, while underestimating them results in unnecessarily large samples.

2. **Resource Constraints**: Achieving the desired sample size may be impractical due to time, budget, or logistical limitations. Researchers must balance statistical requirements with real-world constraints.

3. **Multiple Comparisons**: Studies involving multiple tests or comparisons increase the risk of Type I errors. Adjusting for this (e.g., using Bonferroni correction) impacts power and sample size requirements.

4. **Variability in Data**: High variability increases sample size requirements, making studies in diverse populations or noisy environments more demanding.

Enhancing Power Without Increasing Sample Size

When increasing sample size is impractical, researchers can enhance power through other means:

1. **Reduce Variability**: Improve measurement precision or control for confounding variables to lower the standard error.
2. **Increase Effect Size**: Use stronger interventions or focus on larger differences to improve detectability.
3. **Choose One-Tailed Tests**: When appropriate, a one-tailed test requires fewer participants than a two-tailed test.

Chapter 9: Inferential Statistics

Confidence Intervals: Interpreting Margins of Error

Confidence intervals are a fundamental concept in inferential statistics, providing a range of values within which a population parameter is likely to lie. They are used to estimate unknown quantities, such as the population mean or proportion, based on sample data. Confidence intervals combine the sample statistic with a margin of error, which accounts for sampling variability. This approach allows researchers to make informed statements about population parameters without measuring the entire population.

What is a Confidence Interval?

A confidence interval (CI) is a range of values calculated from sample data, expressed as:

$$\text{Point Estimate} \pm \text{Margin of Error}$$

The **point estimate** is the sample statistic (e.g., mean, proportion), while the **margin of error** reflects the variability in the estimate due to sampling. The margin of error depends on the standard error, the sample size, and the desired confidence level.

For example, if the mean height of a sample of 50 people is 170 cm, with a standard error of 2 cm and a 95% confidence level, the confidence interval is:

$$170 \pm (1.96 \times 2) = 170 \pm 3.92 = (166.08, 173.92)$$

This means we are 95% confident that the true population mean lies between 166.08 cm and 173.92 cm.

Confidence Levels

The confidence level represents the proportion of confidence intervals, constructed in the same way from repeated samples, that would contain the true population parameter. Common confidence levels are 90%, 95%, and 99%.

- A 90% confidence level indicates a 10% chance that the interval does not contain the population parameter.
- A 95% confidence level reduces this chance to 5%.
- A 99% confidence level further reduces the risk to 1%, but the interval becomes wider, reflecting increased uncertainty.

The confidence level determines the critical value (z or t) used in the margin of error. For a 95% confidence level, the critical z-value is 1.96 in a standard normal distribution.

Components of a Confidence Interval

1. **Point Estimate**: The point estimate is the best single-value estimate of the population parameter. For example, the sample mean (x̄) estimates the population mean (μ), and the sample proportion (p̂) estimates the population proportion (p).

2. **Margin of Error**: The margin of error quantifies the uncertainty in the estimate. It is calculated as:
   Margin of Error = Critical Value × Standard Error
   The **standard error (SE)** depends on the sample size and the variability in the data:

   - For means: SE = σ ÷ √n (when σ is known) or SE = s ÷ √n (when σ is unknown).
   - For proportions: SE = √[p̂ × (1 - p̂) ÷ n].

3. **Critical Value**: The critical value corresponds to the desired confidence level and the distribution of the test statistic. For normal distributions, z-values are used. For small samples or unknown population standard deviations, t-values are applied.

Interpreting a Confidence Interval

A confidence interval provides a range of plausible values for a population parameter. However, it does not guarantee that the true parameter lies within the interval for a specific sample. Instead, it reflects the confidence that this method will produce intervals containing the parameter in repeated sampling.

For example, a 95% confidence interval does not imply a 95% probability that the parameter is in the interval for a single sample. Instead, if 100 confidence intervals are constructed from 100 random samples, approximately 95 of them will contain the true parameter.

Factors Affecting Confidence Intervals

1. **Sample Size**: Larger samples produce smaller standard errors, narrowing the confidence interval. For example, doubling the sample size reduces the margin of error by about 30%.
   Suppose a sample of size 25 yields a 95% confidence interval for the mean of (60, 70). Increasing the sample size to 100 reduces the standard error, resulting in a narrower interval, such as (63, 67).

2. **Variability in the Data**: Higher variability increases the standard error, widening the confidence interval. For instance, data with a standard deviation of 10 will produce wider intervals than data with a standard deviation of 5, given the same sample size.

3. **Confidence Level**: Higher confidence levels (e.g., 99% vs. 95%) require larger critical values, resulting in wider intervals. While this increases certainty, it also reduces precision.
   For example, with a sample mean of 50 and a standard error of 2:
   - At 95% confidence, the interval is $50 \pm (1.96 \times 2) = (46.08, 53.92)$.
   - At 99% confidence, the interval widens to $50 \pm (2.58 \times 2) = (44.84, 55.16)$.

Constructing Confidence Intervals

1. **For Means**: When the population standard deviation (σ) is known and the sample size is large ($n \geq 30$), use the z-distribution: $CI = \bar{x} \pm (z \times SE)$
   When σ is unknown or the sample size is small ($n < 30$), use the t-distribution:
   $CI = \bar{x} \pm (t \times SE)$
   For example, in a sample of 20 students with a mean test score of 75, a standard deviation of 10, and a 95% confidence level: $SE = s \div \sqrt{n} = 10 \div \sqrt{20} \approx 2.24$ t for df = 19 at 95% confidence ≈ 2.093 (from t-table)
   $CI = 75 \pm (2.093 \times 2.24) = 75 \pm 4.69 = (70.31, 79.69)$

2. **For Proportions**: When estimating a population proportion: $CI = \hat{p} \pm (z \times SE)$
   For example, if 60 out of 200 survey respondents prefer a product: $\hat{p} = 60 \div 200 = 0.30$ $SE = \sqrt{[\hat{p} \times (1 - \hat{p}) \div n]} = \sqrt{[0.3 \times 0.7 \div 200]} \approx 0.0324$
   At 95% confidence, z = 1.96: $CI = 0.30 \pm (1.96 \times 0.0324) \approx (0.236, 0.364)$
   This indicates that the true proportion of product preference is likely between 23.6% and 36.4%.

Applications of Confidence Intervals

1. **Healthcare**: Confidence intervals help estimate treatment effects, such as the mean reduction in blood pressure after using a new drug. For instance, if a drug trial produces a 95% confidence interval of (5 mmHg, 10 mmHg), researchers are confident that the true mean reduction lies in this range.

2. **Business**: Companies use confidence intervals to estimate customer satisfaction, sales figures, or market share. For example, a survey might show that 70% of customers are satisfied, with a 95% confidence interval of ±5%.

3. **Quality Control**: Manufacturers construct confidence intervals to ensure product specifications meet quality standards. For example, a 95% confidence interval for the mean weight of packaged goods might be (499 g, 501 g), confirming compliance with the target weight of 500 g.

4. **Environmental Studies**: Confidence intervals estimate pollution levels, species populations, or climate trends. For instance, a study might report that the mean air pollutant concentration is 30 μg/m^3, with a 95% confidence interval of (28 μg/m^3, 32 μg/m^3).

Challenges and Misinterpretations

1. **Misunderstanding Confidence**: A 95% confidence level does not mean there is a 95% chance the true parameter lies in the interval. It refers to the long-term success rate of the interval estimation method.

2. **Dependence on Sample Quality**: Confidence intervals are only valid if the sample is random and representative of the population. Biased or non-random samples can produce misleading intervals.

3. **Ignoring Practical Significance**: Narrow confidence intervals may be statistically precise but practically meaningless. For example, an interval for mean income might be precise but unhelpful if it ignores income inequality.

4. **Overreliance on Large Samples**: While larger samples improve precision, they do not address underlying issues like bias or measurement errors.

t-Tests: Comparing Two Groups

The t-test is a statistical method used to compare the means of two groups to determine whether the observed differences are statistically significant. It is widely applied across various fields, such as medicine, psychology, and business, to test hypotheses about group differences. The t-test is especially useful when the sample size is small, and the population standard deviation is unknown.

Types of t-Tests

There are three main types of t-tests, each suited for specific scenarios:

1. **Independent Samples t-Test**: Compares the means of two independent groups, such as male vs. female test scores or treatment vs. control groups.

2. **Paired Samples t-Test**: Used when the same individuals are measured under two conditions, such as before and after an intervention.

3. **One-Sample t-Test**: Compares the sample mean to a known or hypothesized population mean, such as testing whether the average daily temperature deviates from a historical average.

Assumptions of the t-Test

For valid results, the t-test relies on specific assumptions:

1. **Normality**: The data in each group should be approximately normally distributed. This assumption is less strict for larger samples due to the Central Limit Theorem.

2. **Independence**: Observations within each group should be independent. For example, data from individuals in one group should not influence data in the other group.

3. **Homogeneity of Variance**: For independent samples t-tests, the variances of the two groups should be approximately equal. If this assumption is violated, a variation of the t-test, such as Welch's t-test, can be used.

4. **Scale of Measurement**: The dependent variable should be measured on an interval or ratio scale (e.g., weight, height, or temperature).

Independent Samples t-Test

The independent samples t-test is used to determine whether two unrelated groups have significantly different means. For example, you might test whether students taught with two different methods score differently on a standardized test.

The test statistic (t) is calculated as:

$$t = (\bar{x}_1 - \bar{x}_2) \div \sqrt{[(s_1^2 / n_1) + (s_2^2 / n_2)]}$$

Where:

- $\bar{x}_1$ and $\bar{x}_2$ are the sample means,
- s_1^2 and s_2^2 are the sample variances,
- n_1 and n_2 are the sample sizes.

The degrees of freedom (df) for this test are calculated as:

$$df = n_1 + n_2 - 2$$

Example: Independent Samples t-Test

Suppose a researcher wants to test whether two teaching methods produce different average test scores. The scores for 10 students taught with Method A are: 85, 88, 84, 90, 87, 82, 89, 91, 83, 86.

The scores for 12 students taught with Method B are: 78, 80, 79, 77, 82, 81, 75, 76, 84, 80, 83, 78.

1. **Calculate Group Means**:

    - Mean for Method A ($\bar{x}_1$): 85.5
    - Mean for Method B ($\bar{x}_2$): 79.25

2. **Calculate Group Variances**:

    ○ Variance for Method A (s_1^2): 9.72
    ○ Variance for Method B (s_2^2): 8.25

3. **Calculate the t-Statistic**: $t = (85.5 - 79.25) \div \sqrt{[(9.72 / 10) + (8.25 / 12)]}$ $t \approx 6.25 \div \sqrt{[0.972 + 0.6875]}$ $t \approx 6.25 \div \sqrt{1.6595}$ $t \approx 6.25 \div 1.288$ $t \approx 4.85$

4. **Determine Degrees of Freedom**: $df = n_1 + n_2 - 2 = 10 + 12 - 2 = 20$

5. **Compare t-Statistic with Critical Value**: For $\alpha = 0.05$ (two-tailed test) and $df = 20$, the critical value is approximately ±2.086. Since t = 4.85 is greater than the critical value, the researcher rejects the null hypothesis. This suggests that the teaching methods produce significantly different test scores.

Paired Samples t-Test

The paired samples t-test is used when the same individuals are measured under two conditions, such as before and after an intervention. It evaluates whether the mean difference between paired observations is statistically significant.

The test statistic (t) for paired data is:

$$t = \bar{d} \div (sd \div \sqrt{n})$$

Where:

- $\bar{d}$ is the mean of the differences between paired observations,
- sd is the standard deviation of the differences,
- n is the number of pairs.

Example: Paired Samples t-Test

A fitness instructor tests whether a 4-week program improves push-up performance. Ten participants record their push-ups before and after the program:

- Before: 20, 22, 25, 18, 21, 24, 19, 20, 23, 22.
- After: 24, 26, 28, 21, 24, 28, 22, 23, 27, 25.

1. **Calculate Differences**: Differences (After - Before): 4, 4, 3, 3, 3, 4, 3, 3, 4, 3.

2. **Calculate Mean and Standard Deviation of Differences**:

    ○ Mean difference ($\bar{d}$): 3.4
    ○ Standard deviation of differences (sd): 0.52

3. **Calculate t-Statistic**: $t = 3.4 \div (0.52 \div \sqrt{10})$ $t \approx 3.4 \div 0.164$ $t \approx 20.73$

4. **Determine Degrees of Freedom**: df = n - 1 = 10 - 1 = 9

5. **Compare t-Statistic with Critical Value**: For α = 0.05 (two-tailed test) and df = 9, the critical value is approximately ±2.262. Since t = 20.73 is greater than the critical value, the null hypothesis is rejected. The fitness program significantly improved push-up performance.

One-Sample t-Test

The one-sample t-test compares the sample mean to a known population mean. It evaluates whether the sample mean differs significantly from the hypothesized population mean.

The test statistic (t) is:

$$t = (\bar{x} - \mu) \div (s \div \sqrt{n})$$

Where:

- $\bar{x}$ is the sample mean,
- μ is the population mean,
- s is the sample standard deviation,
- n is the sample size.

Applications of t-Tests

1. **Medicine**: Comparing the effectiveness of two drugs or treatments, such as testing whether a new medication reduces cholesterol levels more effectively than an existing one.

2. **Education**: Evaluating differences in teaching methods or educational interventions, such as comparing test scores between experimental and control groups.

3. **Psychology**: Assessing the impact of therapies, such as comparing pre- and post-treatment anxiety scores for a group of patients.

4. **Business**: Analyzing consumer behavior, such as testing whether a new advertising campaign increases sales compared to a previous campaign.

5. **Environmental Studies**: Comparing pollutant levels between two regions or before and after implementing an environmental regulation.

Limitations of t-Tests

1. **Sensitivity to Assumptions**: Violations of normality or equal variances can affect the validity of t-tests. Transforming data or using nonparametric alternatives (e.g., Mann-Whitney U test) may be necessary.

2. **Small Sample Sizes**: Small samples increase variability and reduce the test's reliability. For very small samples, bootstrapping can provide additional insights.

3. **Multiple Comparisons**: Conducting multiple t-tests increases the risk of Type I errors. Using corrections like the Bonferroni method is recommended.

By understanding and applying t-tests effectively, researchers can make robust comparisons between groups and draw meaningful conclusions across a wide range of disciplines.

ANOVA: Analyzing Differences Among Multiple Groups

Analysis of Variance (ANOVA) is a statistical technique used to compare means across three or more groups to determine whether at least one group mean significantly differs from the others. Unlike the t-test, which compares only two groups, ANOVA is designed to handle multiple groups simultaneously, reducing the risk of Type I errors that arise from conducting multiple pairwise comparisons.

The Basics of ANOVA

ANOVA assesses whether observed differences in sample means are due to genuine group differences or merely random variation. It does this by analyzing two sources of variability:

1. **Between-Group Variability**: Differences in means between the groups being compared.
2. **Within-Group Variability**: Differences among individuals within each group.

The fundamental question in ANOVA is whether the variability between groups is large enough relative to the variability within groups to conclude that the group means are not equal.

The test statistic for ANOVA is the **F-ratio**, calculated as:

F = Variance between groups ÷ Variance within groups

A larger F-ratio indicates that the between-group differences are substantial compared to the within-group variability, suggesting that at least one group mean is significantly different.

Assumptions of ANOVA

For valid results, ANOVA relies on several assumptions:

1. **Normality**: The dependent variable should be approximately normally distributed within each group.
2. **Homogeneity of Variance**: The variances of the groups should be roughly equal. This can be tested using Levene's test or Bartlett's test.
3. **Independence**: Observations must be independent of one another. This assumption is critical for accurate F-ratios.

Violations of these assumptions may require alternative approaches, such as nonparametric tests (e.g., Kruskal-Wallis test) or Welch's ANOVA for unequal variances.

One-Way ANOVA

One-way ANOVA is the simplest form, used when comparing a single independent variable with multiple levels (groups). For example, a researcher might compare the effectiveness of three diets (Diet A, Diet B, Diet C) on weight loss.

Steps in One-Way ANOVA

1. **State the Hypotheses**:
    - Null Hypothesis (H_0): All group means are equal ($\mu_1 = \mu_2 = \mu_3$).
    - Alternative Hypothesis (H_a): At least one group mean is different.

2. **Calculate the F-Ratio**: ANOVA partitions the total variability into between-group and within-group variability, using the following formulas:
    - **Between-Group Variability**: Based on the differences between group means and the overall mean.
    - **Within-Group Variability**: Based on the differences between individual data points and their respective group means.

3. **Determine the Critical F-Value**: Use the F-distribution table and the degrees of freedom for the numerator (between groups) and denominator (within groups).

4. **Make a Decision**: If the calculated F-value exceeds the critical F-value or if the p-value is less than the chosen significance level (e.g., $\alpha = 0.05$), reject the null hypothesis.

Example: One-Way ANOVA

A researcher tests whether three teaching methods (A, B, C) yield different exam scores. The scores are:

- Method A: 85, 90, 88

- Method B: 78, 82, 79
- Method C: 92, 95, 93

1. **Calculate Group Means**:

    - Method A: Mean = (85 + 90 + 88) ÷ 3 = 87.67
    - Method B: Mean = (78 + 82 + 79) ÷ 3 = 79.67
    - Method C: Mean = (92 + 95 + 93) ÷ 3 = 93.33

2. **Overall Mean**: Overall Mean = (85 + 90 + 88 + 78 + 82 + 79 + 92 + 95 + 93) ÷ 9 = 86.89

3. **Partition Variability**:

    - Between-Group Sum of Squares (SSB): Measures variability due to differences in group means.
    - Within-Group Sum of Squares (SSW): Measures variability within each group.

4. These are used to calculate the Mean Squares for between and within groups:

    - MSB = SSB ÷ df_between
    - MSW = SSW ÷ df_within

5. **Calculate the F-Ratio**: F = MSB ÷ MSW

6. **Compare to Critical Value**: If F exceeds the critical value from the F-distribution table (based on df), the null hypothesis is rejected.

Two-Way ANOVA

Two-way ANOVA extends the analysis by including two independent variables and examining their interaction. For example, a study might test the effects of diet (A, B, C) and exercise (low, high) on weight loss. Two-way ANOVA answers three questions:

1. Does diet affect weight loss?
2. Does exercise affect weight loss?
3. Is there an interaction between diet and exercise?

The interaction effect tests whether the effect of one variable depends on the level of the other.

Post Hoc Tests

When ANOVA indicates significant differences, it does not specify which groups differ. Post hoc tests, such as Tukey's HSD (Honestly Significant Difference) or Bonferroni correction, identify the specific group differences while controlling for multiple comparisons.

For example, if a one-way ANOVA finds a significant F-ratio for three groups, Tukey's HSD might reveal that Method C is significantly better than Method B but not significantly different from Method A.

Applications of ANOVA

1. **Healthcare**: Comparing the effectiveness of multiple treatments, such as testing three drugs for blood pressure reduction, with one-way ANOVA or examining the interaction of treatment and dosage levels with two-way ANOVA.

2. **Education**: Evaluating teaching methods or curricula. For instance, testing whether lecture, discussion, and hands-on methods produce different test scores.

3. **Marketing**: Analyzing the effects of advertising strategies on sales or customer engagement. For example, a company might use ANOVA to test the effectiveness of online, TV, and radio ads.

4. **Agriculture**: Testing the effects of fertilizers or irrigation methods on crop yields.

5. **Psychology**: Studying the effects of interventions, such as comparing cognitive-behavioral therapy, mindfulness, and medication for anxiety reduction.

Challenges and Limitations of ANOVA

1. **Sensitivity to Assumptions**: Violations of normality or homogeneity of variance can affect results. Transforming data or using nonparametric alternatives (e.g., Kruskal-Wallis test) may be necessary.

2. **Interpretation of Interactions**: Interpreting interaction effects in two-way ANOVA can be complex, especially with more than two levels for each factor.

3. **Multiple Comparisons**: Post hoc tests are essential to avoid inflated Type I error rates when multiple groups are compared.

4. **Overreliance on p-Values**: ANOVA detects statistical significance but does not measure practical significance. Reporting effect sizes (e.g., eta-squared or partial eta-squared) alongside p-values provides a more comprehensive analysis.

Z-Tests: Comparing Means with Large Sample Sizes

A z-test is a statistical method used to determine whether there is a significant difference between a sample statistic and a known population parameter, or between two sample statistics. Z-tests are particularly useful when dealing with large sample sizes (n ≥ 30) and when the population standard deviation is known. They are among the simplest and most widely used tools in inferential statistics.

Key Features of Z-Tests

Z-tests are based on the standard normal distribution, which has a mean of 0 and a standard deviation of 1. The test statistic, called the z-score, measures how many standard deviations a sample statistic is from the population parameter under the null hypothesis. The z-score is calculated as:

$$z = (\bar{x} - \mu) \div (\sigma \div \sqrt{n})$$

Where:

- $\bar{x}$ is the sample mean,
- μ is the population mean,
- σ is the population standard deviation,
- n is the sample size.

The z-score is then compared to critical values from the standard normal distribution table or converted into a p-value for hypothesis testing.

Types of Z-Tests

1. **One-Sample Z-Test**: Compares a sample mean to a known population mean. For example, testing whether the average height of students in a school differs from the national average.

2. **Two-Sample Z-Test**: Compares the means of two independent samples. For instance, comparing the average salaries of employees in two different companies.

3. **Z-Test for Proportions**: Tests whether the proportion in a sample differs from a known population proportion or whether two sample proportions differ. For example, testing whether the proportion of voters favoring a candidate in a survey matches the proportion in the general population.

Assumptions of Z-Tests

Z-tests rely on specific assumptions:

1. **Normality**: The population from which the sample is drawn should be normally distributed. For large sample sizes (n ≥ 30), the Central Limit Theorem ensures that the sampling distribution of the mean is approximately normal.

2. **Known Population Standard Deviation (σ)**: The population standard deviation must be known. If σ is unknown, a t-test is more appropriate.

3. **Independence**: Observations must be independent. For example, the sample should be randomly selected, and one observation should not influence another.

One-Sample Z-Test

The one-sample z-test evaluates whether the sample mean ($\bar{x}$) differs significantly from the population mean (μ). It is commonly used when the population mean and standard deviation are known.

Example: One-Sample Z-Test

A researcher claims that the average height of adult men in a population is 175 cm. To test this claim, a sample of 100 men is taken, and the sample mean height is found to be 177 cm, with a known population standard deviation of 10 cm. The researcher performs a one-sample z-test at $\alpha = 0.05$.

1. **Formulate Hypotheses**:
    - H_0: $\mu = 175$ (The mean height is 175 cm).
    - H_a: $\mu \neq 175$ (The mean height is not 175 cm).

2. **Calculate the Test Statistic**: $z = (\bar{x} - \mu) \div (\sigma \div \sqrt{n})$ $z = (177 - 175) \div (10 \div \sqrt{100})$ $z = 2 \div (10 \div 10)$ $z = 2 \div 1 = 2$

3. **Determine the Critical Value**: For a two-tailed test at $\alpha = 0.05$, the critical z-values are ± 1.96.

4. **Compare z-Statistic to Critical Values**: Since $z = 2$ is greater than 1.96, the null hypothesis is rejected. The researcher concludes that the mean height of adult men is significantly different from 175 cm.

Two-Sample Z-Test

The two-sample z-test compares the means of two independent samples to determine if they are significantly different. It is used when the population standard deviations of both groups are known.

The formula for the two-sample z-test is:

$$z = (\bar{x}_1 - \bar{x}_2) \div \sqrt{[(\sigma_1^2 / n_1) + (\sigma_2^2 / n_2)]}$$

Where:

- $\bar{x}_1$ and $\bar{x}_2$ are the sample means,

- σ_1 and σ_2 are the population standard deviations,
- n_1 and n_2 are the sample sizes.

Example: Two-Sample Z-Test

A company wants to compare the average salaries of employees in two departments. In Department A, 50 employees have a mean salary of $60,000 with a standard deviation of $5,000. In Department B, 40 employees have a mean salary of $62,000 with a standard deviation of $6,000. The test is conducted at $\alpha = 0.05$.

1. **Formulate Hypotheses**:
    - H_0: $\mu_1 = \mu_2$ (The mean salaries are equal).
    - H_a: $\mu_1 \neq \mu_2$ (The mean salaries are not equal).

2. **Calculate the Test Statistic**: $z = (\bar{x}_1 - \bar{x}_2) \div \sqrt{[(\sigma_1^2 / n_1) + (\sigma_2^2 / n_2)]}$ $z = (60{,}000 - 62{,}000) \div \sqrt{[(5{,}000^2 / 50) + (6{,}000^2 / 40)]}$ $z = -2{,}000 \div \sqrt{[(25{,}000{,}000 / 50) + (36{,}000{,}000 / 40)]}$ $z = -2{,}000 \div \sqrt{[500{,}000 + 900{,}000]}$ $z = -2{,}000 \div \sqrt{1{,}400{,}000}$ $z = -2{,}000 \div 1{,}183.22 \approx -1.69$

3. **Determine the Critical Value**: For a two-tailed test at $\alpha = 0.05$, the critical z-values are ± 1.96.

4. **Compare z-Statistic to Critical Values**: Since $z = -1.69$ does not exceed the critical values, the null hypothesis is not rejected. The company concludes there is no significant difference in salaries between the two departments.

Z-Test for Proportions

When comparing proportions, the z-test evaluates whether the observed proportion in a sample differs from a known population proportion or whether two sample proportions are significantly different. The formula for comparing two proportions is:

$$z = (\hat{p}_1 - \hat{p}_2) \div \sqrt{[\hat{p}(1 - \hat{p}) \times (1/n_1 + 1/n_2)]}$$

Where:

- $\hat{p}_1$ and $\hat{p}_2$ are the sample proportions,
- $\hat{p}$ is the pooled proportion,
- n_1 and n_2 are the sample sizes.

Example: Z-Test for Proportions

A survey finds that 48% of 1,000 voters in Region A and 52% of 900 voters in Region B support a candidate. Is the difference significant?

1. **Calculate the Pooled Proportion**: $\hat{p} = (x_1 + x_2) \div (n_1 + n_2)$ $\hat{p} = (480 + 468) \div (1{,}000 + 900)$ $\hat{p} = 948 \div 1{,}900 \approx 0.498$

2. **Calculate the Test Statistic**: $z = (\hat{p}_1 - \hat{p}_2) \div \sqrt{[\hat{p}(1 - \hat{p}) \times (1/n_1 + 1/n_2)]}$ $z = (0.48 - 0.52) \div \sqrt{[0.498 \times 0.502 \times (1/1{,}000 + 1/900)]}$ $z = -0.04 \div \sqrt{[0.498 \times 0.502 \times 0.002122]}$ $z = -0.04 \div \sqrt{0.000529} \approx -0.04 \div 0.023 \approx -1.74$

3. **Determine the Critical Value**: For $\alpha = 0.05$ (two-tailed test), critical z-values are ± 1.96.

4. **Decision**: Since $z = -1.74$ is within the critical range, the null hypothesis is not rejected. The difference in proportions is not statistically significant.

Applications of Z-Tests

1. **Business**: Comparing average sales, customer satisfaction scores, or market shares across regions or time periods.

2. **Healthcare**: Testing whether a treatment group's mean blood pressure differs from a control group's mean or a standard threshold.

3. **Education**: Analyzing test scores to evaluate curriculum effectiveness or differences between schools.

4. **Environmental Studies**: Comparing pollutant levels in different regions or times.

Limitations

1. **Dependency on Known σ**: Z-tests require the population standard deviation, which is often unknown in real-world scenarios.

2. **Unsuitability for Small Samples**: For small samples, t-tests are more appropriate due to the additional variability.

3. **Sensitivity to Assumptions**: Violations of normality or independence can invalidate results.

Applying z-tests correctly, researchers can make meaningful comparisons and draw reliable conclusions across a range of disciplines.

Chapter 10: Correlation and Regression Analysis

Pearson's Correlation Coefficient: Measuring Relationships

Pearson's correlation coefficient is a statistical measure that quantifies the strength and direction of a linear relationship between two continuous variables. Denoted by **r**, the coefficient ranges from -1 to 1, where the sign indicates the direction of the relationship and the magnitude represents its strength. Pearson's correlation is widely used in various fields, from psychology and biology to economics and engineering, as it provides a simple yet effective way to summarize the degree of linear association between variables.

What is Pearson's Correlation Coefficient?

The formula for Pearson's correlation coefficient is:

$$r = \Sigma((x_i - \bar{x})(y_i - \bar{y})) \div \sqrt{[\Sigma(x_i - \bar{x})^2 \times \Sigma(y_i - \bar{y})^2]}$$

Where:

- x_i and y_i are individual data points for variables X and Y,
- $\bar{x}$ and $\bar{y}$ are the means of X and Y, respectively.

This formula can also be expressed as the covariance of X and Y divided by the product of their standard deviations:

$$r = \text{Cov}(X, Y) \div (\sigma_x \times \sigma_y)$$

Pearson's r measures how well the data points fit a straight line. If all data points lie perfectly on a straight line with a positive slope, r = 1. If they lie perfectly on a line with a negative slope, r = -1. A value of r = 0 indicates no linear relationship between the variables.

Interpreting Pearson's Correlation

1. **Direction**:
    - **Positive Correlation**: When one variable increases, the other tends to increase as well. For example, hours studied and exam scores might show a positive correlation.
    - **Negative Correlation**: When one variable increases, the other tends to decrease. For instance, the speed of a car and travel time might show a negative correlation.

2. **Strength**:
    - **Strong Correlation**: r close to ±1 (e.g., r = 0.9 or r = -0.8) indicates a strong relationship.
    - **Moderate Correlation**: r between ±0.5 and ±0.7 suggests a moderate relationship.
    - **Weak Correlation**: r near 0 (e.g., r = 0.1 or r = -0.2) implies a weak linear relationship.
3. **Linearity**: Pearson's correlation only measures linear relationships. A non-linear relationship, such as a parabolic trend, may yield r = 0 even if the variables are strongly related.

Assumptions of Pearson's Correlation

To interpret r accurately, the following assumptions should hold:

1. **Linearity**: The relationship between the variables should be approximately linear.
2. **Continuous Data**: Both variables must be measured on interval or ratio scales.
3. **Homoscedasticity**: The variability of one variable should remain constant across the range of the other.
4. **Normality**: Both variables should follow approximately normal distributions for statistical inference based on r.

Violations of these assumptions can distort the value of r or make it less meaningful.

Example: Calculating Pearson's r

Suppose a researcher wants to examine the relationship between hours spent exercising per week (X) and body fat percentage (Y) among 10 individuals. The data are:

X (hours)	Y (body fat %)
2	25
4	22
6	18
8	16
10	15

4. **Calculate Means**:
    - Mean of X ($\bar{x}$) = (2 + 4 + 6 + 8 + 10) ÷ 5 = 6

- Mean of Y ($\bar{y}$) = (25 + 22 + 18 + 16 + 15) ÷ 5 = 19.2

2. **Compute Deviations**: For each pair (xi, yi), calculate (xi - $\bar{x}$), (yi - $\bar{y}$), and their product (xi - $\bar{x}$)(yi - $\bar{y}$).

X	Y	xi - $\bar{x}$	yi - $\bar{y}$	(xi - $\bar{x}$)(yi - $\bar{y}$)
2	25	-4	5.8	-23.2
4	22	-2	2.8	-5.6
6	18	0	-1.2	0
8	16	2	-3.2	-6.4
10	15	4	-4.2	-16.8

3. **Calculate r**:

    - Covariance: Cov(X, Y) = Σ((xi - $\bar{x}$)(yi - $\bar{y}$)) ÷ n = -51.2 ÷ 5 = -10.24
    - Standard deviations:
        - σx = √[Σ(xi - $\bar{x}$)² ÷ n] = √[(16 + 4 + 0 + 4 + 16) ÷ 5] = √8 = 2.83
        - σy = √[Σ(yi - $\bar{y}$)² ÷ n] = √[(33.64 + 7.84 + 1.44 + 10.24 + 17.64) ÷ 5] = √14.56 ≈ 3.82
    - Correlation: r = Cov(X, Y) ÷ (σx × σy) r = -10.24 ÷ (2.83 × 3.82) ≈ -0.95

4. The strong negative correlation (r ≈ -0.95) suggests that as exercise hours increase, body fat percentage decreases significantly.

Hypothesis Testing for Pearson's r

To test whether the correlation is significant, calculate the t-statistic:

$$t = r\sqrt{(n - 2)} ÷ \sqrt{(1 - r^2)}$$

For n = 5 and r = -0.95: t = -0.95√(5 - 2) ÷ √(1 - (-0.95)²) t ≈ -0.95√3 ÷ √(1 - 0.9025) t ≈ -0.95 × 1.732 ÷ √0.0975 t ≈ -5.02

Compare this t-value to the critical value for df = n - 2 at the chosen significance level (e.g., α = 0.05). If |t| exceeds the critical value, reject the null hypothesis of no correlation.

Applications of Pearson's Correlation

1. **Healthcare**: Pearson's r is used to explore relationships such as the correlation between cholesterol levels and heart disease risk or physical activity and body weight.

2. **Education**: Researchers analyze correlations between study hours and academic performance, or attendance and grades.

3. **Business**: Companies use Pearson's correlation to examine relationships between advertising expenditure and sales revenue or customer satisfaction and retention rates.

4. **Environmental Studies**: Correlation measures help analyze relationships like temperature and crop yields or pollution levels and health outcomes.

5. **Social Sciences**: Psychologists and sociologists study correlations between variables such as stress levels and productivity or social media usage and self-esteem.

Limitations of Pearson's Correlation

1. **Only Measures Linearity**: Pearson's r does not capture non-linear relationships. A strong curved relationship may yield r = 0, suggesting no association despite clear patterns.

2. **Influence of Outliers**: Outliers can disproportionately affect r, making the relationship appear stronger or weaker than it truly is.

3. **No Causation**: A significant correlation does not imply causation. For example, a strong positive correlation between ice cream sales and drowning incidents does not mean one causes the other; a lurking variable, such as temperature, may explain both.

4. **Assumption Violations**: Violations of normality or homoscedasticity can distort the interpretation of r.

Enhancing Interpretation

To gain deeper insights into relationships, combine Pearson's correlation with scatterplots and additional statistical methods such as regression analysis. A scatterplot reveals the pattern and strength of the relationship visually, helping to identify non-linearity or outliers.

Simple Linear Regression: Prediction with One Variable

Simple linear regression is a statistical method used to model the relationship between a single independent variable (predictor) and a dependent variable (outcome). The goal is to predict the dependent variable based on the independent variable or assess the strength and direction of their relationship. The method assumes a linear relationship between the variables, meaning the change in the dependent variable is proportional to the change in the independent variable.

The Simple Linear Regression Equation

The relationship between the independent variable (X) and the dependent variable (Y) is expressed as:

$$Y = \beta_0 + \beta_1 X + \varepsilon$$

Where:

- **Y**: Dependent variable (response variable),
- **X**: Independent variable (predictor variable),
- β_0: Intercept (the value of Y when X = 0),
- β_1: Slope (the change in Y for a one-unit change in X),
- ε: Error term (the difference between observed and predicted Y values).

The intercept and slope are estimated from the data using the least squares method, which minimizes the sum of squared differences between the observed and predicted Y values.

Fitting the Regression Line

The regression line is fitted to the data by calculating the slope (β_1) and intercept (β_0) using the formulas:

$$\beta_1 = \Sigma((x_i - \bar{x})(y_i - \bar{y})) \div \Sigma(x_i - \bar{x})^2$$
$$\beta_0 = \bar{y} - \beta_1 \bar{x}$$

Here:

- x_i and y_i are individual data points,
- $\bar{x}$ and $\bar{y}$ are the means of X and Y, respectively.

The slope β_1 represents the rate of change in Y for each one-unit increase in X. The intercept β_0 indicates the predicted value of Y when X is zero.

Example: Simple Linear Regression

A researcher wants to examine the relationship between the number of study hours (X) and test scores (Y) among 10 students. The data are:

X (hours)	Y (score)
2	65
4	70
6	78
8	85
10	90

5. **Calculate Means**:

    - Mean of X ($\bar{x}$): $(2 + 4 + 6 + 8 + 10) \div 5 = 6$
    - Mean of Y ($\bar{y}$): $(65 + 70 + 78 + 85 + 90) \div 5 = 77.6$

2. **Compute the Slope (β_1)**: $\beta_1 = \Sigma((x_i - \bar{x})(y_i - \bar{y})) \div \Sigma(x_i - \bar{x})^2$ $\beta_1 = [(2 - 6)(65 - 77.6) + (4 - 6)(70 - 77.6) + \ldots + (10 - 6)(90 - 77.6)] \div [(2 - 6)^2 + (4 - 6)^2 + \ldots + (10 - 6)^2]$ $\beta_1 = 40 \div 40 = 1$

3. **Compute the Intercept (β_0)**: $\beta_0 = \bar{y} - \beta_1 \bar{x}$ $\beta_0 = 77.6 - (1 \times 6) = 71.6$

4. **Regression Equation**: $Y = 71.6 + 1X$

This equation predicts that for every additional hour of study, the test score increases by 1 point.

Making Predictions

Using the regression equation, the researcher can predict test scores for any given number of study hours. For example:

- If a student studies for 5 hours (X = 5), the predicted score is: $Y = 71.6 + (1 \times 5) = 76.6$

Assessing the Fit of the Model

1. **Coefficient of Determination (R^2)**: R^2 measures the proportion of variability in the dependent variable explained by the independent variable. It ranges from 0 to 1, where higher values indicate a better fit. R^2 is calculated as:
$R^2 = 1 - (SS_{res} / SS_{tot})$

    - SSres (Residual Sum of Squares): $\Sigma(y_i - \hat{y}_i)^2$, where $\hat{y}_i$ are predicted values.
    - SStot (Total Sum of Squares): $\Sigma(y_i - \bar{y})^2$.

2. For example, if R² = 0.85, the model explains 85% of the variation in test scores.

3. **Standard Error of the Estimate**: The standard error measures the average distance between observed and predicted values. Smaller values indicate a better fit.

4. **Significance of Regression Coefficients**: Hypothesis tests assess whether the slope (β_1) differs significantly from zero. The null hypothesis (H₀) states that β_1 = 0 (no relationship), and the alternative hypothesis (Hₐ) states that $\beta_1 \neq 0$.
The t-statistic for the slope is calculated as: **t = β_1 ÷ SE(β_1)**
If the p-value is less than the chosen significance level (e.g., 0.05), the null hypothesis is rejected, indicating a significant relationship.

Assumptions of Simple Linear Regression

1. **Linearity**: The relationship between X and Y should be linear.

2. **Independence**: Observations should be independent of each other.

3. **Homoscedasticity**: The variance of residuals (errors) should be constant across all levels of X.

4. **Normality of Residuals**: Residuals should follow a normal distribution.

5. **No Multicollinearity**: This assumption applies only in multiple regression but is not relevant for simple linear regression.

Applications of Simple Linear Regression

1. **Education**: Predicting student performance based on study hours or attendance rates.

2. **Healthcare**: Analyzing the relationship between exercise duration and cholesterol levels or predicting patient outcomes based on treatment duration.

3. **Business**: Estimating sales based on advertising expenditure or analyzing the relationship between price and demand.

4. **Environmental Studies**: Examining the impact of temperature on energy consumption or rainfall on crop yields.

Limitations

1. **Linear Relationship**: Simple linear regression only models linear relationships. If the relationship is non-linear, other techniques, such as polynomial regression, are more appropriate.

2. **One Predictor**: It only considers one independent variable. For more complex relationships, multiple regression is needed.

3. **Influence of Outliers**: Outliers can disproportionately affect the slope and intercept, distorting predictions.

4. **Causal Inference**: Regression shows association, not causation. For instance, a positive relationship between study hours and test scores does not imply that studying more directly causes better scores without controlling for other factors.

Enhancing Model Accuracy

To improve predictions and ensure valid interpretations:

1. Visualize the data using scatterplots to confirm linearity.
2. Remove or account for outliers that distort the relationship.
3. Check residuals for patterns that indicate violations of assumptions.
4. Use additional predictors in a multiple regression model when appropriate.

Multiple Regression: Expanding the Model

Multiple regression is an extension of simple linear regression that allows for the inclusion of two or more independent variables to predict a dependent variable. This method is invaluable when outcomes are influenced by multiple factors, and it provides a more comprehensive understanding of complex relationships. By simultaneously analyzing the effects of multiple predictors, multiple regression can isolate the contribution of each variable while accounting for the others.

The Multiple Regression Equation

The relationship between the dependent variable (Y) and multiple independent variables ($X_1, X_2, ..., X_k$) is expressed as:

$$Y = \beta_0 + \beta_1 X_1 + \beta_2 X_2 + ... + \beta_k X_k + \varepsilon$$

Where:

- Y: Dependent variable (response variable),
- $X_1, X_2, ..., X_k$: Independent variables (predictors),
- β_0: Intercept (value of Y when all Xs are 0),
- $\beta_1, \beta_2, ..., \beta_k$: Regression coefficients for the predictors,
- ε: Error term (the difference between observed and predicted Y).

Each coefficient (β_i) represents the average change in Y for a one-unit increase in X_i, holding all other predictors constant.

Purpose of Multiple Regression

1. **Prediction**: Multiple regression is used to predict outcomes based on several predictors. For example, predicting house prices based on square footage, number of bedrooms, and location.

2. **Understanding Relationships**: The method helps identify and quantify the relationship between the dependent variable and each independent variable while controlling for others.

3. **Testing Hypotheses**: Multiple regression allows researchers to test the significance of individual predictors and assess whether they contribute to explaining variability in the dependent variable.

Fitting a Multiple Regression Model

1. **Estimate Coefficients**: Coefficients (βs) are estimated using the least squares method, which minimizes the sum of squared residuals (differences between observed and predicted Y values).

2. **Compute Predicted Values**: Predicted values ($\hat{Y}$) are calculated by plugging the predictors into the regression equation.

3. **Assess Model Fit**: The overall fit of the model is evaluated using metrics like R^2 and adjusted R^2, which indicate how well the predictors explain the variability in Y.

Example: Multiple Regression

A real estate analyst wants to predict house prices (Y) based on square footage (X_1), number of bedrooms (X_2), and distance from the city center (X_3). The data are:

Square Footage (X_1)	Bedrooms (X_2)	Distance (X_3, miles)	Price (Y, $1000s)
1500	3	5	250
2000	4	10	300
2500	4	8	350
1800	3	6	275
2200	5	12	320

5. **Regression Equation**: The fitted regression model might be: $Y = 50 + 0.1X_1 + 20X_2 - 2X_3$

- Intercept ($\beta_0 = 50$): The base price is $50,000 when all predictors are zero (hypothetical scenario).
- Coefficient for square footage ($\beta_1 = 0.1$): Each additional square foot adds $100 to the price.
- Coefficient for bedrooms ($\beta_2 = 20$): Each additional bedroom adds $20,000 to the price.
- Coefficient for distance ($\beta_3 = -2$): Each additional mile from the city reduces the price by $2,000.

2. **Prediction**: For a 2000 sq. ft. house with 4 bedrooms located 10 miles from the city, the predicted price is: Y = 50 + (0.1 × 2000) + (20 × 4) - (2 × 10) = 50 + 200 + 80 - 20 = $310,000

Key Metrics for Evaluating Model Fit

1. **R^2 (Coefficient of Determination)**: R^2 measures the proportion of variability in Y explained by the predictors. For example, if $R^2 = 0.85$, the model explains 85% of the variation in house prices.

2. **Adjusted R^2**: Unlike R^2, adjusted R^2 accounts for the number of predictors and adjusts for overfitting. Adding irrelevant predictors can increase R^2 but decrease adjusted R^2.

3. **F-Statistic**: The F-test evaluates whether the model as a whole is statistically significant. A significant F-statistic suggests that at least one predictor contributes to explaining Y.

4. **Standard Error of the Estimate**: This metric measures the average distance between observed and predicted Y values. Smaller values indicate better fit.

Testing the Significance of Predictors

Each predictor's significance is assessed using a t-test for its coefficient:

- Null Hypothesis (H_0): $\beta_i = 0$ (the predictor has no effect on Y).
- Alternative Hypothesis (H_a): $\beta_i \neq 0$ (the predictor has an effect on Y).

The t-statistic is calculated as: $t = \beta_i \div SE(\beta_i)$

If the p-value for the t-statistic is less than the significance level (e.g., 0.05), the predictor is deemed significant.

Assumptions of Multiple Regression

1. **Linearity**: The relationship between each predictor and the dependent variable must be linear.

2. **Independence**: Observations must be independent of each other.

3. **Homoscedasticity**: The variance of residuals should be constant across all levels of the predictors.

4. **Normality of Residuals**: Residuals should follow a normal distribution.

5. **No Multicollinearity**: Predictors should not be highly correlated with each other. High multicollinearity inflates standard errors, making it difficult to assess individual predictor significance. Variance inflation factor (VIF) is used to detect multicollinearity, with VIF > 10 indicating a problem.

Applications of Multiple Regression

1. **Healthcare**: Predicting patient outcomes based on variables like age, treatment type, and comorbidities.

2. **Education**: Analyzing the impact of study hours, attendance, and socioeconomic status on student performance.

3. **Business**: Forecasting sales based on advertising spend, market size, and competition levels.

4. **Environmental Studies**: Estimating crop yields based on rainfall, temperature, and soil quality.

5. **Real Estate**: Predicting house prices using factors like location, size, and amenities.

Limitations

1. **Overfitting**: Including too many predictors can make the model overly complex and less generalizable to new data.

2. **Multicollinearity**: High correlations among predictors complicate interpretation and reduce model reliability.

3. **Non-Linearity**: Multiple regression assumes linear relationships. Non-linear relationships require transformations or other modeling techniques.

4. **Outliers**: Extreme values can disproportionately influence coefficients and predictions.

5. **Causation vs. Correlation**: Multiple regression identifies associations, not causation. For example, a model predicting higher sales with increased advertising spend cannot confirm causality without additional analysis.

Enhancing Model Reliability

1. **Check Residuals**: Residual plots can reveal patterns, indicating violations of assumptions like linearity or homoscedasticity.
2. **Transform Variables**: Non-linear relationships can be addressed through transformations (e.g., log or square root).
3. **Use Regularization**: Techniques like ridge or lasso regression reduce overfitting by penalizing large coefficients.
4. **Cross-Validation**: Splitting the data into training and testing sets ensures that the model generalizes well to unseen data.

Applying multiple regression correctly and understanding its nuances, researchers can analyze complex relationships, make accurate predictions, and gain deeper insights into their data across various disciplines.

Residual Analysis: Diagnosing Model Fit

Residual analysis is a critical step in regression modeling that helps assess the fit of the model and verify whether its assumptions are met. Residuals, the differences between observed and predicted values, contain valuable information about the relationship between predictors and the dependent variable. By analyzing residuals, researchers can identify patterns, detect violations of assumptions, and refine their models for better accuracy.

What Are Residuals?

A residual is the difference between the observed value (y_i) and the predicted value ($\hat{y}_i$) for a given data point:

$$\text{Residual} = y_i - \hat{y}_i$$

Residuals represent the portion of the observed value not explained by the regression model. Ideally, residuals should be randomly distributed, small in magnitude, and free from systematic patterns. When residuals deviate from these characteristics, it suggests that the model may not adequately represent the data.

Key Assumptions Checked Through Residual Analysis

Residual analysis is used to test several fundamental assumptions of regression:

1. **Linearity**: The relationship between predictors and the dependent variable should be linear. Non-linearity in the data will result in residuals that exhibit patterns, such as curves or clusters.

2. **Homoscedasticity**: Residuals should have constant variance across all levels of predicted values. If residual variance increases or decreases systematically, the assumption of homoscedasticity is violated.

3. **Independence**: Residuals should be independent of one another. Correlated residuals, often observed in time series data, indicate a violation of this assumption.

4. **Normality**: Residuals should follow a normal distribution. This assumption is particularly important for hypothesis testing and constructing confidence intervals in regression.

Methods of Residual Analysis

1. **Residual Plots**: Residual plots visually display residuals (y-axis) against predicted values (x-axis) or an independent variable. These plots help identify patterns or trends that indicate assumption violations.

    - A random scatter of points around zero suggests a good fit.
    - A curved pattern suggests non-linearity.
    - A funnel shape indicates heteroscedasticity, where residual variance increases or decreases with predicted values.

2. **Normal Probability Plot (Q-Q Plot)**: This plot compares the distribution of residuals to a theoretical normal distribution. If the residuals follow a straight diagonal line, the normality assumption is likely met. Deviations from this line indicate non-normality.

3. **Histogram of Residuals**: A histogram of residuals provides a quick visual check of their distribution. Ideally, the histogram should resemble a bell curve, indicating normality.

4. **Leverage and Influence Measures**: Residual analysis often includes identifying influential observations or outliers. Leverage measures (e.g., Cook's Distance, DFBETAS) help identify points that have a disproportionate impact on the regression model.

Example of Residual Analysis

A real estate analyst fits a regression model to predict house prices (Y) based on square footage (X_1) and number of bedrooms (X_2). After fitting the model, residuals are calculated for each data point.

1. **Residual Plot**: The analyst plots residuals against predicted prices. A random scatter around zero suggests a good fit. However, if a curved pattern emerges, it may indicate that a variable was omitted or that a transformation is needed.

2. **Normal Q-Q Plot**: The analyst examines the Q-Q plot of residuals. If most points fall along the diagonal line, the normality assumption is satisfied. Outliers or deviations at the tails suggest non-normality.

3. **Histogram**: A histogram of residuals shows whether the distribution is approximately symmetric and bell-shaped. Skewed or multi-modal distributions indicate potential issues with the model.

4. **Cook's Distance**: The analyst calculates Cook's Distance to identify influential observations. If Cook's Distance for any data point exceeds a threshold (e.g., 4/n, where n is the number of observations), it may disproportionately influence the model and warrant further investigation.

Addressing Issues Identified Through Residual Analysis

1. **Non-Linearity**:

    - **Transform Variables**: Apply transformations (e.g., log, square root) to the independent or dependent variable to linearize the relationship.
    - **Add Non-Linear Terms**: Include polynomial terms or interaction terms to capture non-linear effects.

2. **Heteroscedasticity**:

    - **Weighted Least Squares (WLS)**: Assign weights to observations to address unequal variance.
    - **Transform the Dependent Variable**: Apply a log or square root transformation to stabilize variance.

3. **Non-Normality**:

    - **Transform Residuals**: Use transformations to make residuals more normal.
    - **Robust Regression**: Apply robust regression techniques that are less sensitive to non-normality.

4. **Outliers and Influential Points**:

    - **Remove Outliers**: Exclude points with high leverage or influence after verifying their validity.
    - **Robust Methods**: Use methods like Huber regression that minimize the impact of outliers.

Practical Applications of Residual Analysis

1. **Quality Control**: Residual analysis is used to assess whether a manufacturing process is stable and consistent. Patterns in residuals can reveal systematic errors or variability in production.

2. **Economics**: Economists use residual analysis to identify omitted variables or structural changes in economic models.

3. **Healthcare**: In clinical studies, residual analysis ensures that regression models accurately capture the relationship between treatments and outcomes without bias or unaccounted variability.

4. **Environmental Science**: Researchers analyzing pollution data use residual plots to detect seasonality or other patterns that may affect model accuracy.

5. **Marketing**: Marketers evaluating the impact of advertising spend on sales rely on residual analysis to verify model assumptions and adjust for anomalies.

Limitations of Residual Analysis

1. **Subjectivity**: Visual methods, such as residual plots, rely on subjective interpretation. What appears as a random scatter to one analyst may seem patterned to another.

2. **Sensitivity to Sample Size**: Small sample sizes limit the reliability of residual analysis, as patterns may emerge purely by chance.

3. **Complexity**: Residual analysis becomes more challenging with multiple predictors, as relationships among variables may obscure residual patterns.

Enhancing Model Fit with Residual Analysis

Residual analysis is not merely a diagnostic tool; it is a guide for iterative improvement. By identifying and addressing model shortcomings, researchers can refine their regression models to achieve greater accuracy and validity.

For example:

- If residuals show a curved pattern, a quadratic term might be added to capture non-linear effects.
- If residual variance increases with predicted values, a log transformation of the dependent variable can stabilize variance.

Through careful examination and interpretation of residuals, analysts can ensure that their models provide reliable, unbiased predictions and insights, regardless of the complexity of the data.

Chapter 11: Chi-Square Tests

Chi-Square Goodness-of-Fit Test

The chi-square goodness-of-fit test evaluates whether a set of observed categorical data matches an expected distribution. It is particularly useful when testing hypotheses about proportions in a single categorical variable. By comparing observed frequencies to expected frequencies, this test determines if discrepancies are due to random variation or if they suggest a significant difference from the hypothesized distribution.

Purpose of the Test

The test checks if the observed data distribution aligns with a theoretical or expected distribution. For example:

- Does a six-sided die produce equal outcomes for each face (fair die)?
- Are customer preferences consistent with market share predictions?

Test Statistic and Formula

The chi-square test statistic is calculated as:

$$\chi^2 = \Sigma((O_i - E_i)^2 \div E_i)$$

Where:

- O_i is the observed frequency for category i,
- E_i is the expected frequency for category i,
- Σ represents the sum across all categories.

The statistic measures the total squared difference between observed and expected frequencies, scaled by the expected frequencies. Larger χ^2 values indicate greater deviation from the expected distribution.

Steps for Conducting the Chi-Square Goodness-of-Fit Test

1. **Define Hypotheses**:

    - Null Hypothesis (H₀): The observed data follow the expected distribution.
    - Alternative Hypothesis (Hₐ): The observed data do not follow the expected distribution.

2. **Calculate Expected Frequencies**: Based on the null hypothesis, compute the expected frequencies for each category. If all categories are equally likely, divide the total sample size by the number of categories.

3. **Compute the Chi-Square Statistic**: Use the formula to calculate χ^2 by summing the squared differences between observed and expected frequencies, divided by the expected frequencies.

4. **Determine Degrees of Freedom**: Degrees of freedom (df) for the test are given by: df = k - 1 Where k is the number of categories.

5. **Compare to the Critical Value or Find the p-Value**: Compare the calculated χ^2 to the critical value from the chi-square distribution table, or use the p-value. If χ^2 exceeds the critical value or if the p-value is less than the chosen significance level (e.g., α = 0.05), reject H_0.

Example: Chi-Square Goodness-of-Fit Test

A company claims that their candy is equally distributed among five colors: red, blue, green, yellow, and orange. To test this claim, a researcher samples 200 candies and observes the following frequencies:

- Red: 36
- Blue: 44
- Green: 38
- Yellow: 40
- Orange: 42

1. **Set Hypotheses**:
    - H_0: The candies are equally distributed across colors.
    - H_a: The candies are not equally distributed across colors.

2. **Calculate Expected Frequencies**: If the distribution is equal, the expected frequency for each color is: E_i = Total candies ÷ Number of categories = 200 ÷ 5 = 40

3. **Compute χ^2**: $\chi^2 = \Sigma((O_i - E_i)^2 \div E_i)$ $\chi^2 = ((36 - 40)^2 \div 40) + ((44 - 40)^2 \div 40) + ((38 - 40)^2 \div 40) + ((40 - 40)^2 \div 40) + ((42 - 40)^2 \div 40)$ $\chi^2 = (16 \div 40) + (16 \div 40) + (4 \div 40) + (0 \div 40) + (4 \div 40)$ $\chi^2 = 0.4 + 0.4 + 0.1 + 0 + 0.1 = 1.0$

4. **Determine Degrees of Freedom**: df = k - 1 = 5 - 1 = 4

5. **Compare to Critical Value**: For α = 0.05 and df = 4, the critical value from the chi-square table is approximately 9.49. Since χ^2 = 1.0 is less than 9.49, we fail to reject H_0. The data do not provide evidence that the candy distribution deviates from equal proportions.

Applications of the Test

1. **Quality Control**: Manufacturers use the chi-square goodness-of-fit test to check whether production outputs (e.g., defective and non-defective items) match expected proportions.

2. **Biology**: Geneticists test hypotheses about inheritance patterns, such as whether observed offspring ratios align with Mendelian predictions.

3. **Market Research**: Businesses evaluate whether customer preferences align with market share projections.

4. **Gaming**: The fairness of dice, roulette wheels, or other gaming devices can be tested using this method.

Limitations

1. **Sample Size Requirements**: The chi-square test may be unreliable with small expected frequencies ($E_i < 5$). In such cases, data should be combined into fewer categories or alternative methods (e.g., exact tests) should be used.

2. **Categorical Data Only**: The test is limited to categorical data and cannot be used for continuous variables without binning them into categories.

3. **Sensitivity to Sample Size**: Large sample sizes can result in significant χ^2 values even for small, practically meaningless differences.

4. **Assumes Independence**: Observations must be independent. Dependence among data points invalidates the test results.

Enhancing the Test's Utility

To improve the reliability of the chi-square goodness-of-fit test:

1. Ensure sufficient sample size to meet the expected frequency condition.
2. Use graphical methods (e.g., bar charts) alongside the test to visualize discrepancies.
3. Apply exact tests or simulation methods when sample sizes are small or assumptions are questionable.

Overall, by understanding and correctly applying the chi-square goodness-of-fit test, researchers can rigorously evaluate whether observed categorical data align with theoretical expectations in a wide range of contexts.

Chi-Square Test of Independence

The chi-square test of independence determines whether two categorical variables are associated or independent. It is one of the most widely used tests in statistics for analyzing contingency tables, where the frequencies of different combinations of categories are tabulated. This test is useful for a variety of applications, such as examining relationships between gender and voting preferences, treatment type and recovery rates, or product features and consumer preferences.

Purpose of the Test

The chi-square test of independence evaluates whether the distribution of one variable is independent of the other. For example:

- Does gender (male, female) influence voting preference (Candidate A, Candidate B)?
- Is there a relationship between exercise frequency (low, medium, high) and diet type (vegan, non-vegan)?

Test Statistic and Formula

The chi-square statistic is calculated as:

$$\chi^2 = \Sigma((O_i - E_i)^2 \div E_i)$$

Where:

- O_i is the observed frequency for a cell in the contingency table,
- E_i is the expected frequency for that cell,
- Σ represents the sum over all cells.

The test statistic measures the total squared difference between observed and expected frequencies, scaled by the expected frequencies. Larger χ^2 values suggest a stronger deviation from independence.

Steps for Conducting the Chi-Square Test of Independence

1. **Define Hypotheses**:
    - Null Hypothesis (H_0): The two variables are independent.
    - Alternative Hypothesis (H_a): The two variables are not independent (they are associated).

2. **Create a Contingency Table**: Organize the data into a table showing the frequency of each category combination.

3. **Calculate Expected Frequencies**: For each cell, the expected frequency is calculated as: E_i = (Row Total × Column Total) ÷ Grand Total

4. **Compute the Chi-Square Statistic**: Use the formula to calculate χ^2 by summing the squared differences between observed and expected frequencies, divided by the expected frequencies.

5. **Determine Degrees of Freedom**: Degrees of freedom (df) are calculated as: df = (Number of Rows - 1) × (Number of Columns - 1)

6. **Compare to the Critical Value or Find the p-Value**: Compare the calculated χ^2 value to the critical value from the chi-square distribution table, or use the p-value. If χ^2 exceeds the critical value or the p-value is less than the chosen significance level (e.g., $\alpha = 0.05$), reject H_0.

Example: Chi-Square Test of Independence

A marketing team wants to determine whether gender (male, female) influences preference for three product designs (A, B, C). A survey collects the following data:

	Design A	Design B	Design C	Row Total
Male	30	25	15	70
Female	20	35	25	80
Column Total	50	60	40	150

7. **Set Hypotheses**:

    ○ H_0: Gender and product design preference are independent.
    ○ H_a: Gender and product design preference are not independent.

2. **Calculate Expected Frequencies**: For each cell, calculate E_i = (Row Total × Column Total) ÷ Grand Total. For example:

    ○ Expected frequency for males preferring Design A: $E_{11} = (70 \times 50) \div 150 = 23.33$
    ○ Expected frequency for females preferring Design B: $E_{22} = (80 \times 60) \div 150 = 32.00$

3. The expected frequencies for the table are:

Gender	Design A	Design B	Design C
Male	23.33	28.00	18.67
Female	26.67	32.00	21.33

4. **Compute χ^2**: $\chi^2 = \Sigma((O_i - E_i)^2 \div E_i)$ $\chi^2 = ((30 - 23.33)^2 \div 23.33) + ((25 - 28.00)^2 \div 28.00) + ... + ((25 - 21.33)^2 \div 21.33)$ $\chi^2 \approx 1.91 + 0.32 + 0.72 + 1.67 + 0.28 + 0.65$ $\chi^2 \approx 5.55$

5. **Determine Degrees of Freedom**: df = (Rows - 1) × (Columns - 1) = (2 - 1) × (3 - 1) = 2

6. **Compare to Critical Value**: For $\alpha = 0.05$ and df = 2, the critical value from the chi-square table is 5.99. Since $\chi^2 = 5.55 < 5.99$, fail to reject H_0. The data do not provide sufficient evidence to conclude that gender and product design preference are associated.

Applications of the Test

1. **Healthcare**: Evaluating whether treatment outcomes (recovery, no recovery) are associated with treatment types (A, B, C).

2. **Education**: Investigating relationships between study habits (daily, weekly, rarely) and grades (A, B, C).

3. **Business**: Analyzing whether customer demographics (age, gender) influence purchasing decisions (product categories).

4. **Social Science**: Examining relationships between political affiliation (party A, party B) and voting patterns (yes, no).

Limitations

1. **Sample Size**: Small expected frequencies ($E_i < 5$) may render the test unreliable. Fisher's Exact Test is an alternative for small sample sizes.

2. **Assumes Independence**: The test assumes that observations are independent. Violations of this assumption, such as in repeated measures designs, invalidate results.

3. **Categorical Data**: The test is limited to categorical variables. Continuous data must be grouped into categories, potentially losing detail.

4. **Sensitivity to Sample Size**: Large sample sizes can yield significant results for small, practically unimportant differences.

Enhancing the Test's Reliability

1. **Ensure Adequate Sample Size**: Collect enough data to meet the expected frequency condition ($E_i \geq 5$ for all cells).

2. **Combine Categories**: When expected frequencies are too small, merge similar categories to increase expected counts.

3. **Use Graphical Tools**: Visualize the data using stacked bar charts or mosaic plots to complement the test results.

4. **Explore Effect Sizes**: Supplement the test with measures like Cramer's V or Phi coefficient to quantify the strength of association.

Applications in Categorical Data Analysis

Categorical data analysis is essential for examining variables that can be divided into distinct groups or categories. These data types include nominal variables, like gender or product types, and ordinal variables, like customer satisfaction ratings or education levels. Techniques like the chi-square tests of goodness-of-fit and independence, logistic regression, and correspondence analysis provide researchers with ways to analyze relationships, patterns, and distributions in categorical data.

Understanding Categorical Data

Categorical data are non-numeric and fall into discrete groups. These data can be further divided into:

- **Nominal Data**: Categories without a natural order (e.g., colors, brands).
- **Ordinal Data**: Categories with a meaningful order but no fixed intervals (e.g., satisfaction levels: low, medium, high).

Unlike continuous data, categorical data are not measured on a scale and require specialized statistical methods for analysis.

Key Techniques for Analyzing Categorical Data

1. **Chi-Square Tests**:

    - **Goodness-of-Fit**: Tests whether the observed distribution of a single categorical variable matches an expected distribution.
    - **Test of Independence**: Evaluates whether two categorical variables are associated.

2. **Logistic Regression**: Logistic regression models the relationship between one or more predictors (categorical or continuous) and a binary or multinomial outcome. For example, predicting whether a customer will purchase (yes/no) based on age and income.

3. **Correspondence Analysis**: This exploratory technique visualizes relationships between rows and columns in a contingency table, often revealing patterns in complex datasets.

4. **Fisher's Exact Test**: An alternative to the chi-square test for small sample sizes or sparse data, Fisher's test calculates exact probabilities rather than relying on approximations.

5. **Proportional Odds Models**: For ordinal data, these models analyze the relationship between predictors and an ordered categorical response variable.

Applications of Categorical Data Analysis

1. **Healthcare**:
   - **Diagnosis and Treatment**: Analyzing the relationship between symptoms and diagnoses. For example, does the presence of specific symptoms (categorical) correlate with disease type (categorical)?
   - **Drug Trials**: Testing whether treatment types (e.g., placebo, drug A, drug B) influence recovery rates (e.g., recovered, not recovered).

2. Example: A study examines the effectiveness of three medications (A, B, C) on recovery rates in patients with a common cold. Using a chi-square test of independence, researchers determine whether recovery is associated with medication type.

3. **Education**:
   - **Student Performance**: Examining relationships between study habits (daily, weekly, rarely) and academic outcomes (pass, fail).
   - **Program Evaluation**: Determining whether participation in specific programs (e.g., online learning vs. in-person classes) affects student satisfaction levels (e.g., satisfied, neutral, dissatisfied).

4. Example: Researchers analyze survey responses to evaluate whether satisfaction with online learning varies by course type (STEM, humanities, business).

5. **Marketing and Consumer Behavior**:
   - **Preference Analysis**: Understanding consumer preferences for product categories (e.g., electronics, apparel) based on demographic variables (e.g., age, gender).
   - **Purchase Behavior**: Examining whether promotional strategies (e.g., discounts, free shipping) influence purchasing decisions (yes, no).

6. Example: A retailer conducts a chi-square test to determine whether male and female customers prefer different product categories.

7. **Social Sciences**:
    - **Voting Behavior**: Investigating whether political preferences (party affiliation) vary by demographic factors (e.g., age, region).
    - **Public Opinion**: Analyzing survey data to explore relationships between opinions on policy issues and demographic characteristics.
8. Example: A study tests whether support for a new policy (support, oppose) is associated with educational attainment (high school, college, graduate degree).
9. **Quality Control and Manufacturing**:
    - **Defect Analysis**: Testing whether defect rates vary across production lines or shifts.
    - **Product Testing**: Analyzing customer feedback (satisfied, unsatisfied) to identify quality issues.
10. Example: A factory uses a chi-square test to assess whether the proportion of defective items differs by machine.

Advanced Methods for Categorical Data

1. **Log-Linear Models**: Log-linear models analyze multi-way contingency tables, exploring interactions between more than two categorical variables. For example, analyzing how age, gender, and product type jointly influence purchasing behavior.

2. **Cluster Analysis**: When categorical data involve multiple variables, clustering techniques group similar observations. For instance, customer segmentation based on purchase preferences.

3. **Latent Class Analysis**: This method identifies unobserved (latent) groups in categorical data. For example, discovering hidden segments of customers based on survey responses.

4. **Decision Trees**: Algorithms like CART (Classification and Regression Trees) and CHAID (Chi-Square Automatic Interaction Detection) predict outcomes based on categorical predictors, providing interpretable rules.

Challenges in Categorical Data Analysis

1. **Sample Size**: Small sample sizes reduce the reliability of tests like the chi-square test. For sparse data, Fisher's Exact Test or Bayesian methods may be more appropriate.

2. **Loss of Information**: Continuous variables converted into categories lose information about variability and magnitude. For instance, categorizing income into brackets obscures differences within those brackets.

3. **Overfitting**: With many categories or variables, models risk overfitting, particularly in small datasets. Cross-validation or penalization techniques can mitigate this issue.

4. **Interpreting Results**: While statistical significance indicates association, it does not imply causation. For example, finding a relationship between product type and customer demographics does not mean demographics cause preferences.

Best Practices for Analyzing Categorical Data

1. **Preliminary Analysis**: Use bar charts, mosaic plots, or stacked bar graphs to visualize relationships between variables before conducting formal tests.

2. **Check Assumptions**: Ensure assumptions of independence and adequate sample size are met before applying tests like chi-square.

3. **Consider Effect Size**: Statistical significance does not measure the strength of association. Supplement tests with effect size metrics like Cramer's V or the Phi coefficient.

4. **Validate Findings**: Replicate analyses on independent datasets or use cross-validation for predictive models.

Using the appropriate techniques and adhering to best practices, researchers can extract meaningful insights from categorical data and apply them effectively across diverse domains.

Chapter 12: Nonparametric Statistics

Introduction to Nonparametric Methods

Nonparametric methods are statistical techniques that do not rely on specific assumptions about the distribution of the data. Unlike parametric methods, which often assume a normal distribution or require other strict conditions, nonparametric methods are more flexible and can be applied to a wider variety of data types. These methods are especially useful when dealing with ordinal data, ranked data, or datasets that violate key assumptions such as normality or homogeneity of variance.

Why Use Nonparametric Methods?

Nonparametric methods are particularly advantageous when:

1. **Data Distributions Are Unknown or Non-Normal**: Parametric methods like the t-test or ANOVA require data to follow a normal distribution. Nonparametric tests work regardless of the shape of the distribution.

2. **Small Sample Sizes**: When sample sizes are too small to reliably estimate parameters, nonparametric methods provide robust alternatives.

3. **Ordinal Data or Ranks**: Nonparametric methods handle ordinal data directly, such as satisfaction ratings (low, medium, high) or rankings in a competition.

4. **Presence of Outliers**: Nonparametric methods are less sensitive to outliers and skewed data because they often rely on medians or ranks instead of means.

Characteristics of Nonparametric Methods

1. **Focus on Ranks and Medians**: Many nonparametric methods convert data into ranks or compare medians, rather than means, to assess differences or relationships.

2. **Distribution-Free**: These methods do not assume a specific probability distribution, making them adaptable to a variety of datasets.

3. **Robustness**: Nonparametric methods are resistant to violations of assumptions, such as non-normality or unequal variances.

Common Nonparametric Methods

1. **Tests for Two Groups**:

- **Mann-Whitney U Test**: Compares two independent groups.
- **Wilcoxon Signed-Rank Test**: Compares two related groups or matched pairs.

2. **Tests for Multiple Groups**:

    - **Kruskal-Wallis Test**: Nonparametric equivalent of ANOVA for more than two independent groups.
    - **Dunn's Test**: Post-hoc analysis for identifying differences between specific groups.
    - **Friedman Test**: Nonparametric test for more than two related groups.

3. **Tests for Relationships**:

    - **Spearman's Rank Correlation**: Measures the strength and direction of a monotonic relationship between two variables.
    - **Kendall's Tau**: Another method for assessing rank correlation, particularly for small datasets.

4. **Goodness-of-Fit Tests**:

    - **Kolmogorov-Smirnov Test**: Compares a sample's distribution to a theoretical distribution.
    - **Chi-Square Goodness-of-Fit Test**: Tests whether observed frequencies match expected frequencies.

Examples of When to Use Nonparametric Methods

1. **Medical Research**: A study aims to compare pain relief scores (on a 1–10 scale) between two treatments. Since the data are ordinal and do not follow a normal distribution, the Mann-Whitney U test is appropriate.

2. **Ecology**: Researchers want to determine whether plant heights differ across three soil types. If the data are skewed or include outliers, the Kruskal-Wallis test provides a robust alternative to ANOVA.

3. **Psychology**: A psychologist measures stress levels (low, medium, high) before and after a mindfulness program. The Wilcoxon Signed-Rank Test can assess changes without assuming normality.

Strengths of Nonparametric Methods

1. **Flexibility**: They work well across diverse data types, including ordinal, ranked, or continuous data.

2. **Robustness**: Nonparametric methods remain reliable under assumption violations, such as non-normality or unequal variances.

3. **Simplicity**: These methods are straightforward to compute and interpret, particularly for small datasets or exploratory analyses.

4. **Versatility**: Many nonparametric tests have both independent and paired versions, making them adaptable to various study designs.

Limitations of Nonparametric Methods

1. **Lower Power**: Nonparametric tests are generally less powerful than parametric tests when assumptions for the latter are met. This means they may require larger sample sizes to detect significant differences.

2. **Loss of Information**: Converting data to ranks can lead to a loss of information, especially for continuous variables.

3. **No Confidence Intervals**: Some nonparametric methods do not provide confidence intervals, limiting their ability to quantify effect sizes.

4. **Interpretation**: While nonparametric tests are robust, interpreting the results in terms of practical significance can be challenging, especially when ranks are used instead of raw data.

How Nonparametric Methods Work

Nonparametric tests often replace raw data with ranks or categories. For example, in the Mann-Whitney U test, all data points from two groups are ranked together, and the test evaluates whether the ranks are distributed equally between the groups. This approach eliminates the need for distributional assumptions.

Practical Example: Comparing Two Groups

Suppose researchers want to compare recovery times (in days) between two treatments for a disease. The data are not normally distributed, with one treatment group showing a strong positive skew due to a few patients recovering unusually quickly. A Mann-Whitney U test can be used to determine if there is a significant difference between the two groups.

- **Observed Data**:
    - Group A: 5, 7, 8, 9, 12
    - Group B: 6, 6, 8, 10, 15

- **Ranks**: Combine all observations, rank them from smallest to largest, and assign average ranks for ties:
    - Group A ranks: 1, 3, 5, 6, 8.5
    - Group B ranks: 2, 2, 5, 7, 10

- **Sum of Ranks**: Calculate the sum of ranks for each group:
    - Rank Sum (Group A) = 1 + 3 + 5 + 6 + 8.5 = 23.5
    - Rank Sum (Group B) = 2 + 2 + 5 + 7 + 10 = 26

- **Interpretation**: Using the U statistic and a reference table, researchers determine whether the observed rank distribution indicates a significant difference.

When to Choose Nonparametric Methods

Nonparametric methods should be used when:

- Data violate normality assumptions or contain significant outliers.
- The sample size is small, making parametric tests unreliable.
- The data are ordinal or rank-based rather than continuous.

Extending Nonparametric Methods

Nonparametric methods are not limited to basic tests. They can be adapted to regression models (e.g., nonparametric regression), survival analysis, or other advanced statistical techniques. For example, the Kaplan-Meier estimator is a nonparametric method used in survival analysis to estimate the probability of survival over time.

Applications Across Fields

1. **Business**:
    - Analyzing customer satisfaction ratings across different service tiers.
    - Understanding relationships in financial data that don't follow parametric distributions.
    - Comparing sales ranks of products in different regions.

2. **Education**:
    - Testing whether class rankings differ between teaching methods.
    - Analyzing ordinal exam scores (e.g., pass, merit, distinction) across schools.

3. **Public Health**:
    - Examining the effectiveness of health campaigns using ordinal survey responses.
    - Comparing infection rates (low, medium, high) across treatment groups.

4. **Environmental Studies**:
    - Analyzing pollution levels categorized as low, moderate, or severe in different regions.
    - Comparing biodiversity ranks across different habitats.

With nonparametric methods, researchers can overcome the limitations of traditional parametric techniques, ensuring robust and meaningful analyses across diverse datasets. Nonparametric methods provide the flexibility needed for real-world data, where assumptions often fail to hold.

Mann-Whitney U Test and Wilcoxon Signed-Rank Test

The Mann-Whitney U test and the Wilcoxon Signed-Rank test are nonparametric methods used to compare groups. Unlike parametric tests, they do not assume a normal distribution, making them ideal for datasets with skewed distributions, small sample sizes, or ordinal data. Both tests use ranks rather than raw data values, offering a robust way to evaluate group differences while minimizing the impact of outliers.

Mann-Whitney U Test: Comparing Two Independent Groups

The Mann-Whitney U test evaluates whether two independent groups differ in terms of their central tendencies. It is a nonparametric alternative to the independent samples t-test. By comparing ranks, the test determines whether one group tends to have higher or lower values than the other.

Hypotheses:

- Null Hypothesis (H_0): The distributions of the two groups are identical.
- Alternative Hypothesis (H_a): The distributions of the two groups differ (or one group tends to have larger values).

Assumptions:

1. The data are ordinal, interval, or ratio-level.
2. Observations are independent within and between groups.
3. The two samples come from populations with the same shape (for meaningful comparisons of medians).

Test Statistic: The Mann-Whitney U statistic is based on ranks assigned to the combined data from both groups. The ranks are summed for each group, and the U statistic is calculated using the formula:

$$U = n_1 n_2 + (n_1(n_1 + 1) \div 2) - R_1$$

Where:

- n_1 and n_2 are the sample sizes of the two groups,
- R_1 is the sum of ranks for the first group.

Alternatively, the smaller U value from the two groups can be used, with smaller U values indicating stronger group differences.

Example: A researcher compares recovery times (in days) for two treatments. The data are:

- Treatment A: 5, 7, 8, 9, 12
- Treatment B: 6, 6, 8, 10, 15

1. Combine the data and rank all observations:
    - Combined ranks: 1, 2.5, 2.5, 4, 5, 6, 7, 8, 9, 10
    - Ranks for Treatment A: 1, 4, 6, 7, 9 (Sum = 27)
    - Ranks for Treatment B: 2.5, 2.5, 5, 8, 10 (Sum = 28)

2. Calculate U for each group:
    - U for Treatment A = (5 × 5) + (5 × 6 ÷ 2) - 27 = 12.5
    - U for Treatment B = (5 × 5) + (5 × 6 ÷ 2) - 28 = 11.5

3. Select the smaller U value: U = 11.5

4. Compare to the critical value: For $n_1 = n_2 = 5$ and $\alpha = 0.05$ (two-tailed), the critical value of U is 2. Since 11.5 > 2, we fail to reject H_0. There is no significant difference in recovery times between the treatments.

Wilcoxon Signed-Rank Test: Comparing Two Related Groups

The Wilcoxon Signed-Rank test is used to compare two related samples or matched pairs. It assesses whether the median difference between pairs is zero, making it a nonparametric alternative to the paired t-test.

Hypotheses:

- Null Hypothesis (H_0): The median difference between paired observations is zero.
- Alternative Hypothesis (H_a): The median difference is not zero.

Assumptions:

1. The data are ordinal, interval, or ratio-level.
2. Observations within pairs are dependent, but pairs are independent of each other.
3. The differences between paired observations are symmetrically distributed.

Test Statistic: The test uses the ranks of the absolute differences between paired observations. The test statistic, W, is the smaller of the sums of ranks for positive and negative differences.

Steps:

1. Calculate the differences between paired observations.
2. Assign ranks to the absolute differences, ignoring signs.
3. Sum the ranks for positive and negative differences.
4. Use the smaller rank sum as the test statistic (W).

Example: A study measures stress levels (on a 1–10 scale) before and after a mindfulness program for 10 participants. The data are:

Participant	Before	After	Difference	Rank	Signed Rank
1	7	5	-2	4	-4
2	8	7	-1	3	-3
3	6	5	-1	3	-3
4	9	8	-1	3	-3
5	10	8	-2	4	-4
6	7	6	-1	3	-3
7	8	6	-2	4	-4
8	6	5	-1	3	-3
9	9	7	-2	4	-4
10	7	6	-1	3	-3

5. Calculate rank sums:

    ◦ Positive differences: None
    ◦ Negative differences: Sum of ranks = -34

2. Determine the test statistic:

    ◦ W = 34 (absolute value of smaller rank sum)

3. Compare to critical value: For n = 10 and $\alpha = 0.05$ (two-tailed), the critical value of W is 8. Since 34 > 8, fail to reject H_0. The data do not suggest a significant change in stress levels.

Key Differences Between the Tests

1. **Type of Data**:
    - Mann-Whitney U: Independent groups.
    - Wilcoxon Signed-Rank: Paired or related groups.

2. **Hypothesis**:
    - Mann-Whitney U: Tests whether one group tends to have higher or lower values than the other.
    - Wilcoxon Signed-Rank: Tests whether the median difference between pairs is zero.

3. **Data Handling**:
    - Mann-Whitney U: Uses ranks of combined data.
    - Wilcoxon Signed-Rank: Uses ranks of paired differences.

Applications

1. **Healthcare**:
    - Mann-Whitney U: Comparing recovery times for two treatments.
    - Wilcoxon Signed-Rank: Assessing pain reduction before and after medication.

2. **Education**:
    - Mann-Whitney U: Comparing test scores between two teaching methods.
    - Wilcoxon Signed-Rank: Evaluating pre- and post-test scores for the same group.

3. **Business**:
    - Mann-Whitney U: Comparing customer satisfaction scores between two brands.
    - Wilcoxon Signed-Rank: Assessing changes in sales before and after a marketing campaign.

4. **Social Sciences**:
    - Mann-Whitney U: Analyzing differences in income levels between two demographics.
    - Wilcoxon Signed-Rank: Measuring changes in attitudes after an intervention.

Kruskal-Wallis Test for Group Comparisons

The Kruskal-Wallis test is a nonparametric method used to compare three or more independent groups to determine if they originate from the same population. As a nonparametric equivalent to one-way ANOVA, it evaluates differences in medians without assuming normality or equal variances. This test is ideal for ordinal data, small sample sizes, or datasets with outliers or skewed distributions.

Purpose of the Kruskal-Wallis Test

The Kruskal-Wallis test examines whether the ranks of observations differ significantly across groups. For example:

- Do satisfaction ratings differ between customers of three service providers?
- Is there a difference in recovery times for three types of treatments?

The test does not require interval or ratio-level data, making it suitable for ordinal data or ranks.

Hypotheses

1. Null Hypothesis (H_0): The distributions of the groups are identical (no significant differences in medians).
2. Alternative Hypothesis (H_a): At least one group has a different distribution or median.

Test Statistic

The Kruskal-Wallis test statistic (H) is calculated as:

$$H = (12 \div N(N + 1)) \times \Sigma(R_i^2 \div n_i) - 3(N + 1)$$

Where:

- N is the total number of observations,
- n_i is the number of observations in group i,
- R_i is the sum of ranks for group i.

The statistic is approximately chi-square distributed with degrees of freedom equal to the number of groups minus one (k - 1). Larger H values indicate greater differences between groups.

Assumptions of the Kruskal-Wallis Test

1. The data are ordinal, interval, or ratio-level.

2. Observations are independent within and between groups.
3. The groups are independent (e.g., no repeated measures).

Steps for Conducting the Test

1. Combine data from all groups and rank them from smallest to largest. Assign tied ranks as averages.
2. Calculate the sum of ranks (Ri) for each group.
3. Compute the test statistic (H) using the formula.
4. Determine the degrees of freedom (df = k - 1) and find the critical value or p-value from the chi-square distribution.
5. Compare H to the critical value or assess the p-value. If H exceeds the critical value or the p-value is less than the significance level (e.g., 0.05), reject H_0.

Example: Kruskal-Wallis Test

A researcher compares pain relief scores (on a 1–10 scale) for three treatments: A, B, and C. The data are:

- Treatment A: 6, 7, 8
- Treatment B: 5, 6, 7, 7
- Treatment C: 8, 9, 9, 10

Step 1: Rank the Combined Data Rank all observations, assigning tied ranks as averages:

Score	Rank
5	1
6	2.5
6	2.5
7	4.5
7	4.5
7	4.5
8	7.5
8	7.5
9	9.5
9	9.5

	10	11

Step 2: Calculate Group Ranks Sum the ranks for each group:

- Treatment A: 7.5 + 4.5 + 7.5 = 19.5
- Treatment B: 1 + 2.5 + 4.5 + 4.5 = 12.5
- Treatment C: 7.5 + 9.5 + 9.5 + 11 = 37.5

Step 3: Compute H Using N = 11 (total observations) and ni (group sizes):

$H = (12 \div 11(11 + 1)) \times [(19.5^2 \div 3) + (12.5^2 \div 4) + (37.5^2 \div 4)] - 3(11 + 1)$

$H \approx (12 \div 132) \times [(380.25 \div 3) + (156.25 \div 4) + (1406.25 \div 4)] - 36$

$H \approx (0.0909) \times [126.75 + 39.06 + 351.56] - 36$

$H \approx 0.0909 \times 517.37 - 36$

$H \approx 46.99 - 36$

$H \approx 10.99$

Step 4: Determine Critical Value Degrees of freedom = k - 1 = 3 - 1 = 2. For $\alpha = 0.05$, the critical value from the chi-square table is 5.99.

Step 5: Decision Since H = 10.99 > 5.99, reject H_0. There is evidence that at least one treatment group has a different median pain relief score.

Post Hoc Tests

If the Kruskal-Wallis test indicates significant differences, follow-up pairwise comparisons identify which groups differ. Pairwise Mann-Whitney U tests or Dunn's test are common, with adjustments (e.g., Bonferroni correction) to control for multiple comparisons.

Applications of the Kruskal-Wallis Test

1. **Healthcare**:
    - Comparing recovery times for patients treated with three types of therapies.
    - Assessing patient satisfaction ratings across multiple hospitals.

2. **Education**:

- Analyzing test scores across teaching methods (traditional, flipped classroom, online).

3. **Marketing**:
    - Testing customer satisfaction for three product categories.
    - Evaluating marketing tactics for different platforms.
    - Comparing sales performance across regions.

4. **Environmental Science**:
    - Examining pollution levels across three industrial zones.
    - Comparing biodiversity indices across ecosystems.

Strengths of the Kruskal-Wallis Test

1. **Flexibility**: It handles ordinal data, skewed distributions, and outliers.

2. **No Assumptions of Normality**: The test does not require normally distributed data or equal variances.

3. **Adaptability**: It works well with small sample sizes, making it suitable for exploratory studies.

Limitations

1. **Loss of Power**: Compared to one-way ANOVA, the Kruskal-Wallis test may require larger sample sizes to detect differences.

2. **No Effect Size**: The test statistic (H) does not directly quantify the magnitude of group differences.

3. **Identifies Differences, Not Directions**: While the test detects differences, post hoc methods are required to determine which groups differ.

Enhancing the Kruskal-Wallis Test

1. **Visualization**: Boxplots or violin plots alongside the test help interpret group differences.

2. **Effect Size Metrics**: Measures like eta-squared (η^2) or rank-based effect sizes complement the test.

3. **Software Tools**: Statistical software (e.g., SPSS, R, Python) automates calculations and provides p-values for quick decision-making.

Chapter 13: Advanced Topics in Statistics

Factor Analysis: Uncovering Latent Variables

Factor analysis is a statistical method used to identify underlying structures, or latent variables, within a set of observed variables. These latent variables, often called factors, are not directly measured but are inferred from correlations or covariances among the observed variables. Factor analysis is widely used in psychology, sociology, marketing, and other fields where researchers seek to reduce complexity and uncover hidden patterns.

Purpose of Factor Analysis

The primary purpose of factor analysis is to reduce the dimensionality of data while retaining as much information as possible. By grouping correlated variables into factors, it simplifies data interpretation and highlights relationships that may not be immediately apparent. For example, a survey measuring different aspects of customer satisfaction might have overlapping questions. Factor analysis can group these questions into a few broad categories, such as product quality, service, and price.

Types of Factor Analysis

1. **Exploratory Factor Analysis (EFA)**: EFA identifies potential factors in a dataset without prior assumptions about their structure. Researchers use it to explore relationships among variables and generate hypotheses.

2. **Confirmatory Factor Analysis (CFA)**: CFA tests a predefined factor structure to confirm whether the data fit the hypothesized model. It is commonly used when researchers have a theoretical framework guiding their analysis.

Key Concepts in Factor Analysis

1. **Loadings**: Factor loadings represent the strength and direction of the relationship between each observed variable and a factor. Higher loadings indicate a stronger association.

2. **Eigenvalues**: Eigenvalues measure the variance explained by each factor. Factors with eigenvalues greater than 1 are typically considered significant, as they explain more variance than a single variable.

3. **Communality**: Communality indicates how much of an observed variable's variance is explained by the factors. Values close to 1 suggest that most of the variable's variance is accounted for.

4. **Rotation**: Factor rotation simplifies interpretation by adjusting the factor loadings. Common methods include:

    - **Varimax Rotation**: Maximizes variance among factors, making loadings more distinct.
    - **Oblique Rotation**: Allows factors to correlate, which is useful when underlying constructs are related.

Steps in Factor Analysis

1. **Data Preparation**: Ensure that the data are suitable for factor analysis. The sample size should be large enough to produce stable results, with at least 5–10 observations per variable. Examine correlations between variables to verify they are sufficiently related.

2. **Determine the Number of Factors**: Use methods like the **eigenvalue-greater-than-one rule**, **scree plot**, or **parallel analysis** to decide how many factors to retain.

3. **Extract Factors**: Apply a method such as **principal component analysis (PCA)** or **maximum likelihood extraction** to identify factors. PCA reduces data dimensionality by transforming variables into uncorrelated components, while maximum likelihood finds factors that maximize the likelihood of observing the data.

4. **Rotate Factors**: Perform factor rotation to clarify the structure and interpret loadings more easily.

5. **Interpret Factors**: Assign meaningful labels to factors based on the variables that load strongly onto them. For example, a factor with high loadings for "price fairness" and "cost transparency" might be labeled "Perceived Value."

Example of Factor Analysis

A company conducts a survey to measure customer satisfaction using 10 questions on product quality, service, and pricing. Factor analysis is performed to identify latent dimensions.

1. **Correlation Matrix**: A correlation matrix reveals strong correlations among questions related to product quality, service, and price, suggesting latent variables.

2. **Extraction**: PCA identifies three factors with eigenvalues greater than 1, explaining 70% of the variance.

3. **Rotation**: Varimax rotation reveals clearer groupings:

    - Factor 1: Questions about product quality (e.g., "durability," "design").

- Factor 2: Questions about service (e.g., "staff friendliness," "response time").
- Factor 3: Questions about pricing (e.g., "value for money," "affordability").

4. **Interpretation**: The company labels the factors as "Product Quality," "Service," and "Pricing" and uses them to tailor improvement strategies.

Applications of Factor Analysis

1. **Psychology**: Identifying underlying constructs such as intelligence, personality traits, or mental health dimensions. For example, the Big Five personality traits—openness, conscientiousness, extraversion, agreeableness, and neuroticism—were derived through factor analysis.

2. **Market Research**: Simplifying customer feedback into factors like satisfaction, loyalty, and usability. This helps businesses understand consumer behavior and develop targeted marketing strategies.

3. **Education**: Analyzing student performance data to uncover latent dimensions such as motivation, knowledge, and learning styles.

4. **Healthcare**: Identifying symptom clusters in medical research or understanding patient satisfaction dimensions in healthcare services.

5. **Social Sciences**: Grouping survey items related to social attitudes, political preferences, or cultural values.

Advantages of Factor Analysis

1. **Data Reduction**: Factor analysis reduces large datasets into manageable components, making it easier to identify patterns and relationships.

2. **Simplified Interpretation**: Grouping variables into factors provides a clearer understanding of the underlying structure.

3. **Adaptability**: The method works with continuous, ordinal, or even binary data, depending on the extraction technique used.

4. **Robustness to Multicollinearity**: By focusing on shared variance, factor analysis minimizes the impact of multicollinearity among variables.

Limitations of Factor Analysis

1. **Subjectivity**: Decisions about the number of factors, rotation methods, and labeling involve judgment and may vary among researchers.

2. **Large Sample Size Requirements**: Factor analysis is sensitive to sample size, with small samples producing unstable solutions.

3. **Assumption Violations**: Factor analysis assumes linear relationships between variables and adequate correlations. Poorly correlated variables may not yield meaningful factors.

4. **Exploratory Nature**: EFA is data-driven and may not align with theoretical expectations. CFA addresses this by testing predefined models.

Enhancing Factor Analysis

1. **Use Adequate Sample Sizes**: Ensure a sufficient number of observations to achieve stable and reliable results. A common rule is 10 observations per variable.

2. **Test for Suitability**: Apply the **Kaiser-Meyer-Olkin (KMO)** measure and **Bartlett's test of sphericity** to verify that the data are appropriate for factor analysis.

3. **Combine with Other Methods**: Pair factor analysis with cluster analysis or regression to uncover deeper insights or make predictions.

4. **Validate Results**: Use confirmatory factor analysis to test the stability of the factor structure in new datasets.

Time Series Analysis: Trends and Forecasting

Time series analysis focuses on understanding, modeling, and forecasting data points collected or recorded sequentially over time. It is widely used in fields such as finance, economics, meteorology, and engineering to uncover patterns and predict future values. Time series data are characterized by their temporal ordering, which distinguishes them from other types of data.

Components of Time Series

Time series data often exhibit distinct components that can be analyzed separately:

1. **Trend**: The long-term movement in the data, representing an overall increase or decrease over time. For example, housing prices may show a general upward trend over decades.

2. **Seasonality**: Regular, repeating patterns or cycles observed within specific time intervals, such as daily, monthly, or yearly. For instance, retail sales often increase during the holiday season.

3. **Cyclicality**: Fluctuations that occur over longer periods, often tied to economic or business cycles. Unlike seasonality, cyclic patterns do not have fixed intervals.

4. **Noise**: Random, irregular variations in the data that cannot be attributed to trend, seasonality, or cycles. Noise reflects the unpredictable aspects of the data.

Time Series Models

1. **Autoregressive (AR) Models**: AR models predict future values based on past values of the series. The model uses a linear combination of lagged observations. For instance, AR(1) uses one lagged value: **$Yt = \phi_1 Yt\text{-}1 + \varepsilon t$** Here, Yt is the current value, ϕ_1 is the coefficient for the lagged value, and εt is the error term.

2. **Moving Average (MA) Models**: MA models predict future values based on past forecast errors. MA(q) uses q lagged error terms: $Yt = \theta_1 \varepsilon t\text{-}1 + \theta_2 \varepsilon t\text{-}2 + ... + \theta q \varepsilon t\text{-}q + \varepsilon t$

3. **Autoregressive Integrated Moving Average (ARIMA)**: ARIMA combines AR and MA components with differencing to make non-stationary data stationary. It is denoted as ARIMA(p, d, q), where:

    - p: Order of autoregression,
    - d: Degree of differencing,
    - q: Order of the moving average.

4. ARIMA is widely used for forecasting and is particularly effective for data without seasonality.

5. **Seasonal ARIMA (SARIMA)**: SARIMA extends ARIMA by incorporating seasonal components. It is denoted as ARIMA(p, d, q)(P, D, Q)m, where (P, D, Q) represent seasonal parameters and m denotes the seasonality period.

6. **Exponential Smoothing (ETS)**: ETS methods forecast by applying exponentially decreasing weights to past observations. Variants include:

    - Simple Exponential Smoothing: For data with no trend or seasonality.
    - Holt's Method: For data with trends.
    - Holt-Winters Method: For data with both trends and seasonality.

7. **State Space Models**: These models represent time series as a combination of observed and latent states, offering a flexible framework for complex time series.

Stationarity in Time Series

A stationary time series has a constant mean, variance, and autocorrelation over time. Stationarity is crucial for many models, as non-stationary data can lead to unreliable results. Methods to achieve stationarity include:

- **Differencing**: Subtracting consecutive values to remove trends.
- **Log Transformation**: Stabilizing variance.
- **Detrending**: Removing the trend component.

Autocorrelation and Partial Autocorrelation

Autocorrelation measures the correlation between a time series and its lagged values. Partial autocorrelation isolates the relationship between a time series and a specific lag while controlling for other lags. These metrics are visualized using autocorrelation function (ACF) and partial autocorrelation function (PACF) plots, which guide the selection of AR and MA terms in models.

Steps in Time Series Analysis

1. **Data Exploration**: Plot the time series to observe trends, seasonality, and noise. Use line charts, seasonal decomposition, and scatterplots of lagged values.

2. **Stationarity Testing**: Apply tests like the Augmented Dickey-Fuller (ADF) or Kwiatkowski-Phillips-Schmidt-Shin (KPSS) test to assess stationarity.

3. **Model Selection**: Choose appropriate models (e.g., ARIMA, ETS) based on data characteristics. Use ACF and PACF plots for guidance.

4. **Parameter Estimation**: Fit the model by estimating its parameters using techniques like maximum likelihood estimation (MLE).

5. **Model Diagnostics**: Evaluate residuals to ensure they are white noise (random with zero mean and constant variance). Residual plots and statistical tests (e.g., Ljung-Box test) help assess model fit.

6. **Forecasting**: Use the model to predict future values and assess forecast accuracy with metrics like mean absolute error (MAE) or root mean square error (RMSE).

Applications of Time Series Analysis

1. **Finance**:
    - Forecasting stock prices, interest rates, or exchange rates.
    - Modeling market volatility using Generalized Autoregressive Conditional Heteroskedasticity (GARCH) models.

2. **Economics**:

- Analyzing GDP growth, unemployment rates, or inflation trends.
- Studying economic cycles.
- Analyzing seasonal effects.

3. **Retail and E-commerce**:
    - Predicting sales demand to optimize inventory.
    - Analyzing seasonal trends in consumer behavior.

4. **Healthcare**:
    - Monitoring disease outbreaks over time.
    - Forecasting hospital admissions based on historical trends.

5. **Weather and Climate**:
    - Modeling temperature, rainfall, or wind patterns.
    - Predicting extreme weather events.

6. **Energy**:
    - Analyzing electricity demand and supply.
    - Forecasting renewable energy production based on weather conditions.

Example of Time Series Analysis

A retail store wants to forecast monthly sales for the next year based on historical data. The steps are:

1. **Visualize Data**: Plot the sales data to identify trends and seasonality. A clear upward trend and annual seasonal peaks around December are observed.

2. **Stationarity Testing**: The ADF test indicates non-stationarity (p-value > 0.05). Differencing the data once removes the trend, achieving stationarity.

3. **Model Selection**: ACF and PACF plots suggest an ARIMA(1, 1, 1)(0, 1, 1)12 model to account for the trend, seasonal differencing, and autocorrelations.

4. **Fit the Model**: Estimate parameters using MLE. Diagnostic checks confirm that residuals are white noise.

5. **Forecast**: Use the model to predict sales for the next 12 months. The forecast shows a continued upward trend with seasonal peaks.

Strengths of Time Series Analysis

1. **Temporal Focus**: Time series models explicitly account for the order of data points, capturing dependencies over time.

2. **Wide Applicability**: The methods apply to diverse fields, from finance to weather forecasting.

3. **Predictive Power**: Advanced models like SARIMA or state space models provide accurate forecasts for complex data.

Limitations

1. **Assumption Sensitivity**: Many models assume stationarity, which requires careful preprocessing.

2. **Data Requirements**: Time series analysis often requires a long history of observations to produce reliable results.

3. **Complexity**: Models can become intricate, especially for data with multiple seasonal patterns or non-linear relationships.

4. **Uncertainty**: Forecasts are inherently uncertain, particularly for long horizons.

Improving Time Series Models

1. **Feature Engineering**: Incorporate external variables (e.g., holidays, economic indicators) into models to improve accuracy.

2. **Ensemble Methods**: Combine forecasts from multiple models to reduce error and improve reliability.

3. **Machine Learning Integration**: Techniques like Long Short-Term Memory (LSTM) networks can model non-linear and complex dependencies in time series data.

Bayesian Statistics: Updating Beliefs with Data

Bayesian statistics is a paradigm for statistical inference based on Bayes' Theorem, which provides a framework for updating probabilities as new evidence becomes available. Unlike classical or frequentist approaches, Bayesian methods incorporate prior knowledge or beliefs into the analysis, combining them with observed data to generate a posterior distribution. This approach is particularly useful when prior information is available or when dealing with complex models.

Bayes' Theorem: The Foundation

Bayes' Theorem is a mathematical formula used to update the probability of a hypothesis (H) given new evidence (E). It is expressed as:

$$P(H \mid E) = [P(E \mid H) \times P(H)] \div P(E)$$

Where:

- P(H | E): Posterior probability (probability of H given E),
- P(E | H): Likelihood (probability of observing E given H),
- P(H): Prior probability (initial belief about H before observing E),
- P(E): Marginal likelihood (probability of the evidence, averaged over all possible hypotheses).

This formula combines the likelihood of the observed data with the prior probability to produce the posterior probability, which reflects updated beliefs.

Key Components of Bayesian Statistics

1. **Prior Distribution**: The prior reflects initial beliefs about a parameter or hypothesis before observing data. For example, a prior might express the belief that a coin is fair (P(heads) = 0.5).
   Priors can be:

   - **Informative**: Incorporates specific knowledge or expertise (e.g., historical data).
   - **Non-informative**: Expresses minimal prior knowledge, such as a uniform distribution.

2. **Likelihood Function**: The likelihood quantifies how well the observed data support a specific hypothesis or parameter value. For example, if a coin lands heads 8 out of 10 times, the likelihood of the data given a fair coin can be calculated using the binomial distribution.

3. **Posterior Distribution**: The posterior combines the prior and likelihood to provide an updated probability distribution for the parameter or hypothesis. It forms the basis for inference in Bayesian analysis.

4. **Marginal Likelihood**: Also known as the evidence, it normalizes the posterior distribution, ensuring that probabilities sum to 1. While essential, it is often challenging to compute in complex models.

Bayesian Inference Process

1. **Define the Prior**: Specify the prior distribution for the parameter(s) of interest. For example, if analyzing the probability of heads for a coin, the prior might be a Beta(1, 1) distribution (uniform between 0 and 1).

2. **Formulate the Likelihood**: Define the likelihood function based on the data-generating process. For a coin toss, the likelihood might follow a binomial distribution.

3. **Compute the Posterior**: Use Bayes' Theorem to combine the prior and likelihood, yielding the posterior distribution.

4. **Summarize the Posterior**: Extract meaningful information from the posterior, such as point estimates (mean, median, or mode) or credible intervals.

5. **Make Decisions**: Use the posterior to make probabilistic statements or decisions. For example, determine the probability that the coin is biased or predict the outcome of future tosses.

Example: Bayesian Inference for a Coin Toss

Suppose a coin is tossed 10 times, and it lands heads 8 times. We aim to estimate the probability of heads (θ).

1. **Prior**: Assume a Beta(2, 2) prior, reflecting a weak belief that the coin is likely fair but allowing for some uncertainty.

2. **Likelihood**: The likelihood follows a binomial distribution: $P(data | \theta) = \theta^8(1 - \theta)^2$

3. **Posterior**: Combining the Beta prior and binomial likelihood yields a Beta(10, 4) posterior: $P(\theta | data) \propto \theta^8(1 - \theta)^2 \times \theta^1(1 - \theta)^1$ $P(\theta | data) \propto \theta^9(1 - \theta)^3$
The posterior reflects updated beliefs, favoring higher probabilities of heads.

4. **Inference**:

    ○ Posterior mean: $10 \div (10 + 4) = 0.714$
    ○ 95% credible interval: Use a Beta(10, 4) distribution to compute the interval, approximately [0.47, 0.91].

5. Based on the posterior, we infer that the coin is more likely to land heads than tails, with a 95% credible interval for θ.

Applications of Bayesian Statistics

1. **Medical Research**:

    ○ Estimating treatment effects using prior clinical studies and current trial data.
    ○ Calculating the probability of a patient having a disease given test results and prior prevalence rates.

2. Example: A diagnostic test has 95% sensitivity and 90% specificity. Given a disease prevalence of 5%, Bayesian analysis updates the probability of disease for a positive test result.

3. **Machine Learning**:

- Bayesian networks model complex relationships between variables.
- Bayesian optimization improves hyperparameter tuning for algorithms.

4. Example: Bayesian optimization selects the best parameters for a neural network by balancing exploration and exploitation.

5. **Finance**:
    - Updating forecasts for stock returns based on new economic indicators.
    - Assessing credit risk using historical data and real-time market changes.

6. Example: Bayesian portfolio allocation adjusts weights dynamically as new market data arrive.

7. **Environmental Science**:
    - Predicting climate change impacts using historical and simulated data.
    - Modeling species distribution with ecological and environmental variables.

8. **Industrial Applications**:
    - Reliability analysis for predicting equipment failure rates.
    - Quality control processes based on historical defect rates.

Advantages of Bayesian Statistics

1. **Incorporation of Prior Knowledge**: Bayesian methods explicitly incorporate prior information, making them especially useful in areas with extensive historical data.

2. **Probabilistic Interpretation**: Results are expressed as probabilities, providing a natural and intuitive way to interpret uncertainty.

3. **Flexibility**: Bayesian models handle complex problems, including hierarchical models and missing data, more easily than frequentist methods.

4. **Sequential Updating**: Bayesian inference allows for continuous updating of beliefs as new data become available, enabling dynamic decision-making.

Challenges and Limitations

1. **Subjectivity of Priors**: The choice of prior can influence results, especially with limited data. Sensitivity analysis is essential to assess the impact of priors.

2. **Computational Intensity**: Bayesian methods often involve complex integrals or simulations, requiring advanced computational tools like Markov Chain Monte Carlo (MCMC).

3. **Interpretation Complexity**: Bayesian results, such as posterior distributions and credible intervals, can be challenging to interpret for non-statisticians.

4. **Slow Convergence**: For large datasets or intricate models, MCMC algorithms may take considerable time to converge.

Modern Computational Tools

Advances in computing have made Bayesian analysis more accessible:

- **MCMC Algorithms**: Techniques like Gibbs sampling and the Metropolis-Hastings algorithm approximate posterior distributions.
- **Software**: Tools such as R (e.g., Stan, JAGS), Python (e.g., PyMC, TensorFlow Probability), and specialized platforms facilitate Bayesian modeling.
- **Variational Inference**: An alternative to MCMC, it approximates posterior distributions using optimization, offering faster convergence.

Enhancing Bayesian Analysis

1. **Use Informative Priors**: When possible, incorporate domain knowledge to improve inference accuracy.

2. **Perform Sensitivity Analysis**: Test how results change with different priors to ensure robustness.

3. **Combine with Machine Learning**: Bayesian methods complement machine learning, enhancing interpretability and probabilistic predictions.

4. **Educate Stakeholders**: Communicate Bayesian results clearly, emphasizing probabilistic reasoning to aid understanding.

Monte Carlo Simulations: Modeling Uncertainty

Monte Carlo simulations are a computational method for modeling and analyzing uncertainty in complex systems. By simulating random samples from known probability distributions, Monte Carlo methods estimate the likelihood of different outcomes and assess the impact of uncertainty on a process. These simulations are widely used in finance, engineering, physics, and many other fields to solve problems that are analytically intractable.

What Are Monte Carlo Simulations?

Monte Carlo simulations rely on random sampling to approximate solutions to problems that involve uncertainty or variability. The process involves creating a model of the system, running repeated simulations using random inputs, and analyzing the resulting outputs to draw conclusions.

For example, consider a scenario where you want to estimate the probability of a company's project exceeding its budget. With Monte Carlo simulations, you would model the project costs using probability distributions for factors like labor, materials, and overhead. By simulating thousands of potential outcomes, you could estimate the likelihood of going over budget.

Key Steps in Monte Carlo Simulations

1. **Define the Problem**: Identify the system or process to be modeled. Specify the inputs, outputs, and relationships among variables.

2. **Assign Probability Distributions**: Model uncertain inputs using appropriate probability distributions. For example:

    - Costs might follow a normal distribution.
    - Completion times could follow a triangular or uniform distribution.

3. **Generate Random Samples**: Use random number generators to create values for the inputs based on their probability distributions.

4. **Simulate the Model**: Run the simulation by plugging the random inputs into the model and calculating the output. Repeat this process thousands or even millions of times.

5. **Analyze Results**: Summarize the simulation outcomes using statistics like means, medians, standard deviations, and percentiles. Create visualizations such as histograms, box plots, or cumulative probability plots to interpret the results.

Example of Monte Carlo Simulation

Imagine a manufacturing company wants to estimate the likelihood of meeting a production deadline. The project has three stages:

1. **Raw Material Delivery**: Estimated to take 4–7 days (uniform distribution).

2. **Production**: Normally distributed with a mean of 15 days and standard deviation of 3 days.

3. **Shipping**: Triangular distribution with a minimum of 2 days, most likely value of 4 days, and a maximum of 8 days.

4. **Model the System**: Total production time = Delivery time + Production time + Shipping time.

5. **Assign Distributions**:
    - Delivery time: Uniform(4, 7)
    - Production time: Normal(15, 3)
    - Shipping time: Triangular(2, 4, 8)

6. **Simulate**: Generate 10,000 random samples for each stage, calculate the total production time for each iteration, and store the results.

7. **Analyze**:
    - Mean total time: 23.5 days.
    - 90th percentile: 27 days (90% of projects finish within this time).
    - Probability of finishing within 25 days: ~75%.

Applications of Monte Carlo Simulations

1. **Finance**:
    - **Portfolio Risk Assessment**: Estimate potential losses under varying market conditions.
    - **Option Pricing**: Simulate stock price paths to calculate derivative values.

2. Example: A financial analyst uses Monte Carlo methods to model the impact of interest rate fluctuations on bond prices.

3. **Engineering**:
    - **Reliability Analysis**: Evaluate the probability of system failure under different stress conditions.
    - **Optimization**: Simulate multiple designs to identify the best-performing configuration.

4. Example: An aerospace engineer assesses the likelihood of component failure due to temperature variations.

5. **Healthcare**:
    - **Clinical Trials**: Model patient outcomes under varying treatment regimens.
    - **Epidemiology**: Simulate the spread of infectious diseases and evaluate intervention strategies.

6. Example: Researchers estimate the effect of vaccination campaigns on reducing COVID-19 cases.

7. **Energy**:

- ○ **Power Grid Management**: Assess the reliability of energy supplies under fluctuating demand.
- ○ **Renewable Energy**: Model solar or wind power generation based on weather data.

8. Example: A utility company simulates energy demand during extreme weather events to plan resource allocation.

9. **Project Management**:

    - ○ **Schedule Risk Analysis**: Estimate the likelihood of project delays.
    - ○ **Cost Estimation**: Model the probability of exceeding budget constraints.

10. Example: A construction firm evaluates the probability of finishing a project within the allocated timeline, given uncertainties in material delivery and labor availability.

Advantages of Monte Carlo Simulations

1. **Flexibility**: Monte Carlo simulations can model systems with complex, nonlinear relationships, multiple variables, and varying distributions.

2. **Realistic Uncertainty Representation**: By sampling from probability distributions, Monte Carlo methods provide a realistic depiction of variability and randomness.

3. **Versatility**: They are applicable across industries and disciplines, making them a go-to tool for uncertainty analysis.

4. **Scalability**: Advances in computational power enable simulations with millions of iterations, improving the precision of results.

Limitations

1. **Computational Intensity**: Large-scale simulations require significant computational resources, especially for high-dimensional models.

2. **Model Accuracy**: The quality of the results depends on the accuracy of the underlying model and input distributions. Poorly specified distributions can lead to misleading conclusions.

3. **Interpretation Challenges**: Understanding and communicating probabilistic results to non-experts can be difficult.

4. **Randomness**: The method relies on random sampling, which can introduce variability in results. Larger sample sizes reduce this effect.

Enhancing Monte Carlo Simulations

1. **Select Appropriate Distributions**: Carefully choose distributions that match the characteristics of the uncertain variables.

2. **Increase Sample Size**: Use more iterations to improve result stability and precision.

3. **Validate Models**: Compare simulation outcomes to real-world data or analytical results to ensure accuracy.

4. **Parallel Computing**: Leverage parallel processing to reduce computation time for large simulations.

5. **Scenario Analysis**: Run simulations under different scenarios (e.g., best-case, worst-case) to evaluate system robustness.

Monte Carlo Simulations in Decision-Making

Monte Carlo simulations empower decision-makers by quantifying uncertainty and enabling risk-based decisions. For example, a business may use simulations to determine whether to launch a new product, considering market uncertainties. By analyzing the probability of success under varying conditions, they can make informed choices about resource allocation and timing.

Monte Carlo simulations bridge the gap between theory and practice, offering a powerful method for analyzing uncertainty in diverse and complex systems.

Optimization: Achieving Optimal Results

Optimization involves finding the best possible solution to a problem within a set of constraints. Whether maximizing efficiency, minimizing costs, or balancing trade-offs, optimization is a cornerstone of decision-making in fields ranging from engineering and economics to logistics and artificial intelligence. At its core, optimization uses mathematical models to determine the most advantageous outcome under given circumstances.

Types of Optimization Problems

Optimization problems can be classified based on their structure, constraints, and decision variables:

1. **Linear Optimization (Linear Programming)**: Linear programming (LP) optimizes a linear objective function subject to linear equality and inequality constraints. For example:

- Minimize cost = $c_1x_1 + c_2x_2$
- Subject to: $a_{11}x_1 + a_{12}x_2 \leq b_1, x_1, x_2 \geq 0$

2. LP is widely used in resource allocation, transportation, and production scheduling.

3. **Nonlinear Optimization**: Nonlinear programming (NLP) deals with problems where the objective function or constraints are nonlinear. For example:

   - Maximize profit = $\log(x_1) + x_2^2$
   - Subject to: $x_1x_2 \leq 10, x_1, x_2 \geq 0$

4. NLP is essential for complex systems like chemical processes or energy optimization.

5. **Integer Programming**: Integer programming (IP) restricts some or all decision variables to integer values. Applications include facility location and workforce scheduling.

6. **Mixed-Integer Programming (MIP)**: MIP combines continuous and integer variables, expanding the range of practical applications.

7. **Stochastic Optimization**: Stochastic models account for uncertainty in parameters, such as demand or weather conditions, making them ideal for supply chain and risk management.

8. **Multi-Objective Optimization**: Multi-objective problems involve optimizing two or more conflicting objectives simultaneously. For example, minimizing cost while maximizing quality. These problems often use Pareto efficiency to identify solutions where no objective can be improved without worsening another.

Key Components of Optimization

1. **Objective Function**: The objective function represents the goal of the optimization problem, such as minimizing costs or maximizing profits. It quantifies what needs to be optimized.

2. **Decision Variables**: These are the unknowns the optimization model seeks to determine. For example, x_1 and x_2 could represent the quantities of two products to produce.

3. **Constraints**: Constraints define the feasible region, limiting the values of decision variables. For instance, production capacity or budget constraints ensure solutions remain realistic.

4. **Feasible Region**: The feasible region is the set of all points that satisfy the constraints. The optimal solution lies within this region.

Optimization Techniques

1. **Gradient Descent**: Gradient descent is an iterative method for finding the minimum of a function. It updates variables in the direction of the negative gradient (steepest descent).
    Example:

    - Objective: Minimize $f(x) = x^2$
    - Update rule: $x_{k+1} = x_k - \alpha \nabla f(x_k)$, where α is the learning rate.

2. **Simplex Method**: The simplex method solves linear programming problems by systematically moving along the edges of the feasible region to find the optimal vertex.

3. **Interior-Point Methods**: These methods navigate the interior of the feasible region, offering an alternative to simplex for large-scale problems.

4. **Genetic Algorithms (GAs)**: GAs mimic natural selection to solve optimization problems, using crossover, mutation, and selection to evolve solutions.

5. **Simulated Annealing**: This probabilistic technique explores the solution space, allowing occasional uphill moves to escape local minima.

6. **Dynamic Programming**: Dynamic programming breaks problems into smaller subproblems, solving each recursively. It is effective for sequential decision-making tasks.

7. **Convex Optimization**: Convex optimization focuses on problems where the objective function and feasible region are convex. Such problems guarantee a global optimum.

8. **Heuristics and Metaheuristics**: Heuristic methods, like tabu search or particle swarm optimization, provide approximate solutions to complex problems where exact methods are infeasible.

Applications of Optimization

1. **Engineering**:
    - Designing energy-efficient buildings by optimizing materials and insulation.
    - Determining the optimal shape of an aircraft wing to minimize drag.

2. **Supply Chain and Logistics**:
    - Optimizing warehouse locations to minimize transportation costs.
    - Determining the best delivery routes to reduce fuel consumption.

3. **Finance**:
   - Portfolio optimization to balance risk and return.
   - Finding allocations between different asset classes.
   - Hedging strategies to minimize financial risk.

4. **Healthcare**:
   - Allocating medical resources, such as ventilators or ICU beds, during crises.
   - Scheduling operating rooms to maximize patient throughput.

5. **Manufacturing**:
   - Determining production schedules to minimize downtime.
   - Optimizing assembly line configurations for efficiency.

6. **Artificial Intelligence**:
   - Training machine learning models by minimizing loss functions.
   - Hyperparameter tuning to improve algorithm performance.

7. **Environmental Science**:
   - Identifying optimal locations for renewable energy installations.
   - Balancing conservation efforts with land use for agriculture.

Example of Optimization in Practice

A company produces two products, P_1 and P_2, using limited resources. The objective is to maximize profit:

1. **Objective Function**: Maximize profit = $40x_1 + 30x_2$

2. **Constraints**:
   - Resource A: $2x_1 + x_2 \leq 100$
   - Resource B: $x_1 + 2x_2 \leq 80$
   - Non-negativity: $x_1, x_2 \geq 0$

3. **Solution**:
   - Graphically or using the simplex method, the optimal solution is $x_1 = 30$, $x_2 = 20$.
   - Maximum profit: $40(30) + 30(20) = 1{,}800$.

Strengths of Optimization

1. **Efficiency**: Optimization identifies the best solution with minimal waste of resources.

2. **Versatility**: It applies to diverse domains, from industrial processes to scientific research.

3. **Quantifiable Outcomes**: Optimization provides clear, actionable results supported by mathematical rigor.

4. **Cost Savings**: By identifying the most efficient solutions, organizations can reduce costs and improve productivity.

Limitations

1. **Complexity**: Real-world problems often involve nonlinear, high-dimensional systems with many constraints.

2. **Data Dependence**: The accuracy of optimization outcomes depends on the quality of input data and model assumptions.

3. **Computational Demands**: Large-scale problems require significant computational resources, especially for stochastic or multi-objective models.

4. **Local Optima**: Nonlinear problems may converge to local rather than global optima.

Improving Optimization Outcomes

1. **Refine Models**: Incorporate realistic constraints and objective functions to better reflect real-world conditions.

2. **Leverage Advanced Algorithms**: Use state-of-the-art techniques like deep reinforcement learning for highly complex problems.

3. **Perform Sensitivity Analysis**: Assess how changes in parameters affect solutions, ensuring robustness under uncertainty.

4. **Combine Methods**: Hybrid approaches, such as combining genetic algorithms with gradient-based methods, can exploit the strengths of multiple techniques.

Future of Optimization

With advancements in computational power and algorithms, optimization continues to evolve. Quantum computing promises to revolutionize optimization by solving problems previously considered intractable. Fields like autonomous systems and smart cities increasingly rely on optimization to make data-driven, efficient decisions.

Chapter 14: Real-World Applications of Statistics

Business Analytics: Driving Decisions with Data

Business analytics involves using statistical methods and tools to extract actionable insights from data. By analyzing historical trends, identifying patterns, and making predictions, businesses can make informed decisions that optimize performance, reduce costs, and enhance customer satisfaction. In today's competitive landscape, leveraging data effectively is essential for achieving strategic goals.

The Foundation of Business Analytics

Business analytics typically encompasses three types of analyses:

1. **Descriptive Analytics**: Summarizes historical data to understand past performance. For example, analyzing sales data to determine which products performed best during a specific period.

2. **Predictive Analytics**: Uses statistical models and machine learning algorithms to forecast future outcomes. For instance, predicting customer churn based on behavioral patterns.

3. **Prescriptive Analytics**: Recommends optimal actions based on predictions and simulations. For example, determining the best pricing strategy for maximizing revenue.

Each of these stages relies heavily on statistical techniques, from hypothesis testing to regression analysis.

Data Sources in Business Analytics

Businesses use diverse data sources to fuel analytics:

- **Transactional Data**: Sales, purchases, and customer interactions recorded in databases.
- **Customer Feedback**: Surveys, reviews, and social media posts that reveal customer preferences.
- **Market Data**: Competitor pricing, industry trends, and economic indicators.
- **Operational Data**: Metrics like inventory levels, production efficiency, and logistics performance.

Combining these data types provides a comprehensive view of business operations and market dynamics.

Statistical Methods in Business Analytics

1. **Regression Analysis**: Regression is used to identify relationships between variables and predict outcomes. For example, a retailer might use regression to predict future sales based on advertising spend, pricing, and seasonal effects.

2. **Time Series Analysis**: Time series methods analyze trends and seasonality in data collected over time. Businesses apply these techniques to forecast sales, optimize inventory, and manage supply chains.

3. **Cluster Analysis**: Clustering segments customers into groups based on similarities in behavior or demographics. For instance, an e-commerce platform might group customers into frequent shoppers, deal-seekers, and casual browsers to personalize marketing campaigns.

4. **A/B Testing**: Also known as split testing, A/B testing compares two versions of a variable (e.g., a website layout) to determine which performs better. Statistical significance testing ensures that observed differences are not due to random chance.

5. **Logistic Regression**: Logistic regression predicts binary outcomes, such as whether a customer will make a purchase (yes/no) or churn (stay/leave). It is widely used in customer retention strategies.

Applications of Business Analytics

1. **Customer Relationship Management (CRM)**: Businesses analyze customer data to improve retention and loyalty. For example, loyalty programs are tailored using statistical models that predict which rewards will resonate most with different customer segments.

2. **Pricing Optimization**: Statistical models help businesses determine the optimal price point that maximizes revenue while remaining competitive. Elasticity analysis evaluates how changes in price affect demand.

3. **Supply Chain Management**: Analytics enhances supply chain efficiency by predicting demand, optimizing inventory levels, and improving delivery schedules. For instance, predictive models estimate seasonal demand surges, ensuring adequate stock availability.

4. **Marketing Campaign Effectiveness**: Businesses evaluate the performance of advertising campaigns using metrics like conversion rates and return on investment (ROI). Multivariate analysis identifies the factors that contribute most to campaign success.

5. **Human Resources**: Workforce analytics uses statistics to improve hiring, training, and retention. For example, predictive models identify employees at risk of leaving and recommend interventions.

Case Study: Retail Analytics

A national retail chain seeks to optimize its marketing efforts. By analyzing customer transaction data, the company segments its customers into three groups: high spenders, occasional shoppers, and deal-seekers. It implements targeted marketing campaigns for each group:

- High spenders receive personalized product recommendations based on past purchases.
- Occasional shoppers are offered loyalty rewards to encourage more frequent visits.
- Deal-seekers are informed about sales and promotions.

The company tracks campaign performance using A/B testing, finding that personalized recommendations increase purchase frequency by 20% among high spenders. Statistical analysis ensures that observed effects are statistically significant, enabling data-driven decisions.

Emerging Trends in Business Analytics

1. **Machine Learning Integration**: Machine learning enhances traditional statistical methods by uncovering non-linear patterns and complex interactions. For example, recommendation engines use algorithms like collaborative filtering to predict customer preferences.

2. **Real-Time Analytics**: Businesses increasingly use real-time data streams to make immediate decisions. For instance, online retailers adjust prices dynamically based on demand and competitor pricing.

3. **Big Data and Cloud Computing**: The rise of big data enables businesses to analyze massive datasets from multiple sources. Cloud computing provides scalable storage and processing power, making analytics accessible to organizations of all sizes.

4. **Ethical Analytics**: With growing concerns about privacy and data misuse, businesses are adopting ethical practices in data collection and analysis. Transparent reporting and adherence to regulations like GDPR are becoming standard.

Challenges in Business Analytics

1. **Data Quality**: Inaccurate or incomplete data can lead to flawed analyses and misguided decisions. Businesses must invest in robust data cleaning and validation processes.

2. **Integration Across Departments**: Siloed data systems hinder the ability to gain a unified view of operations. Effective analytics require seamless data integration across departments.

3. **Interpreting Results**: Statistical results can be complex and challenging to communicate to non-technical stakeholders. Visualizations and clear narratives help bridge this gap.

4. **Scalability**: As businesses grow, their data needs expand. Ensuring that analytics systems can handle increasing data volumes and complexity is essential.

Enhancing Business Analytics

1. **Invest in Training**: Equip employees with the skills to interpret statistical results and apply them to decision-making. Training in tools like Python, R, or Tableau empowers teams to leverage analytics effectively.

2. **Adopt Advanced Tools**: Use cutting-edge statistical software and machine learning frameworks to enhance analytical capabilities. Tools like TensorFlow and SAS provide advanced modeling features.

3. **Focus on Actionable Insights**: Analytics should always tie back to business objectives. Reports should emphasize actionable recommendations, not just descriptive statistics.

4. **Collaborate Across Teams**: Encourage collaboration between data scientists, business leaders, and domain experts to ensure that analytics aligns with organizational goals.

Economics and Finance: Probability Applications in Markets and Economies

Statistics and probability are foundational to economics and finance. They enable analysts, policymakers, and businesses to model uncertainty, forecast trends, and make decisions. From assessing market risk to studying economic fluctuations, probabilistic methods provide the tools to analyze complex systems and predict outcomes with precision.

Probability in Financial Markets

1. **Risk Assessment**: Financial markets involve uncertainty, and probability helps quantify risk. Analysts calculate the likelihood of adverse events, such as defaults, market crashes, or losses in portfolio value.

- **Value at Risk (VaR)** estimates the maximum loss a portfolio might experience over a specific period with a given confidence level. For example, a 1-day VaR of $1 million at 95% confidence means there is only a 5% chance of losing more than $1 million in one day.

- **Expected Shortfall (ES)**, or Conditional VaR, measures the average loss in the worst-case scenarios beyond the VaR threshold.

2. **Option Pricing**: Derivatives like options depend on underlying assets' future behavior, modeled probabilistically. The **Black-Scholes model** uses stochastic calculus to estimate an option's fair price. The model assumes:

    - Asset prices follow a geometric Brownian motion.
    - Volatility, risk-free rate, and other parameters remain constant over the option's life.

3. Example: A call option on a stock priced at $100 with a strike price of $110 uses probability to estimate whether the stock will exceed the strike price before expiry.

4. **Portfolio Diversification**: Probability helps assess how assets in a portfolio are correlated. Diversification minimizes risk by investing in assets with low or negative correlations, reducing the likelihood of simultaneous losses.

    - **Covariance** quantifies how two assets move together.
    - **Correlation coefficient** (ranging from -1 to 1) measures the strength of their relationship. A value close to 0 suggests weak correlation, while -1 indicates perfect negative correlation.

5. **Monte Carlo Simulations in Finance**: Monte Carlo methods simulate various scenarios to estimate the probability of different outcomes, such as portfolio returns or option prices. For instance, an investor might simulate stock price movements under varying market conditions to assess portfolio performance.

Economic Applications of Probability

1. **Macroeconomic Forecasting**: Probabilistic models predict macroeconomic indicators such as GDP growth, inflation, and unemployment. For example:

    - **Bayesian Vector Autoregressions (BVAR)** incorporate prior information to improve forecast accuracy.
    - **Scenario Analysis** evaluates the probabilities of different economic outcomes under alternative policy scenarios.

2. **Policy Impact Evaluation**: Economists use probability to assess the effects of fiscal or monetary policies. For instance:

    - What is the probability that a tax cut will boost consumption?

- How likely is an interest rate hike to curb inflation?

3. Probabilistic methods enable policymakers to weigh the likelihood of achieving desired outcomes against potential risks.

4. **Income Distribution and Inequality**: Probability distributions describe income levels across populations. Common models include:

    - **Log-normal distribution**: Often used for income data, as it accounts for skewness caused by high-income outliers.
    - **Pareto distribution**: Models the top end of wealth distributions, highlighting inequality.

5. Metrics like the **Gini coefficient** summarize income inequality, with values closer to 1 indicating greater disparity.

6. **Behavioral Economics**: Probability underpins models of decision-making under uncertainty, such as **prospect theory**, which describes how individuals evaluate risks and rewards. For example, people tend to overweight low probabilities (e.g., lottery odds) and underweight high probabilities (e.g., winning a small prize).

Case Study: Predicting Recessions

Economists use probability models to estimate the likelihood of recessions. A popular tool is the **yield curve**, which compares short-term and long-term interest rates. An inverted yield curve (when short-term rates exceed long-term rates) historically signals an increased probability of recession.

1. **Data Collection**: Gather data on 10-year Treasury yields and 3-month Treasury bill rates.

2. **Modeling**: Use logistic regression to estimate the probability of a recession based on the yield curve spread.

3. **Output**: The model predicts a 40% chance of recession within the next year if the yield curve remains inverted for three consecutive months.

4. **Policy Implications**: Central banks might adjust monetary policy to mitigate risks, such as lowering interest rates to stimulate economic activity.

Statistical Models in Finance and Economics

1. **Time Series Models**: Time series techniques, like ARIMA or GARCH, forecast economic indicators and financial market volatility. For example, GARCH models predict changes in stock price volatility based on past behavior.

2. **Game Theory**: Game theory uses probability to model strategic interactions between economic agents. Applications range from pricing strategies in oligopolies to negotiations in international trade.

3. **Markov Chains**: Markov processes model systems that transition between states based on probabilities. For instance, Markov chains can represent credit rating transitions, such as the likelihood of a company moving from "A" to "BBB."

4. **Regression Analysis**: Regression estimates relationships between variables. For example:

    - Economists might regress GDP on investment, consumption, and exports.
    - Financial analysts could examine how stock returns depend on market indices, sector performance, and macroeconomic indicators.

Challenges in Probability Applications

1. **Model Assumptions**: Many models rely on assumptions, such as normality or constant volatility, which may not hold in real-world scenarios. For instance, market returns often exhibit **fat tails**, meaning extreme outcomes occur more frequently than predicted by normal distributions.

2. **Uncertainty in Parameters**: Estimating probabilities depends on accurate parameter values, such as volatilities or correlations. Errors in these estimates can lead to flawed predictions.

3. **Dynamic Systems**: Economic and financial systems evolve over time, making static models insufficient. Adaptive methods, like machine learning, are increasingly used to address these challenges.

4. **Black Swan Events**: Rare, unpredictable events, such as the 2008 financial crisis, challenge probabilistic models. Traditional models often underestimate the likelihood of such extreme outcomes.

Emerging Trends

1. **Machine Learning in Finance**: Machine learning algorithms analyze large datasets to identify patterns and predict probabilities. For example:

    - Neural networks forecast stock prices based on historical data.
    - Clustering algorithms segment customers for targeted marketing.

2. **Behavioral Probability Models**: Advances in behavioral finance incorporate psychological factors into probabilistic models, improving predictions of market behavior.

3. **Sustainability Metrics**: Probability models assess environmental, social, and governance (ESG) risks. For instance, Monte Carlo simulations estimate the probability of meeting carbon emission targets under varying policy scenarios.

4. **Decentralized Finance (DeFi)**: Probabilistic models support risk assessment in decentralized lending, trading, and investment platforms powered by blockchain technology.

Enhancing Probability Models

1. **Robustness Testing**: Validate models using out-of-sample data and stress testing to ensure reliability under different scenarios.

2. **Incorporate Real-World Complexity**: Use techniques like stochastic differential equations or agent-based modeling to capture non-linearities and dynamic interactions.

3. **Focus on Explainability**: Complex models must balance accuracy with interpretability to ensure stakeholders understand the implications of probabilistic predictions.

Health and Medical Research: Evidence-Based Practice

Statistics underpin evidence-based practice in health and medical research. From clinical trials to public health studies, statistical methods help researchers design experiments, analyze data, and draw valid conclusions. By quantifying uncertainty and identifying patterns, statistics ensure that medical decisions are informed by reliable evidence rather than anecdotal observations.

Statistical Foundations in Medical Research

1. **Study Design**:
    - **Randomized Controlled Trials (RCTs)**: RCTs are the gold standard for evaluating the efficacy of treatments. Participants are randomly assigned to treatment or control groups to minimize bias.
    - **Cohort Studies**: These studies follow groups of individuals over time to observe outcomes based on exposure to risk factors.
    - **Case-Control Studies**: Case-control studies compare individuals with a condition (cases) to those without it (controls) to identify potential causes.

2. **Hypothesis Testing**: Medical research often involves testing hypotheses, such as whether a new drug reduces symptoms more effectively than a placebo.

Statistical tests, like t-tests or chi-square tests, determine whether observed differences are significant or due to random variation.

3. **Estimation**: Confidence intervals provide a range of values within which the true effect size is likely to lie. For example, a confidence interval for a vaccine efficacy estimate might indicate that the true effectiveness is between 85% and 95%.

4. **Probability and Risk**:

    - **Absolute Risk**: The probability of an event occurring in a population.
    - **Relative Risk (RR)**: The ratio of the probability of an event in the treatment group to that in the control group.
    - **Odds Ratio (OR)**: The ratio of the odds of an event occurring in one group to the odds in another.

Applications in Health and Medicine

1. **Clinical Trials**: Clinical trials assess the safety and efficacy of treatments, drugs, and medical devices. Statistics guide every phase:

    - **Phase I**: Small trials to evaluate safety and dosage.
    - **Phase II**: Intermediate trials to assess efficacy and side effects.
    - **Phase III**: Large-scale trials to confirm effectiveness and monitor adverse reactions.
    - **Phase IV**: Post-marketing surveillance to detect long-term effects.

2. Example: In a vaccine trial, researchers compare the incidence of infection between vaccinated and unvaccinated groups. A chi-square test might reveal whether the vaccine significantly reduces infection rates.

3. **Epidemiology**: Epidemiologists use statistics to study the distribution and determinants of health conditions in populations. Common methods include:

    - **Survival Analysis**: Examining time-to-event data, such as time until disease onset or death.
    - **Regression Models**: Identifying associations between risk factors and health outcomes.

4. Example: A study on smoking and lung cancer might use logistic regression to quantify the relationship between smoking intensity and cancer risk.

5. **Public Health Interventions**: Statistics evaluate the impact of health policies and programs. For instance:

    - Analyzing trends in vaccination coverage to identify underserved populations.

- Modeling the spread of infectious diseases to predict outbreaks and allocate resources.

6. Example: During the COVID-19 pandemic, statistical models estimated the basic reproduction number (R0) to guide containment measures.

7. **Medical Imaging**: Advanced statistical techniques analyze medical images, such as X-rays or MRIs, to assist in diagnosis. Machine learning algorithms, powered by statistical models, detect anomalies and classify images with high accuracy.

8. **Genetics and Genomics**: Biostatistics is critical in studying genetic data to identify disease-causing mutations. Techniques like genome-wide association studies (GWAS) identify genetic variants associated with specific conditions. Example: A GWAS might reveal that a particular gene variant increases the risk of developing Alzheimer's disease by 30%.

Case Study: Evaluating a New Drug

A pharmaceutical company tests a new drug for lowering blood pressure. The study involves 200 participants, randomly assigned to either the drug group or the placebo group.

1. **Data Collection**: Measure systolic blood pressure (SBP) before and after treatment.

2. **Statistical Analysis**:
   - Calculate the mean SBP reduction in both groups.
   - Perform a two-sample t-test to determine whether the drug group shows a significantly greater reduction than the placebo group.

3. **Results**:
   - Drug group: Mean reduction = 15 mmHg, SD = 5.
   - Placebo group: Mean reduction = 8 mmHg, SD = 4.
   - p-value = 0.001, indicating a statistically significant difference.

4. **Interpretation**: The drug reduces SBP significantly more than the placebo. Researchers calculate a 95% confidence interval for the mean difference (5.5 to 9.5 mmHg) to quantify the effect size.

Emerging Trends in Medical Research

1. **Big Data in Healthcare**: Electronic health records, wearable devices, and genomic databases generate vast amounts of data. Statistical methods analyze these datasets to uncover trends, predict outcomes, and personalize treatments.

2. **Artificial Intelligence (AI) and Machine Learning**: AI-powered models, such as neural networks, enhance diagnostic accuracy and predict patient outcomes. For example, predictive models estimate hospital readmission risks based on patient history.

3. **Bayesian Methods**: Bayesian statistics update prior knowledge with new evidence, enabling dynamic decision-making. For instance, Bayesian models help monitor clinical trials in real-time, adjusting sample sizes or stopping trials early if results are conclusive.

4. **Real-World Evidence (RWE)**: RWE complements clinical trials by analyzing data from routine clinical practice. Statistical methods handle observational data, addressing biases and confounding factors.

Challenges in Medical Statistics

1. **Bias in Study Design**: Selection bias, measurement bias, or confounding can skew results. Randomization and blinding reduce these risks, but careful statistical adjustment is often necessary.

2. **Small Sample Sizes**: Rare diseases or early-phase trials often involve small samples, limiting statistical power. Advanced methods, such as bootstrapping, address this challenge by estimating confidence intervals through resampling.

3. **Multiple Testing**: Analyzing multiple outcomes or subgroups increases the risk of false positives. Adjustments like the Bonferroni correction control the family-wise error rate.

4. **Interpreting P-Values**: P-values indicate statistical significance but not clinical importance. For instance, a small p-value might reflect a trivial difference if the sample size is large.

Improving Statistical Practices in Medicine

1. **Transparent Reporting**: Use reporting guidelines like CONSORT (for RCTs) or STROBE (for observational studies) to ensure clarity and reproducibility.

2. **Focus on Effect Sizes**: Emphasize effect sizes and confidence intervals over p-values to convey the magnitude and precision of findings.

3. **Pre-Registration**: Register study protocols and analysis plans in advance to prevent selective reporting or data dredging.

4. **Collaborative Teams**: Involve biostatisticians early in the research process to ensure rigorous study design and analysis.

Social Sciences: Understanding Human Behavior

Statistics is central in social sciences by enabling researchers to analyze, interpret, and draw conclusions about human behavior. From understanding voting patterns to measuring the impact of education policies, statistical methods provide a structured approach to exploring complex social phenomena. By quantifying relationships and patterns in data, social scientists can make informed decisions, validate theories, and guide policy-making.

Statistical Foundations in Social Science Research

1. **Descriptive Statistics**: Descriptive statistics summarize data to reveal patterns and trends. Measures like mean, median, and standard deviation provide insights into central tendencies and variability. For example, the average income of a population might highlight economic disparities across regions.

2. **Inferential Statistics**: Inferential methods allow researchers to generalize findings from a sample to a broader population. Techniques like confidence intervals and hypothesis testing estimate population parameters and assess the significance of observed differences.

3. **Probability in Social Behavior**: Probabilistic models describe the likelihood of events, such as voter turnout or adoption of technology. For example, logistic regression might estimate the probability that an individual supports a specific policy based on demographic factors.

4. **Correlation and Causation**: Statistical tools, such as correlation coefficients and regression analysis, quantify relationships between variables. While correlation measures association, experimental designs or advanced methods like structural equation modeling (SEM) assess causation.

Applications of Statistics in Social Sciences

1. **Sociology**:
    - **Social Inequality**: Researchers measure income inequality using metrics like the Gini coefficient or Lorenz curve.
    - **Cultural Studies**: Cluster analysis identifies cultural groupings based on shared values, practices, or beliefs.
2. Example: A study examines the relationship between education level and job satisfaction. Regression analysis reveals that higher education correlates with increased job satisfaction, controlling for age and income.
3. **Psychology**:

- **Experimental Studies**: Randomized experiments test hypotheses about cognitive processes, behavior, or emotions.
- **Survey Analysis**: Factor analysis identifies latent variables, such as personality traits or mental health dimensions.

4. Example: A psychologist uses ANOVA to compare memory retention between three groups exposed to different learning techniques. The results show that interactive methods significantly improve retention compared to traditional lectures.

5. **Political Science**:

   - **Election Studies**: Statistical models predict voter turnout and preferences based on demographics and historical data.
   - **Policy Analysis**: Regression models evaluate the impact of policies, such as changes in tax rates on public approval.

6. Example: A logistic regression predicts the probability of voting based on age, income, and political affiliation. Results suggest that younger, lower-income individuals are less likely to vote.

7. **Education**:

   - **Student Performance**: Multilevel modeling analyzes factors influencing academic achievement, accounting for individual and school-level effects.
   - **Program Evaluation**: Propensity score matching assesses the effectiveness of interventions like tutoring programs or curriculum changes.

8. Example: A study evaluates the impact of a bilingual education program on language proficiency. Matching students in the program with similar students not in the program reveals significant improvements in language skills.

9. **Economics**:

   - **Labor Market Analysis**: Time series models forecast unemployment trends.
   - **Behavioral Economics**: Statistical experiments test theories about decision-making, such as loss aversion or anchoring effects.

10. Example: An economist uses a difference-in-differences approach to measure the effect of minimum wage increases on employment levels. The analysis suggests minimal negative impact on jobs in low-wage sectors.

Common Statistical Techniques in Social Sciences

1. **Survey Sampling**: Surveys collect data from representative samples to generalize findings to larger populations. Techniques like stratified sampling ensure diverse subgroups are adequately represented.

2. **Multivariate Analysis**: Methods like multiple regression or principal component analysis (PCA) explore relationships between multiple variables simultaneously. For example, PCA might reduce a large set of survey items into key factors.

3. **Time Series Analysis**: Social scientists analyze temporal data to study trends and cycles. For instance, researchers might use ARIMA models to forecast crime rates based on historical data.

4. **Structural Equation Modeling (SEM)**: SEM combines factor analysis and regression to test complex relationships between observed and latent variables. It is widely used in psychology and sociology to validate theoretical models.

5. **Network Analysis**: Network analysis examines relationships between individuals, groups, or organizations. Metrics like centrality measure the influence of actors within a network.
   Example: A study maps social connections in a workplace to identify influential employees or potential bottlenecks in communication.

Case Study: Analyzing Social Mobility

A sociologist investigates intergenerational income mobility, exploring whether children earn more than their parents. The study uses survey data from 5,000 families.

1. **Data Collection**: Gather data on parental income and children's income at similar ages.

2. **Statistical Analysis**:
   - Compute correlation coefficients to measure the strength of the relationship between parental and child income.
   - Use regression analysis to estimate the intergenerational elasticity of income (IGE). An IGE of 0.5 suggests that 50% of income differences persist across generations.

3. **Findings**: The analysis reveals significant regional variations in mobility, with urban areas showing higher mobility than rural areas.

4. **Policy Implications**: Results inform policies aimed at reducing barriers to upward mobility, such as improving access to education or addressing housing segregation.

Challenges in Social Science Research

1. **Measurement Bias**: Social phenomena are often difficult to measure precisely. For example, self-reported data may suffer from recall bias or social desirability bias.

2. **Causality vs. Correlation**: Observational studies often struggle to establish causation. Confounding variables may obscure true relationships.

3. **Complex Interactions**: Social systems involve dynamic, non-linear interactions that are difficult to model using traditional methods.

4. **Ethical Concerns**: Protecting participant privacy and ensuring informed consent are critical in studies involving sensitive topics.

Emerging Trends

1. **Big Data in Social Sciences**: Social media platforms, online interactions, and administrative records generate massive datasets. Advanced analytics, including natural language processing, reveal insights into human behavior at scale. Example: Sentiment analysis of Twitter data tracks public opinion during elections or crises.

2. **Agent-Based Modeling**: Agent-based models simulate interactions among individuals to study emergent social phenomena, such as crowd behavior or the spread of misinformation.

3. **Machine Learning**: Machine learning enhances traditional statistical methods by identifying non-linear patterns and interactions. For example, clustering algorithms segment populations based on behavioral traits.

4. **Interdisciplinary Collaboration**: Collaboration between social scientists, data scientists, and statisticians enriches research by combining domain expertise with advanced analytical methods.

Improving Statistical Practices in Social Sciences

1. **Use Robust Methods**: Apply techniques like sensitivity analysis to test the robustness of findings against different assumptions or models.

2. **Incorporate Mixed Methods**: Combine quantitative analysis with qualitative approaches, such as interviews or ethnography, to provide a richer understanding of social phenomena.

3. **Transparent Reporting**: Follow reporting guidelines to ensure clarity and reproducibility. For example, specify data sources, statistical methods, and limitations.

4. **Engage Diverse Perspectives**: Include diverse populations in studies to improve generalizability and address potential biases.

Statistics are essential for understanding and interpreting human behavior in complex social contexts. Social scientists can use statistics to generate evidence that informs policies, shapes societal norms, and advances our understanding of the human experience.

Engineering and Technology: Optimizing Systems

Statistics in engineering and technology is essential for designing, testing, and optimizing systems. From manufacturing processes to software development, statistical methods allow engineers and technologists to make data-driven decisions, improve efficiency, and ensure quality. These methods are embedded in disciplines such as mechanical engineering, electrical engineering, software engineering, and systems optimization.

The Role of Statistics in Engineering

Engineering involves solving real-world problems under constraints like cost, time, and resources. Statistics aids engineers in:

1. **Modeling Systems**: Mathematical models describe physical, chemical, or computational systems. For example, regression models can predict material properties under varying stress conditions.

2. **Quality Control**: Statistical tools like control charts monitor and maintain the quality of production processes. For instance, Six Sigma methodologies use statistical techniques to reduce defects.

3. **Risk Assessment**: Engineers assess the probability of system failures using reliability analysis. Probability distributions, such as the Weibull distribution, model time-to-failure data.

4. **Optimization**: Optimization techniques identify the best parameters for a system to maximize performance or minimize costs. For example, statistical experiments determine the optimal mix of materials for construction.

Statistical Techniques in Engineering

1. **Design of Experiments (DOE)**: DOE involves planning and conducting experiments systematically to study the effects of multiple factors. Engineers use DOE to:
    - Identify key factors influencing a system.
    - Optimize processes by determining the best combination of variables.

2. Example: A chemical engineer might use DOE to optimize the temperature, pressure, and catalyst concentration in a reaction to maximize yield.

3. **Statistical Process Control (SPC)**: SPC monitors production processes using control charts to identify variability and prevent defects. Common control charts include:

    - **X-bar and R charts**: Monitor process means and ranges.
    - **P-charts**: Track proportions of defective items in a sample.

4. Example: In a car manufacturing plant, SPC ensures that components meet specifications, reducing the likelihood of recalls.

5. **Reliability Engineering**: Reliability engineering evaluates the likelihood of a system performing without failure for a specified time. Techniques include:

    - **Fault Tree Analysis (FTA)**: Identifies potential failure pathways.
    - **Mean Time Between Failures (MTBF)**: Estimates average time between system breakdowns.

6. Example: An aerospace engineer uses reliability analysis to ensure critical components of an aircraft meet safety standards.

7. **Regression Analysis**: Regression models quantify relationships between variables. For example, a regression model might predict the strength of a material based on its composition and manufacturing conditions.

8. **Monte Carlo Simulations**: Monte Carlo simulations model uncertainty by running repeated simulations with random inputs. For instance, an electrical engineer might simulate circuit performance under varying conditions to assess reliability.

Applications in Engineering and Technology

1. **Mechanical Engineering**:

    - **Finite Element Analysis (FEA)**: Combines numerical methods with statistical techniques to simulate physical systems and predict stress, strain, and deformation.
    - **Material Testing**: Statistical models evaluate properties like tensile strength, elasticity, and fatigue life.

2. Example: A bridge designer uses FEA and statistical models to ensure that the structure can withstand extreme weather conditions and heavy traffic loads.

3. **Electrical Engineering**:

- **Signal Processing**: Statistical methods, such as Fourier analysis, process and filter noisy signals in communication systems.
- **Circuit Design**: Reliability analysis ensures that electronic components meet performance criteria under varying environmental conditions.

4. Example: A telecommunications engineer uses time series analysis to optimize signal transmission in a cellular network.

5. **Software Engineering**:

    - **Performance Testing**: Statistical tools evaluate system performance, such as response time or throughput, under different workloads.
    - **Defect Prediction**: Regression models estimate the likelihood of bugs in software modules, enabling targeted testing.

6. Example: A software engineer uses machine learning algorithms to predict which parts of a codebase are most prone to errors, improving testing efficiency.

7. **Civil Engineering**:

    - **Structural Analysis**: Statistical models assess the probability of failure in buildings, bridges, and dams.
    - **Traffic Flow Modeling**: Regression and simulation techniques analyze and optimize traffic patterns.

8. Example: A traffic engineer uses statistical simulations to design an intersection that minimizes congestion during peak hours.

9. **Manufacturing**:

    - **Lean Manufacturing**: Statistical tools identify inefficiencies and eliminate waste.
    - **Robotics**: Machine learning and statistics improve the accuracy and precision of automated systems.

10. Example: In an automotive factory, engineers use SPC to monitor robot assembly lines, ensuring consistent quality.

Case Study: Optimizing a Renewable Energy System

A renewable energy company aims to optimize the performance of a wind farm. The objective is to maximize energy output while minimizing maintenance costs.

1. **Data Collection**: Sensors record wind speed, turbine rotation, and power output over a year.

2. **Data Analysis**:

- Regression analysis identifies how wind speed affects energy output.
- Reliability analysis estimates the probability of turbine failure under different operating conditions.

3. **Optimization**: Engineers use DOE to identify the best settings for blade angle and rotation speed.

4. **Simulation**: Monte Carlo simulations assess the system's performance under varying weather conditions.

5. **Results**: Optimized turbine settings increase energy output by 12% and reduce maintenance costs by 8%.

Challenges in Engineering and Technology Statistics

1. **High Dimensionality**: Engineering datasets often involve numerous variables. Dimensionality reduction techniques, like principal component analysis (PCA), simplify analysis while retaining critical information.

2. **Uncertainty in Data**: Measurement errors, missing data, or environmental variability can affect statistical models. Robust methods, such as Bayesian analysis, address these uncertainties.

3. **Complex Interactions**: Systems often exhibit non-linear or multi-factor interactions. Advanced techniques, like machine learning, model these relationships more effectively than traditional methods.

4. **Computational Complexity**: Simulating or optimizing large-scale systems requires significant computational resources. Parallel computing and cloud-based solutions address these demands.

Emerging Trends in Engineering and Technology

1. **Artificial Intelligence (AI)**: AI and machine learning algorithms enhance predictive modeling and optimization. For example, neural networks predict equipment failures, while reinforcement learning optimizes robotic systems.

2. **Digital Twins**: Digital twins are virtual replicas of physical systems that simulate performance under various conditions. Statistical models power these simulations, enabling real-time monitoring and optimization.
   Example: A digital twin of a power grid predicts failures and suggests preventive measures, improving reliability.

3. **IoT and Big Data**: The Internet of Things (IoT) generates vast amounts of sensor data. Statistical methods analyze these data streams to improve system performance and detect anomalies.

4. **Sustainability Metrics**: Engineers use statistical models to evaluate the environmental impact of projects, such as carbon footprint analysis or life cycle assessment.

Improving Statistical Applications in Engineering

1. **Integrate Data Sources**: Combining data from sensors, simulations, and experiments enhances model accuracy.

2. **Invest in Training**: Equip engineers with statistical knowledge and tools to interpret results and make informed decisions.

3. **Leverage Advanced Software**: Use specialized tools like MATLAB, R, or Python for statistical modeling and optimization.

4. **Collaborate Across Disciplines**: Collaboration between engineers, data scientists, and statisticians encourages innovative solutions to complex problems.

Statistics and engineering are deeply intertwined, enabling the design and optimization of systems that drive progress across industries. With statistical methods, engineers and technologists create efficient, reliable, and innovative solutions to meet the challenges of the modern world.

Appendix

Terms and Definitions

- **Population**: The entire group of individuals or items that a researcher wants to study.
- **Sample**: A subset of the population selected for analysis.
- **Parameter**: A numerical value summarizing a characteristic of a population.
- **Statistic**: A numerical value summarizing a characteristic of a sample.
- **Descriptive Statistics**: Methods for summarizing and organizing data.
- **Inferential Statistics**: Techniques for making predictions or inferences about a population based on a sample.
- **Variable**: A characteristic or property that can take on different values.
- **Quantitative Variable**: A variable that represents numerical data.
- **Qualitative Variable**: A variable that represents categorical data.
- **Discrete Variable**: A variable that takes on a finite or countable number of values.
- **Continuous Variable**: A variable that can take any value within a given range.
- **Nominal Level of Measurement**: Data categorized without a natural order (e.g., gender, colors).
- **Ordinal Level of Measurement**: Data categorized with a meaningful order but without consistent intervals (e.g., rankings).
- **Interval Level of Measurement**: Data with ordered values and consistent intervals but no true zero (e.g., temperature in Celsius).
- **Ratio Level of Measurement**: Data with ordered values, consistent intervals, and a true zero point (e.g., weight, height).
- **Mean**: The average of a set of values.
- **Median**: The middle value in an ordered data set.
- **Mode**: The most frequently occurring value in a data set.
- **Range**: The difference between the highest and lowest values in a data set.
- **Variance**: A measure of the dispersion of data points around the mean.
- **Standard Deviation**: The square root of the variance, indicating the average deviation from the mean.
- **Interquartile Range (IQR)**: The difference between the first quartile (Q1) and third quartile (Q3).
- **Percentile**: A value below which a given percentage of data falls.
- **Probability**: The likelihood of an event occurring, ranging from 0 to 1.
- **Random Variable**: A variable whose values are determined by the outcomes of a random experiment.
- **Probability Distribution**: A function that describes the probabilities of possible values of a random variable.
- **Binomial Distribution**: A discrete probability distribution for a fixed number of independent trials with two possible outcomes.
- **Normal Distribution**: A continuous probability distribution that is symmetric and bell-shaped.
- **Poisson Distribution**: A distribution that models the number of occurrences of an event in a fixed interval of time or space.

- **Skewness**: A measure of the asymmetry of a data distribution.
- **Kurtosis**: A measure of the "tailedness" of a data distribution.
- **Null Hypothesis (H_0)**: The hypothesis that there is no effect or difference in a study.
- **Alternative Hypothesis (H_a)**: The hypothesis that there is an effect or difference in a study.
- **p-Value**: The probability of obtaining a result at least as extreme as the observed result, assuming H_0 is true.
- **Significance Level (α)**: The threshold for rejecting the null hypothesis, commonly set at 0.05.
- **Type I Error**: Rejecting the null hypothesis when it is true.
- **Type II Error**: Failing to reject the null hypothesis when it is false.
- **Confidence Interval**: A range of values within which the true parameter is likely to fall with a specified confidence level.
- **Correlation Coefficient**: A statistic that measures the strength and direction of a linear relationship between two variables.
- **Regression**: A statistical method for modeling relationships between variables.
- **Simple Linear Regression**: Models the relationship between two variables with a straight line.
- **Multiple Regression**: Models the relationship between one dependent variable and two or more independent variables.
- **Residual**: The difference between observed and predicted values in a regression model.
- **Chi-Square Test**: A test for independence or goodness-of-fit in categorical data.
- **t-Test**: A test comparing the means of two groups.
- **ANOVA (Analysis of Variance)**: A test comparing the means of three or more groups.
- **Z-Test**: A test comparing a sample mean to a population mean when the population variance is known.
- **Sampling**: The process of selecting a subset from a population.
- **Random Sampling**: A sampling method where each member of the population has an equal chance of being selected.
- **Stratified Sampling**: Dividing the population into subgroups and sampling from each subgroup.
- **Cluster Sampling**: Dividing the population into clusters and randomly selecting entire clusters for sampling.
- **Systematic Sampling**: Selecting every nth individual from a list or population.
- **Central Limit Theorem**: The principle that the sampling distribution of the sample mean approaches a normal distribution as the sample size increases.
- **Sampling Distribution**: The probability distribution of a sample statistic.
- **Nonparametric Statistics**: Statistical methods that do not assume a specific data distribution.
- **Bootstrap Method**: A resampling technique for estimating the sampling distribution of a statistic.
- **Monte Carlo Simulation**: A computational method using random sampling to solve problems or model systems.
- **Factor Analysis**: A method for identifying underlying relationships between variables.
- **Principal Component Analysis (PCA)**: A technique for reducing the dimensionality of data while retaining variability.

- **Time Series**: Data collected or recorded sequentially over time.
- **Autocorrelation**: The correlation of a variable with its past values.
- **Stationarity**: A property of a time series where statistical properties remain constant over time.
- **Heteroscedasticity**: A condition where the variability of a variable is unequal across values of another variable.
- **Multicollinearity**: A situation where two or more independent variables in a regression model are highly correlated.
- **Bayesian Statistics**: A framework for statistical inference based on updating probabilities with new evidence.
- **Posterior Probability**: The updated probability of a hypothesis after considering new evidence.
- **Likelihood**: The probability of observing the data given a particular model or parameter value.
- **Marginal Probability**: The probability of an event occurring, regardless of other variables.
- **Joint Probability**: The probability of two or more events occurring together.
- **Conditional Probability**: The probability of an event occurring given that another event has occurred.
- **Entropy**: A measure of uncertainty or randomness in a system.
- **Overfitting**: A modeling error where the model captures noise instead of the underlying pattern.
- **Underfitting**: A modeling error where the model is too simple to capture the underlying pattern in the data.
- **Cross-Validation**: A method for evaluating the performance of a statistical model using multiple subsets of the data.
- **Outliers**: Data points that differ significantly from the rest of the data.
- **Missing Data**: Data that is absent or unavailable in a dataset.
- **Imputation**: The process of replacing missing data with estimated values.
- **Censoring**: When the value of an observation is only partially known.
- **Survival Analysis**: Techniques for analyzing time-to-event data.
- **Latent Variable**: A variable that is not directly observed but inferred from other variables.
- **Effect Size**: A measure of the magnitude of a relationship or difference between groups.

Afterword

Thank you for joining me on this look through *Statistics Step by Step*. I hope this book has helped you build a solid foundation in statistics, demystifying concepts that might have once felt intimidating and showing you how statistics isn't just a subject, but an important framework for understanding the world around us.

As you've seen throughout these chapters, statistics is much more than numbers and equations. It's a way of thinking—a structured approach to analyzing data, uncovering patterns, and making informed decisions. Whether you're planning to use statistics in your career, your studies, or your personal life, I hope you've gained both confidence and curiosity in exploring this fascinating field.

We started with the basics—understanding the purpose of statistics, the types of data, and how to organize and visualize it effectively. From there, we went into measures of central tendency, variability, probability, and distributions. We then moved on to advanced topics like inferential statistics, hypothesis testing, and regression analysis. Each step along the way, we built on the previous ones, gradually expanding your knowledge and skill set.

More than anything, I hope you've come to appreciate how statistics connects theory with practice. It's not just about getting through math problems, but using calculations to tell meaningful stories, solve real-world problems, and answer important questions.

Of course, learning statistics doesn't end here. The field is constantly evolving, with new techniques, tools, and technologies emerging all the time. Whether you're interested in mastering advanced topics like machine learning and big data analytics or simply staying informed about how statistics is used in different industries, the possibilities are endless.

As you continue exploring, remember that the principles you've learned in this book—critical thinking, attention to detail, and a healthy skepticism of data—will serve you well. Keep practicing, stay curious, and don't be afraid to make mistakes. Every challenge is an opportunity to deepen your understanding.

I wrote this book with the hope of making statistics accessible, practical, and even enjoyable for readers like you. If this book has sparked your interest in the subject or made statistics feel less intimidating, then I consider it a success.

Thank you for taking the time to read and learn with me. Statistics has the power to transform the way we see and understand the world, and I'm thrilled to have shared that with you.

Here's to continued learning, curiosity, and the amazing insights waiting to be discovered —one step at a time.

Printed in Great Britain
by Amazon